THE FOUR PEAKS

By the same author

Teach Yourself Squash (with Leslie Hamer)

The Tennis Set

Squash, A History

The Peak District Companion

Walking The Tops

Game, Set and Deadline

Love Thirty

THE FOUR PEAKS

One man's journey to
the summits of
Ireland, Scotland, Wales and England

REX BELLAMY

Macdonald

A Macdonald Book

First published in Great Britain in 1992 by
Macdonald & Co (Publishers) Ltd
London & Sydney

Copyright © Rex Bellamy 1992

The right of Rex Bellamy to be identified as author
of this work has been asserted by him in accordance with the
Copyright, Designs and Patents Act 1988.

A CIP catalogue record for this book is available
from the British Library.

ISBN 0 356 20024 8

Typeset by Leaper & Gard Ltd, Bristol, England
Printed and bound in Great Britain by
BPCC Hazell Books
Aylesbury, Bucks, England
Member of BPCC Ltd.

Macdonald & Co (Publishers) Ltd
165 Great Dover Street
London SE1 4YA
A member of Maxwell Macmillan Publishing Corporation

Contents

Introduction

The blonde next door: 'You must be barmy.'

The blonde at the hairdressers: 'Mad. Totally mad.'

The golf partner: 'Bloody silly, at your age.'

The wife: 'You're not as young as you used to be. Sure you're still up to it? I don't want to be drawing the blinds if they send you back in pieces.'

The literary agent: 'These days, I get knackered just walking around London.'

And so on.

It's fair to say that when my hopes of climbing the highest mountains in England, Ireland, Scotland and Wales became a contractual commitment with the publishers, the local response was not totally encouraging. Mind you, most of the sceptics did not know a lot about mountains and some of them did not know a lot about me. They assumed that going up and down mountains was a strenuous, difficult and hazardous enterprise that made no kind of sense for anyone ticking off a series of birthdays beginning with a six. Wrong. Given reasonable health and a modicum of know-how, it even makes sense if the birthdays begin with a seven. Hill-walkers know that. My brother wrote a delighted and slightly envious note from his home in Toronto (he is older than me but has two canoes,

1

teaches t'ai chi, and is ever looking for new horizons) and I took further comfort from two former Wimbledon champions. Jimmy Connors is fond of telling me that age is just a number. And when I retired from *The Times* in 1989 a note from Billie Jean King popped up during my farewell 'do' at Wimbledon: 'Always follow your dreams.'

That sank in. This 'Four Peaks' venture was not exactly a dream, just a vague stirring of ambition. But after forty-five years of international sport, of typewriters and telephones, airports and hotel rooms, what fun it would be to recapture the joy of roaming about in high places. And why not tackle something worthwhile and a bit different? At this point in the internal debate there came to mind our school motto, *summum petite* (strive for the highest, or go for the top). This had been graphically illustrated by a blazer badge that pictured an eagle soaring towards a star. I was no eagle and the altitudes in mind were way below star level, but when that motto fell off some dusty shelf in my memory the message was clear: go for Corrán Tuathail, Ben Nevis, Snowdon and Scafell Pike. The easy routes, of course. No sweat. No risks. Just get up and down with a minimum of fuss. Vanity suggested that there could not be many sexagenarians who had done all four during October and November (or even wanted to). Nor, in fact, did I. The first go at Scafell Pike had to be aborted because of foul weather and five months were to pass before I tried again.

The question of fitness had to be answered. I had recently given up squash. This may have been connected with the fact that a corpse in transit from an adjacent court was known to me, and about my age. Having moved south from the Peak District and regular hill-walking thirty-seven years earlier, I had only sporadically kept in touch with the finest of all recreations. The waistline was 2 in (5 cm) beyond its prime and I was becoming an easy target for the physical equivalent of rust. The 'Four Peaks' might not have been so comfortably negotiated but for the unwitting aid of an artist and a soldier,

Thomas Keay and 'Barney' Barnett. They persuaded me to take up golf. Serving a golfing novitiate as an instant veteran, I discovered that – the Cowdray Park course being what it is – I was engaged in a stick-and-ball version of hill-walking that was no mean substitute for the real thing. The hills I was heading for simply had bigger bunkers. Golf was not the only conditioning exercise. Around the house I walked on the balls of the feet (good for the calf muscles) and took the stairs two or three at a time. Out shopping, I wore a heavy pair of walking boots. Now and again there was a gentle jog across Midhurst Common before breakfast. This was startling for the squirrels, unaccustomed to taking cover at a time when the sun is still in two minds about getting up. Nothing much. I was just giving the old engine a decoke. And the programme worked out pretty well. Corrán Tuathail hurt, but licked me into shape. The three later climbs were easier.

The build-up became exciting. This was going to be quite an adventure, a neatly dramatic way of rounding off half a century of upwardly mobile leisure. Moreover, I was going to share it with you: in a sense, take you with me. That idea had germinated when John Pawsey, my agent, asked if there was a book I really wanted to write: perhaps something more personal than the seven others. This book was the answer. It would satisfy twin compulsions: to climb and to write. As the concept took shape, memories crowded in. Most of them concerned the Peak District. But after reading every moun-taineering book we could lay our hands on, and saving for eighteen months, my brother and I finally got to Switzerland and found out about ropes, crampons, ice axes, and those mountain huts with unisex dormitories. Our guide put it this way: 'There are no men and women here – only moun-taineers.' He was pleased with 'les frères' because, thanks to that Peak District grounding, we were at ease on rock. At any moment one expected to hear the time-honoured cliché: '*M'sieu est – je vous dis franchement – un véritable chamois.*'

That trip inspired a long flirtation with rock-climbing. At

the time I was working at weekends but climbed in midweek with a chimney sweep. He had muscles and, in an emergency, had scrambled from drainpipe to roof and back again, to rescue his gear. For two years we tackled easy climbs on a variety of Peak District crags. Resting contentedly, we propped our backs against warm rock and ate sandwiches, our legs stretched in the heather, fresh moorland breezes around us, and curlews crying sadly in that dreamy wilderness of heath and gritstone. Then Harry Ward emigrated to Canada and bigger and better chimneys. My companions of the hills share an inconvenient habit of fleeing to Canada.

Two South African friends once took me to see the Voortrekker Monument, near Pretoria. They knew me well and saw the look in my eyes as we stood at the foot of 260 steps. There was no question, just an answer: 'We'll wait...' Two colleagues, plus a baffled but patient taxi-driver, let me talk them into a tour of the lovely heights around Sofia. In Palm Springs I went up and down the aerial tramway so often that the crew got to know me by name. The odd memory of Palm Springs concerns a pick-up mixed doubles match. My partner, a beefy and boisterous black lady, suddenly turned to me and said: 'Man, it don't matter how long your pencil is. It's how well you write with it...' As double meanings go, that scored well. From Vancouver I went up Grouse Mountain. But you have the picture. The compulsion to climb was inborn.

Many of the memories in this book will be yours as well as mine. Many of the thoughts and feelings and opinions, too, will be familiar in kind if not in the form in which they are expressed. But this story will, I hope and suggest, be funnier and more anecdotal than most of its kind. Mountain books and magazines tend to take themselves rather seriously, and gravity can be dull company unless one is falling off a cliff. True, there is a lot here that should kindle fires in the young and point them in the right direction. But the spirit of laughter will never be far from the surface and together we are going to meet some interesting characters: among them a slightly alarming Irish giant; the couple who run the Glen Nevis Centre and have a love story to tell; a mountaineer who keeps in trim by abseiling down oil-rigs; a ratcatcher; a lady who makes bobble hats and lives in the shadow of Mont Blanc when she is not living in the shadow of Snowdon; a CID man; the greatest of fell-runners; and a Geordie who became an athlete when he discovered that he was diabetic. All these, plus the ghosts of long-dead, legendary figures.

Yes, this is a rambling sort of book for rambling people. But in two ways it is disciplined and single-minded. Everything hangs on the basic structure, which consists of getting safely up and down four famous mountains. And it has been written for the pleasure of hill-walkers, of all ages and every level of ability and experience. Rock-climbers and mountaineers – who combine hill-walking with rock-climbing, in all weathers – are welcome to the party but it has not been organized for their benefit. Theirs are specialized crafts. We are concerned here simply with the upper crust (that's a metaphor, not a social comment) of those engaged in our most popular recreation, walking in the countryside. Hill-walking has become the best kind of epidemic. Those who have yet to tread the heights – and that can only be for reasons of geography, disability or perversity – would be astonished if they could see the summer swarms on Snowdon, Ben Nevis or Scafell Pike.

The *raison d'être* for this book exists mainly in words rather than photographs, because I happen to be a writer rather than a photographer. Moreover, whereas expert and enthusiastic photographers like to hang about until conditions are right for them, I was briskly engaged in climbing mountains and, in any case, had only a compact camera. But even my own pictures will, I hope, reinforce the spirit of the book. My brother was a constant source of encouragement and advice and our resident professional at Midhurst, Michael Chevis, provided guidance beyond the call of duty. Here, I can do little more than pass on a few hints.

Most of us can make a reasonable shot at composing a

photograph: giving it shape and substance. The novice does not find it easy to do justice to a landscape but can at least try to give his picture a sense of scale by introducing a foreground figure, or perhaps a hut, a rucksack, or a track in the snow. Clouds and water can be useful components. Try to avoid straight lines, especially across the middle of the photograph. Select your main subject and arrange everything else to show it off to the best advantage. Note the position of the sun, because a contrast between light and shadow – most evident when the sun is low – can break up what might otherwise be a 'flat' picture. If you really go into the craft of camera-work you need to know the effect of yellow, orange or red filters. But it is not easy to track down filters to fit a compact camera.

Maybe I missed my vocation. The only time I submitted an illustrated article to a glossy magazine, they paid me more for the photographs than they did for the text...

As Boris Becker was to learn after his first Wimbledon triumph, the highest peak is not necessarily the most difficult to climb. Tackling these four mountains the way I did was child's play compared with the challenges offered by a multitude of other ascents. But getting to the highest points was a richly rewarding experience, within your powers as it was within mine. Granted a car and tolerable weather, the three mainland peaks could be climbed in a week, even from Midhurst. Corrán Tuathail is more awkward to reach but well worth the trouble. There were a couple of odd, personal things about the enterprise as a whole. For most of my hill-walking career summits have been less important than having a good day on the hills. This time it was the other way round but no less enjoyable. The other point is that when returning to the mountains in retirement I found them smaller, less intimidating, than they had been in youth. That comes with growing up. Experience teaches us to see everything in a wider context. I recently bumped into Rod Laver and told him he still looked much the same as the Laver of the 1960s, the greatest tennis player I have ever seen. 'You're looking at me with old eyes,' he said...

This is a book for eyes and hearts of all ages. The writing renewed the exhilaration of the climbing. May the reading do as much for you, reviving cherished memories and holding out exciting promises for the future. There is always another mountain to be climbed.

The Natural Thing To Do

'Thanks for the pictures,' my brother wrote from Toronto. 'They brought back a few memories, good and not so good. There were days when you could feel as if you were walking on air, days that were a heather-scented haze of sheer delight in just being there. You hoped they would never end. The other side of the coin was the drudgery, the wet-footed, rain-soaked misery of plodding on treadmill-like moorland into relentless wind and needle-sharp rain, thinking "I must be crazy to do this – for pleasure". Then there were blisters and aching legs and shoulders, plus feeling like a limp lettuce leaf when it was over. You still went and did it again, though. There must be a masochistic streak in all of us.'

Don's references to wet feet and aching shoulders were reminders of youth, when we walked in nailed boots (less waterproof than today's bonded models, with ridged soles replacing nails) and carried heavy canvas rucksacks. And etched on his mind, no doubt, were recollections of our last joint hill-walking ventures. In 1979, before he defected to Canada, we roamed every corner of the long-familiar Peak District, checking facts for a book that meant much to both of us, *The Peak District Companion*. We already knew the area well but saw it through fresh eyes as a research team: ever

9

curious, ever questioning, ever persistent in tracking down the obscure trivia of history. Our pleasure in all this – in dotting the i's and crossing the t's of memory – was repeatedly immersed in what seemed to be oceans of water. We got wet and wetter, wading through mud and, often, temporary streams gushing down gullies the map insisted were tracks. Like sponges on legs, we hunted this way and that for elusive old farmhouses and other locations that had unusual stories to tell.

As mine was the name on the publisher's contract there was, perhaps, a slight disparity in our obdurate enthusiasm for finding whatever it was we happened to be looking for. But Don's forbearance and fortitude were exemplary. The closest he came to a protest was a comment made in the Woodlands Valley at the end of a tiring day as we sloshed our way up one of those gushing gullies in search of one of those ruined farmhouses. You could say that in heavy rain we were walking up the equivalent of a shallow river.

'The farmhouse,' I suggested, 'can't be far away. Up here and turn left.'

I hate to imagine what Don was thinking, but he permitted himself no more than the bantering comment:

'You should have been born in a bloody submarine.'

Anyway, his letter from Toronto hit a few nails squarely on the heads. Our days on the hills – Don's, mine and yours – are analogies of a Kipling dictum. Kipling, by the way, may have been unique in acquiring his Christian name from a reservoir: that at Rudyard (on the edge of the Peak District), where his parents did their courting. The dictum in question reads: 'There are but two sorts of women – those who take the strength out of a man and those who put it back.' If necessary, make the appropriate adjustments of gender. Even better, revise Kipling to read that there are hill-walking excursions that take the strength out of us and others that put it back. We climb and ramble in the knowledge that physical and mental stress may be involved. If spared an excess of that, we are grateful. If not, we derive satisfaction – rather than enjoyment, which would indeed be masochistic – from fronting up to the rough stuff and struggling through it to the ultimate haven of some pub in the valley. On the bad days, it helps to have been brought up in the North, because from childhood one has been accustomed to hills, wind and rain. The climate in particular has a lot to do with the dogged bloody-mindedness of northern folk and their gift for laconic, doom-laden wit. Live with adversity and you learn to laugh at it.

An Everest mountaineer's response when asked why he wanted to climb to the highest point on Earth, 'Because it's there', was at once the best and worst of answers: the best because there is truth in it, the worst because it implies that climbers cannot adequately explain their motives. The truth in it lies in the fact that climbing is as natural as walking. Consequently the essential question is not why people climb but why some people do not.

Before exploring this controversial vein more deeply one must define the terms. Hill-walking, mountaineering and rock-climbing all, by definition, involve climbing – in the sense of an upward progression. But they are distinct if related and occasionally overlapping branches of the same family. Hill-walking and its extension, mountaineering, are recreations. Rock-climbing is a sport. This book is about hill-walking, which from time to time incorporates scrambling: the use of the hands for balance or support, which is not the same thing as using them for adhesive and ascensive purposes (that is rock-climbing). So let us not make too much of the fact that our primitive ancestors were equipped with prehensile fingers and toes to facilitate their safe progress as they swung from tree to tree or rock to rock. There is no longer any pressing need for us to do that. Rock-climbers are merely gratifying atavistic desiderata.

Walking, which usually involves a gradient of some degree, remains an essential natural function – and walking up hills meets a variety of other inborn needs. Physical and spiritual uplift come in one package. At the same time we satisfy our curiosity, our sense of adventure, and find out more about ourselves and our environment. And on top of all this refreshment for body and soul we can practise, according to individual interests, any one of a host of hobbies: photography, geology, botany, wildlife, bugs, history, or whatever. But all that does no more than gild the lily. Hill-walking is the natural thing to do and does not need rational reinforcement. Walking in the countryside is probably Britain's most popular recreation and its culmination is walking the hills. They give us a wider view, visually and mentally.

Climbing is a necessary component of a full life and, one way or another, we do it all the time. As children we clamber up garden walls and teeter along them, or dare one another to tackle this or that tree. There is nothing mischievous or eccentric about this (though mothers, examining the torn clothing and bloody abrasions, would have us believe so). It is simply a natural response to the basic urge to climb. In adolescence we learn to confuse and mollify maternal concern by disguising that enduring urge under the trappings of dignity: outdoor clothing, boots, perhaps ropes (many young hill-walkers flirt with rock-climbing, as I did, if lucky enough to be within reach of crags). Our instinctive affinity with high places – an affinity which those brought up far from hills may be slow to recognize – stays with us all our lives.

My own hill-walking was restricted by forty-five years as a globe-trotting sports writer but the sight of a decent bump on the Earth's crust always made me check the working schedule to see if three or four hours could be spared for communing with clouds and clearing the mind, either alone or with colleagues susceptible to persuasion. As a result I made my way to tops in fourteen countries on four continents. When I retired from *The Times*, the sports editor, Tom Clarke, invited the fledgling freelance to go to a reservoir, Lake Vyrnwy, on the edge of Snowdonia, to write a piece about the centenary of that renowned fly-fishing venue. I demurred. Fishing is not my scene.

'Let me think about it,' I said. 'I'll call you back.'

Tom did not have to wait long. On consulting the map I discovered that Lake Vyrnwy was handily placed for a half-day on Aran Fawddwy, 2,975 ft (907 m) high. You guess? I instantly realized that fly-fishing was a subject no self-respecting journalist could ignore. And within days I was up among the winds and the sheep again, though (a cautionary note) I was careless on two counts and endured punitive if trivial discomfort. First, I wore a seaman's slick, foul-weather jacket – a strident yellow – that did not breathe. It had some of the qualities of linoleum. And when I discarded this stifling sheath the north-east wind imperilled my pendant manhood. It was a no-win situation. Second, lungs and legs reminded me that the over-sixties should do preparatory fitness training before making a hill-walking comeback. On the other hand I went down as if competing in the Grand National. The incentive was closing time. Repeated references to map and wristwatch confirmed that there could be no slackening of pace. With ten minutes to spare, a restorative pint was working wonders in the Red Lion at Dinas Mawddwy.

You see the point of all this – once bitten by the hill-walking bug, one stays bitten.

I once met my brother in London for an hour or so after our paths had diverged and joint hill-walking ventures had begun to seem no more than a memory (this was pre-1979). I made some comment to the effect that living in the South had one disadvantage: the moorland heights were too far away.

'The mountains,' Don responded, 'are all around us.'

This was pretty deep, but true. The instinctive need to rise in the world has connotations other than physical. Life is a continual quest for improvement in our circumstances – domestic, social, professional – and this desire for betterment is a form of climbing. Essentially we want to make those around us happier and more comfortable. We want to be better people. We want to push our professional talents to the limit. The advancement to higher altitudes, of one sort or another, satisfies a basic need which is yet another reminder that climbing, in every sense, is the natural thing to do.

Would there, one wonders, be life on Earth but for the first spectacular example of a man who put family and flock into intensive care? In this area the biblical theory of natural selection is not entirely at odds with Darwin's. The story goes that when the Lord decided to terminate the world's wickedness by drowning it, He first sorted out a good man who deserved a chance to make a fresh start. The Boss gave Noah precise instructions about boat-building and told him to stock the craft with his entire family, plus a male and female from every species of wildlife. Noah was six hundred years old and well past his sell-by date, but finished the boat with a week to spare. Let us take the six hundred with tongue in cheek: biblical texts are like those TV quiz games that, in the hope of impressing us, insist on adding superfluous noughts to the points won.

Anyway, forty days and nights of rain produced a flood, as you might expect. But the boat floated and, when the waters subsided, found a perch on Ararat, a mountainous chunk of what is now the eastern extremity of Turkey. If you happen to be meticulous about details, note that Noah had his 601st birthday party before floating to the top of his mountain (a means of access that remains unique). Noah has one more claim to our attention. He was a farmer and, taking time off from the chore of supervising the Earth's repopulation with people and livestock, he planted the world's first vineyard – and got drunk on the crop. An accident, no doubt. He had to find out what the grapes had to say to him. This farmer, viniculturist, boat-builder and stud died at the age, we are told, of 950. Delete the noughts from the ages and the story is so good that it ought to be true.

But you knew all that, didn't you? You knew that every living thing owed its survival to a mountain. And you are equally aware that 'The Law' governing every concept of decent society was also born on a mountain: Sinai (of the three possible locations, all in Egypt, Jebel Musa is the most popular choice). Moses went up there to clear his mind, to think straight and think big. He came down with the original code of conduct, the Ten Commandments.

It has become unfashionable to discuss the mysticism of spiritual matters in public. The subject is intensely personal, which may be the main reason why Jehovah's witnesses and the like tend to make us ill at ease and resentful when they turn up on the doorstep. But one has to be insensate – or temporarily bludgeoned into that condition by the babble of a crowd – not to feel the mind broaden when a vista becomes a panorama. Put simply, it has to be good for us when eyes and heart are drawn upwards, when we climb a little closer to the angels and feel those faint stirrings of the spirit inseparable from clouds and silence. An Everest mountaineer, Frank Smythe, wrote an entire book on the subject: *The Spirit of the Hills.* His theme was developed in a discursive, anecdotal way and the book probably sold well (six reprints) mainly because of Smythe's reputation as a mountaineer and writer. There is no Smythe among us today and, even if there was, I doubt whether a book with such a title would find such an eager market.

To boil it down, the loneliness of high places makes us think. Smythe suggested that we had an instinct to investigate our 'relationship with the universe' (hardly felicitous, but try putting it better) and that such investigations were particularly fruitful on mountains – when we were invigorated by exercise, pure air, and the prospect before us. I doubt whether anyone outside the religious orders climbs mountains for spiritual purposes. Equally, I doubt whether anyone climbs a mountain alone without getting some sort of spiritual bonus for his or her labours. The bonus may be dreamy, ingenuous and unrelated to logic. It may do no more than hover around us like a benign ghost. But it gives us a hint, at least, of a wider view – not just of earth and sky, but of the scenery of life as it lies in the mind. One sees more, and more clearly, from high places. This is no time to be flippant about hill-fog.

For this reason, rather than any quest for spiritual guidance, many of us (especially when young) seek the solitude of high, remote moorland when beset by the petty difficulties of earning a living and caring for those dear to us. Like Moses, we want to sort things out, get the day-to-day worries into perspective, and decide what's to be done about it all. As teenagers, in particular, we tend to feel deeply about a host of problems that seem insoluble because of the exaggerated importance we attach to them. They fall into place during a day on the hills. I found that out when serving my novitiate as a journalist and, later, as a husband. Rambling about the Peak District did not solve any problems but it cut them down to size. I was no wiser but I was less confused. If already a hill-walker, you know the truth of all this. If poised on the threshold of the most rewarding of recreations, you will soon discover the truth of it for yourself – and you can bounce it back at me if we should meet over a few leisurely pints in some congenial inn tucked among dusk-laden heights.

By this time, if I have been working well, you will be totally convinced that hill-walking is the natural thing to do. But I have not done with you yet. Are you sensitive to beauty, and continually in search of it? Of course you are. Pretty, lowland places have their charms: flowers and greenery, wildlife and lazy streams, their visual impact enhanced by contrast with flanking heights. But Man has played his part in shaping the splendour of the valleys, a splendour reduced to distant minia-tures when viewed from above. Mountains, on the other hand, give us beauty in its natural form – and on its grandest scale. They develop and expand our powers of perception. More-over, in tackling the hills and mountains we must, of necessity, have it both ways; because unless we do a Noah or borrow a helicopter, every day on the tops begins and ends in the valleys, which can be further explored when particularly bad weather makes the summits a no-go area. You could say that the sight of mountains is an hors-d'oeuvre, the climbing of them a main course, and the ever-changing light and colour a wine so delectable that its effect on the senses challenges belief.

Shying away from the risk of sentimentality, let me introduce a couple of heavyweights whose verse has stayed with me
since youth and may stay with you. We can easily relate to
Shelley's lines...

> And multitudes of dense white fleecy clouds
> Were wandering in thick flocks along the mountains
> Shepherded by the slow, unwilling wind

... because the vision is familiar to all of us. On the other
hand Geoffrey Winthrop Young, while ringing all the right
bells, went farther than most of us would wish to go when he
wrote:

> Only a hill: earth set a little higher
> above the face of earth: a larger view
> of little fields and roads: a little nigher
> to clouds and silence: what is that to you?
> Only a hill; but it's all of life to me,
> up there, between the sunset and the sea

As a professional sports writer who had reported most of the
major sports and, at a modest level, played many of them, I
was often asked which I preferred. The question was particularly prevalent among the parents of sons or daughters they
regarded as multi-talented, and in such cases my response was
usually couched in such terms as these:

Let them try anything and everything they fancy. Tell them
to give it 100 per cent but have fun in the process. They will
sort the sports out and make their own choices. Encourage
them to be doers rather than watchers. Alongside the
conventional sports, make sure they get to the hills. Because
there is no healthier recreation and none that will do as
much to develop character. And hill-walking will last them a

lifetime. Without it they could degenerate, in their thirties, into armchair sportsmen with beer-bellies.

As to character-building, I recall a comment made by James Ramsey Ullman, who achieved the rare feat of writing a memorable novel that was both a mountaineering thriller and a love story: *The White Tower*, which was transformed into a film featuring Glenn Ford and Lloyd Bridges. 'There's one thing a mountain can teach a man better than anything else in the world, except perhaps war,' Ullman wrote, 'and that's the measure of his own strength ... or weakness.' It's an advantage to have that measure, to make that self-assessment, as early in life as possible. And the measure is not merely physical: it is mental and moral, too. There is no need to speculate about the measure, to make assumptions about our abilities or disabilities. On the bulkier bits of our natural environment we put all that to the test and have to live with the answers. The answers we give at sixty may vary slightly from those we gave at twenty, but we do not mind that: because in taking our own measure we have acquired the judgement, the discretion, to temper ambition with prudence and determination with humility.

To paraphrase a note of Frank Smythe's, it is part of our function in life to develop ourselves physically, mentally and spiritually – and the hills are the ideal medium for this development. Another mountaineer, Showell Styles, suggested: 'No other sport so strongly develops those qualities of independence and self-reliance which as a nation we are most in danger of losing.' Can it be wondered at that, on the tops, we sometimes bump into the SAS, the Parachute Regiment, or Army or Police cadets? Almost a decade ago I spent some time on Dartmoor and, later, Tryfan and the Glyders, with Metropolitan Police cadets and their adventure training instructors. One of the latter, Tim Potts, told me that adventure training had advantages both ways: 'They can find out about themselves and we can find out about them.' That cast list – soldiers and policemen – may sound daunting but is introduced simply to point out that hill-walking has the stamp of official approval as a means of testing and developing character. We can all behave well when everything around us looks rosy: in hill-walking terms, when the sun is shining, the going good and the path ahead obvious. But life is not always like that. There are times when we have to struggle through fog and rain on unfamiliar and awkward terrain, perhaps slippery scree, and have doubts about the route. It is then that we find out about ourselves and those around us.

The spirit of adventure, the need to confront challenging circumstances, lurks within most of us. Recreationally, the hills present such a challenge in its most ancient and natural form. But the satisfaction comes not so much from success in our chosen venture (we leave our vanity at home) as from making our best effort within the bounds of prudence. As Smythe put it, 'Good adventure is not to be measured in terms of victory or defeat'. Even when making a tactical withdrawal, or changing the route, we prove something: our common sense. Usually, though, we get to the top, because the task we set ourselves is within our capacities while subjecting them to a reasonably stiff examination. And every time we reach the appointed goal, however modest it may be, we can bask – without being vain-glorious – in the warm glow of success. We feel better for that.

One of the old-timers, Walter Bonatti, admitted: 'I climb mountains because I am afraid of them, and the conquest of fear is one of man's greatest needs'. As a reason for climbing, that was going a bit far. The hill-walking community are aware of fearsome possibilities but carefully avoid them. Any risks we take are trivial and calculated, with a sound margin of safety. At the same time Bonatti's point about the need to conquer fear, to control it, will ring bells in many newcomers to what may be termed the high school. There are not a lot of maternity hospitals on mountains. Most of us are born low-landers and, unless lucky enough to have an early education in hill-craft, have a fear of heights: more precisely, a fear of falling off them. But we can overcome that fear gradually, by practice. Domestically, the ladder exercise is useful. Start by repeatedly climbing ten or a dozen rungs until you think nothing of it. Coming down, look at the rungs – not the ground. Then familiarize yourself with fifteen or twenty until it becomes a bore rather than a thrilling, tentative experience. And so on. You can do the same thing on the hills, gradually increasing the degree of exposure.

In all honesty I have to admit that my wife has just butted in with the comment,

'I wouldn't want to bother overcoming a fear of heights, unless there was something at the top I really wanted. There are plenty of other exciting things to do, like walking through a park...'

That often happens, doesn't it? There we are, flying high on a carefully constructed argument, and somebody shoots us down. Which reminds me of an evening in our favourite local, the Noah's Ark at Lurgashall, when a pilot confessed to a particularly bad landing. The plane hit the ground with a shattering thump and for a few moments there was an awful silence in which everyone offered up prayers of thanks. Then there was a gentle knock on the door of the flight cabin and a steward poked his head in and asked:

'Excuse me. Did we land or were we shot down?'

The fact remains that we all have fears of one sort or another and, in overcoming them, become better prepared to cope with the diversity of life's wider challenges. And to get back to hill-walking, there are people who hold up their hands in horror at the idea of climbing up rocks but would not think it imprudent to walk the streets of Manhattan in the small hours, or cross the Place de la Concorde or the Place de l'Etoile during the rush hour. Give me the mountains, any time. Much safer. Any element of risk is under one's own control.

Talking of Manhattan, I have spent more than a year of my life there, paying the bills for all the good things that have happened to me. Walking up Lexington Avenue one day with a photographer friend, a native New Yorker, I gave vent to what was by then an entrenched loathing for the Big Apple and its man-made canyons. 'To see the sky,' I said, 'you have to risk a crick in the neck or lie flat on your back. It's a totally artificial environment.' Warming to the theme, I insisted that except for Central Park, which was no place for the prudent to take an evening stroll, one seldom saw a tree or heard a bird singing. Whereupon Adam surprised me with the comment that he had a similar feeling of unease in the countryside because of the wide horizons. In each of us, perhaps, lay the germs of the relevant morbid fears: of confined spaces (claustrophobia) and open spaces (agoraphobia). This is relevant to our present discourse because, as with the fear of heights (acrophobia), controlled familiarization is the remedy. There is a wealth of open country when we walk the hills. Often, if briefly, cliffs crowd in on us. The message, in short, is that although hill-walking is not a cure for all ills, it is a cure for many of them.

Most of us spring from the urban masses and seek refreshment for the soul by escaping from the works of Man to the works of Nature. Away from the noise and bustle and teeming humanity and the chore of earning a living, we find recreational contrast and refreshment in wild, high, lonely places. Moreover, we appreciate people more by occasionally getting away from them, by achieving a solitude and an almost-silence in which the mind is at peace and the senses are alert to the beauty of mountains, the subtleties of light and colour playing upon them, the smell of them, and the chuckling, enchanting music of their infantine streams. Nobody can be mean-spirited on a mountain and, once down from them and sucked back into the urban routine, nobody can fail to be better company – or fail to find others better company.

In escaping from the hassle for a while, we become better equipped to deal with it. When reporting at Wimbledon I often had to extemporize a thousand words for the first edition of

The Times within five or ten minutes of leaving some nerve-racking drama on the centre court. One's mind was a whirl. So instead of rushing into the urgent bedlam of the Press Room I spent those precious minutes lighting a pipe and wandering downstairs to commune with the flowers alongside the members' enclosure. Then, emotions under control, I was ready to buy a pint, pick up a telephone, and let the words fly.

A cherished colleague and competitor in those days was Laurie Pignon, a distinguished sports writer and gregarious bon vivant latterly best known as tennis correspondent of the *Daily Mail*. Journalists half his age were put to shame by Laurie's rumbustious zest for his job and for life as a whole. So I should not have been quite so surprised when, not long after his retirement at the age of sixty-five, he suggested a rendezvous in the Peak District. Taking the view that retirement was a continuous holiday, Laurie and his wife Melvyn, formerly England's hockey captain, were playing tennis in summer, 'real' tennis (the original, indoor version) in winter, and now proposed to try hill-walking: an initiative one did not expect from retirees supposedly locked into the comfortable life-style of the Thames Valley. They thought I might be able to give them a few tips. We stayed at one of my old haunts, the Hathersage Inn, and did a 'boomerang' walk around the Derwent Dale tops. Mist and relentless rain made it quite a test for the rookie hill-walkers but they were not put off. Quite the reverse. Since then a series of postcards have arrived from the Lake District and Scotland, and every summer Melvyn and Laurie rent a cottage near Grasmere. As I write, Laurie is seventy-two but still bubbling over with wild-walk projects for Team Pignon:

'We must do the Yorkshire moors, dear boy, and perhaps Wainwright's coast to coast walk...'

You see the point or, rather, points. Life is a series of new beginnings and one can take up hill-walking at any age. There is no need to be an athletic young superman.

In 1982 research work for a book led me to Teesdale for the first time. Jeff Todhunter ('tod' is a dialect word for 'fox'), a kindred spirit in that he is both hill-walker and sports journalist, eased the way by introducing me to the Wainwright of the North-East, Keith Watson, whose most recent books are the two volumes of *North Country Walks* published by Jeff's paper *The Northern Echo*. Keith in turn introduced me to his long-familiar companion on the hills, Brian Hunter, who was soon to demonstrate a rare and hilarious talent for plunging through inches of snow into those funnel-shaped cavities known as swallet-holes or shake-holes: caused either by the erosive sinkage rainwater produces in limestone country, or by a primitive form of opencast mining. But Brian's garrulous sense of humour was irrepressible, even when no more than his head was visible, and he had some fun at my expense by coming on strong with the accent and idiom of the North-East. Until his retirement in 1990, Brian taught at a nursing centre in Sedgefield. And the remarkable thing about the man is that diabetes made him an athlete.

Brian was forty-six when he discovered that he was diabetic: 'Before that I was never an athlete. I was a couch potato, a slob, overweight and smoking fifty cigarettes a day. I could have had a heart attack within a few years. Diabetes may have saved my life. Without it I would not be as fit as I am now' (this was a decade later). 'I've never felt better.' In a period of eight years Brian ran thirty-seven half-marathons, walked the Pennine Way four times, formed a United Kingdom branch of the International Diabetic Athletes Association, and created an official newsletter, Di-Active. Leading diabetic athletes by example, he organized a 1990 programme that included a 10-kilometre road race, a 270-mile trek up the Pennine Way ('My favourite stroll'), a coast-to-coast relay from Stranraer to Whitley Bay, and the first national swimming championships for diabetics. On top of all that, this insulin-dependent human dynamo puts in a lot of time raising funds and travels the country talking to diabetics about the advantages of exercise. 'Regular exercise,' he insists, 'should be an integral part of their care regime.'

Yes, there is a lot more to Brian Hunter than his spectacular knack of 'holing out' when treading the snowfields of upper Teesdale.

An obituary in *The Times* included a sentence that has stayed with me: 'He had much of that quiet confidence and tranquillity of spirit which is often the climber's reward for the discipline and dangers of his calling.' This referred to that renowned mountaineer, Geoffrey Winthrop Young, who is relevant to our present mini-thesis because, having lost one of his original appendages during the First World War, he climbed on a wooden leg. And it was as a convalescent that C.F. Montague produced the funniest essay I have ever read, and repeatedly re-read: 'In Hanging Garden Gully'. Going back to that essay is like opening a fresh bottle of a wine that never fails to charm the palate. And consider the example of Frank Smythe, who went on three Everest expeditions and, during the Second World War, ran a commando mountain warfare school. When invalided out of the RAF and advised to exercise caution when climbing stairs, Smythe went to the Alps and climbed the Aiguille du Plan and, via the Brenva route, Mont Blanc. Not quite what the doctor prescribed.

Young, Montague and Smythe were typical of the up-market, rather exclusive cadre who made rock-climbing and mountaineering recreational pursuits, as distinct from the working chores of sheep farmers, fox-hunters and, later, guides. I mention them here only to underline the point that, as with Laurie Pignon and Brian Hunter (doubtless you can cite other examples), hills and mountains are not the private preserve of the super-fit young. Young, Montague and Smythe also serve as reminders that, since their days, climbing in all its forms has spread into almost every segment of society. It is not for prisoners of convention, because it demands an independence of character alien to those for whom routine is all. But the free spirits among us are not peculiar to this or that social class. An affinity with high places has nothing whatever to do with family or educational background, accent or intellectual capacity. One of the joys of walking the hills is the extraordinary variety of people one meets up there.

It can also be lonely at the top and therein, for many of us, lies part of the satisfaction of getting there. For most of my life I have been closely associated with professional sportsmen and sportswomen. Natural champions are at ease with – even crave for – the inevitable isolation of pre-eminence. The man or woman who insists on being one of the crowd will never be anything else. A tenuous thread therefore links climbers with sports celebrities, but snaps in two places: climbing is no more difficult than we want to make it, and we compete with nobody except ourselves and nothing but the chosen terrain. In conventional sports, by contrast, success can be achieved only at the expense of others. Billie Jean King once said that playing tennis was fun, competing was even more fun, and winning was even greater fun. And when I asked Boris Becker which meant most to him – playing tennis, winning or being a rich celebrity – he did not even pause for reflection. 'Winning,' he said, grinning, 'because that way you have all of it.'

Fair enough. They were talking about their profession, about paying the grocery bills – and when it comes to all that, most of us can be pretty competitive. At the recreational level I have always had reservations about tennis, which seems to me to put too much rotary stress on particular joints and particular groups of muscles and sinews. A similar accusation could be made against other sports, with running the most obvious exception. But although running is as healthy and natural as hill-walking, it does not develop mind and muscle in such a comprehensive way. Even fell-runners miss out in one respect: they have no time to dream.

Now you know why, after that long association with conventional sports, I have reverted to doing rather than watching – and to hill-walking rather than any other recreation. And the next time anybody asks 'Why do you climb?' simply tell them: 'Why doesn't everybody? It's good for you – and it's the natural thing to do.'

Ireland: Corrán Tuathail

3,414 ft (1,040 m)

The natural thing to do first was Corrán Tuathail (say 'C'rawnTOOhill') rather than any peak on my own island. That decision sprang mainly from expedience and curiosity. Expedience because in considering these four ascents I felt much as I do when engaged in man's basic contribution to kitchen craft, washing up: I like to start by getting the fiddly bits, the forks, out of the way. Curiosity because the secluded summit of Ireland had an air of mystery about it that excited the imagination. Moreover, I owed the mountain a debt of conscience because it had won a bet for me before I had any clear idea how to spell – much less, pronounce – its name.

That happened at Wimbledon one day when I was watching a match on court two in the company of an intensely Belfast man, Robert Armstrong of the *Guardian*. Men's tennis on grass lacks the charm of subtlety. Like black and white television, it satisfies us only until we discover something better (that is, colour TV or tennis on almost any surface other than grass). So Robert and I fell to looking at the day and discussing our hopes for the future, which in my case included an ascent to the top of Ireland. Robert insisted that this had to be Brandon, thus implying that natives of Northern Ireland can be vague about the contours of the Republic and may be swayed by reputation rather than the small change of feet and metres. In his eagerness to bet on Brandon, Robert was unfortunate in that he had fallen foul of an Englishman whose knowledge of Irish altitudes surpassed his own. The facts having been checked, he paid up with a bottle of Fitou. Closely related to Minervois, this raised memories of dinner in the enchanting cliff-top village of Minerve during a family holiday near Narbonne. The Fitou also lubricated my growing interest in Corrán Tuathail.

To get back to the expedient reasons for tackling the Irish summit first, I began this project in October and wanted to climb the least accessible peak before the weather turned nasty. It became evident that getting to Corrán Tuathail might be more awkward than getting up it. Like most other places in Britain, Midhurst is not the ideal starting point for anyone *en route* to Killarney; and the map told me that, even from Killarney, Corrán Tuathail could be teasingly remote. True, Ben Nevis is farther away from Midhurst as the crow flies (like the Romans, the intelligent crow travels in straight lines), but one can at least drive all the way to the foot of 'The Ben'. The logistics of the Irish trip are more challenging and more expensive. As for the curiosity factor, for the air of mystery about Corrán Tuathail, the mountain is unfamiliar to most British hill-walkers. It is non-popular – neither popular nor unpopular – because so little is known about it that one can form no preconceptions either way. Even the best maps lack the detail available on maps of Ben Nevis, Snowdon and Scafell Pike. One searches in vain for hints of footpaths and bridges. Many bumps and nooks and crannies have yet to acquire names; and those which have been named tend to confuse us with a variety of spellings because the original cartographers were English and produced anglicized versions of the Gaelic alphabet. (The pertinent example is 'Carrauntoohil' or 'Carrantuohill'.)

The adventurer that lurks within all hill-walkers finds such vagueness irresistible. Nor was I put off when reading some dismissive comments by Showell Styles, who suggested that although Irish mountains were both high and steep by British standards, they tended to be too grassy to tempt the rock-climber. This is relevant to hill-walkers because a staircase of rock is preferable to a slick-surfaced ramp when the angle of ascent or descent is steep. Styles did recommend scrambling along the ridges of the Corrán Tuathail 'horseshoe' and, from what I have since seen of it, that would indeed be an exhilarating day out. But he raised doubts with the presumably exaggerated comment: 'Nature piles on the misery by fencing off all the Irish crags with the blackest and deepest bogs in creation'.

Anyway, my curiosity was aroused, particularly as my previous invasions of the Republic had been restricted to international rugby matches in Dublin. But the logistics were, as I say, challenging, because we are discussing a wild, remote, inadequately labelled area best approached – and that with difficulty – from either Killarney or Killorglin, neither of which is best approached from England. As it happened, only two nights and two days could be spared for what I hoped would be a rapidly consummated courtship with Corrán Tuathail. The weather was incalculable but what a pity it would be to waste any fleeting opportunity on a possibly frustrated assault, perhaps dissipating precious time and energy while improvising a route via inviting knolls and ledges and wrinkles – and doubtless guessing wrong at some time and retreating to try a different tack, while muttering the curses prevalent among all hill-walkers thus forced to concede hard-won height and then regain it. Later I learned that there is an obvious route to the top via the Devil's Ladder: straight ahead from Hag's Glen and turn right on reaching the ridge. But in considering the climb as an innocent, untutored newcomer, I bowed to the need for local knowledge so that I could stay on course and, weather permitting, make a quick kill.

The circle of my acquaintance encompassed Sydney, San Francisco and a variety of intermediate points, including both ends of Africa, but had somehow missed out on Kerry. We journalists, though, even ex-journalists, are hot stuff at tracking down whoever or whatever we need. A series of telephone calls, gradually zeroing in on the target, yielded a unanimous verdict:

'If there's anything you want to know about Corrán Tuathail and Macgillycuddy's Reeks, Con's your man. Con Moriarty. He's got a shop in Killarney. "The Mountain Man", it's called.'

I was soon explaining to this fount of all relevant knowledge that in deference to age (mine) and a handicap of about 10 lb overweight, I was looking for a comparatively easy route to the top. 'You know the type,' I added. 'Reasonably sound in the legs and stamina, given an easy pace, but no longer supple enough or energetic enough to handle the strenuous stuff.' Via the miracle of telephonic communication, Con said he knew just the thing:

'We'll take my four-wheel drive up Hag's Glen. Then we can go up three interesting hanging corries to the ridge and come back down the Devil's Ladder.'

The implications of 'interesting', 'hanging' and 'Devil's Ladder' were not entirely reassuring but Con made the exercise sound like a gentle stroll well within the capacity of wobbly-legged infants, wheezing old dogs and stray sports writers nearing the end of their shelf-life. The really heartening news was Con's ready use of the first person plural. This respected mountain man, who knew Macgillycuddy's Reeks backwards, upwards and sideways, not only had a route suitable for a sexagenarian: he was going with me, to make sure that I didn't flounder about and become a traffic hazard to the sheep unsafely grazing on the steeply sloping greenstuff of his beloved hills. Moreover, there would always be one human figure or another to lend perspective and credibility to photographs. Bare landscapes can be cunningly contrived by the unscrupulous to make molehills look like mountains and puddles like lakes. An intervening body, if obviously perched on some rock or tuft of herbage, gives landscape photographs the stamp of authenticity.

The trip to Killarney can be long and potentially tiring or quick and comfortable. I chose the latter. Kerry airport, at Farranfore, has been commercially developed for international traffic since 1989 and I invested £145 in a Ryanair return flight from Luton. The cost prompted the thought that one could have gone to some tempting spot in mainland Europe for the same price or less. Paris, for example, which never loses its allure. But I worked in Paris for two or three weeks a year for three decades and knew it better (especially its restaurants and watering-holes) than I knew any city in the United Kingdom. Another slog up the hill to the Sacré-Coeur would have been good training, but there was no time for such an inviting digression. For the moment only Kerry mattered, and going there was an exciting prospect because I knew next to nothing about it. Just a vague awareness of the lakes of Killarney, Tralee and those soulful romantic ballads inseparable from a tertiary or quaternary Guinness.

This ignorance of matters Irish – and matters Scottish and Welsh, too – was not entirely my fault. English newspapers, magazines, television and radio tend to concentrate in a blinkered way on English interests and on international politics and disasters, spicing the dish with such items as pay disputes in Estonia, the price of canned peas in Patagonia, or the mating habits of penguins. Curiosity need have no boundaries but frankly I would rather keep in touch with what's going on around me. Ireland, Scotland and Wales seldom get into the act except in terms of death and destruction or as tributaries to the torrent of po-faced political waffle. Reporters cannot neglect the serious stuff that affects our present and future well-being but, at the same time, should always be alert for life's little absurdities. We all like to share a chuckle. We would rather be charmed than alarmed, amused rather than depressed – and the capacity to charm and amuse is more highly developed in the Irish than in any other nation.

All this is to underline the suggestion that the publicity media should keep the English better informed about the 'family' huddled around us on these offshore islands. What mattered, in the days before legs and lungs were tested in the company of Corrán Tuathail and Con Moriarty, was that I should brush up some basic facts about Ireland. Our geography master at school was a former lord mayor of Sheffield (so, for that matter, was the chap who came to read the gas meter) and he did a pretty good job. But the memory is a storeroom and as new stock comes in, the old stuff has to be chucked out or starts gathering dust on a back shelf. For example, I had forgotten that the province of Ulster includes both Northern Ireland ('The Six Counties') and three counties in the Republic; and that the bit of Ireland closest to the Arctic Circle is part of the Republican county of Donegal. In casting such a blinding light on two fruits of scholastic revision I am aware that you may be as underwhelmed as a lady with whom I played a mixed foursome this morning:

'You know, I have lived a long and full life – and could easily have got through the rest of it – without being lumbered with the details of Irish politics and geography.'

Mind you, she had just been hammered 7 and 6 on a bitterly grey morning and was in no mood to get excited about learned intrusions into the badinage that bounces off the walls at the nineteenth. This tends to concern such juicy items as the dilemma of a seventy-year-old spinster who married a man of eighty and, two months later, sued him on the grounds of non-consummation. If you ever need a definition of a frustrated optimist, try that one for size.

The hinterland of the Irish coastline is mostly mountainous or at least hilly. For different reasons three ranges have reputations that have crossed the water. The Mourne Mountains, in the north-east, have been popularized by the heavily emotional ballad that bears their name. South of Dublin are the Wicklow Mountains, the largest visible chunk of granite in either Ireland or Great Britain – and consequently well known to rock-climbers. On a good day they can be faintly seen from Snowdon. In the south-west the delightfully lumpy Dingle

Peninsula has charmed generations of tourists. Its peak is the 'holy' mountain, Brandon, 3,127 ft (953 m) high, named after the part-legendary St Brendan or Brandan. Such records as we have indicate that 'The Navigator' was born in or near Tralee, lived from 484 to 577, and may have spent seven years at sea in search of the mythical 'Land of the Saints'. Then he chose the top of the mountain for his contemplation of the eternal verities and a breathtaking panorama of land and sea. St Brendan was the practical kind of visionary. He founded an abbey and it is estimated that he may have supervised as many as 3,000 monks scattered about the area in remote cells (huts, to you and me), many of which still make a residual impact on the landscape. His was the era in which Ireland had a comparatively advanced civilization and sent missionaries to Britain and the European mainland. Now they send us writers and comedians.

This is one of the loveliest and strangest regions in western Europe, not least because of the almost surrealistic marriage of land and sea. Ireland's jagged south-western coast consists of three peninsulas (five, if we count two smaller invasions of the Atlantic) which jut into the ocean like gigantic, knobbly fingers reaching out towards the distant concrete crags of Manhattan. The biggest and highest land mass is the Iveragh Peninsula, between Dingle Bay and the Kenmare River. Macgillycuddy's Reeks, the crescentic range dominated by Corrán Tuathail, is as close as Ireland gets to communion with the gods, the saints and those halo-powered young ladies in white nighties who have nothing better to do than carry harps about while drifting on air from cloud to cloud.

It is not widely known that Ireland is higher than England and that Macgillycuddy's Reeks incorporate, cheek by jowl on their western flank, the three highest mountains on the island (Brandon comes fourth). These are Corrán Tuathail at 3,414 ft (1,040 m), Beanncaorach at 3,314 ft (1,010 m) and Caher at 3,200 ft (975 m). Corrán Tuathail and Beanncaorach are both higher than the English summit, Scafell Pike. Before going

farther, a note about semantics. Macgillycuddy, like MacCarthy,
O'Sullivan and O'Donaghue, is a family name rooted in the
history of Kerry. I have it on the authority of a professor
of Irish that the word Reeks derives not from smoke or vapour
(the old town of Edinburgh acquired the nickname 'Auld
Reekie' because of the smoke that hovered over it) but from
rick, meaning stack or heap. Rick emerged from the Old
English word hrēak or hrēac. The Irish equivalent is cruach. A
corrán is a sickle or could refer to anything shaped like a
jawbone. The dictionary suggests that Tuathail may be the left-
hand or 'wrong' side but I go along with Con Moriarty ('It's in
the old parish of Tuath, now known as Beaufort, and could be
related to the name of a Celtic tribe, or a man') and the
compatible definition offered by Stella Bond of the Four
Provinces Bookshop in London ('Tuathail is the possessive
case of O'Toole'). Beanncaorach means 'hill of the sheep'.
Caher or the variants cahir or cathair indicates a stone fort and
the mountain may once have had a longer name translated as
'fort of the warrior-hunters'.

The Macgillycuddys and possibly the O'Tooles were presumably big noises here when Ireland's last wild wolf was
killed on or around the Reeks, reportedly in 1700. It remains a
desolate area, for all the grandeur of spectacular scenery. To
the east the Reeks are separated from the Purple Mountain by
a tourist haunt, the awesome glacial cleft of the Gap of Dunloe
in the Black Valley. To the south there is a lesser range of hills.
The western boundary is the River Caragh, which rises south of
the Reeks and runs west and then north into Lough Caragh
and Dingle Bay. In the lowland country north of the Reeks are
the inconveniently distant 'base camps' of Killarney and Killorglin. The quieter of the two is Killorglin except when gypsies
and cattle swarm into it for the annual Puck's Fair. Killarney,
in the valley of the River Flesk, is no great attraction in itself
but is busily geared to the holiday trade. Its romantic associations arose from the beauty of those famous lakes and their
backdrop, Macgillycuddy's Reeks. The flowers around the

lakes are abundant and in many cases unusual and one has to go to the Mediterranean to find the *Arbutus* flourishing as it does here. You may know this better as 'The Strawberry Tree' because of the faint resemblance between unrelated fruits. The gorse, too, can be dazzling. If the lakes and their flora leave you cold and the weather on the Reeks looks unreasonably hostile, you can always play golf or go fishing. The climate? Mild but wet. Which reminds me of a vivid little sentence written by Laurie Pignon after a hill-walking trip: 'The rain was soft on our faces.' Very apt to Kerry.

All this background information came from homework that was verified and expanded during and after my two days and nights in the Republic. Before beginning the 'Four Peaks' enterprise, I also checked the long-neglected contents of the rucksack and relevant areas of the wardrobe, put the legs through a programme of light training, stretched a few other muscles via basic callisthenics, and tried to take off a little weight – which I did, though 2 lb was hardly a triumph for the lip-service paid to the twin tyrants of temperance and exertion. The 32 in waist on my heavy-duty viscose and nylon climbing breeches, unused for seven years, no longer sufficed for the girth it had to contain, so I would have to make do with light-weight golf breeches, 34 in waist. Tight clothing is not recommended for even moderately strenuous activity. Did you know that there are people who head for the hills in skin-tight jeans? When these get wet they affect the legs much as strangulation affects the throat.

A nasty suspicion that one might be inadequately prepared for the demands of Corrán Tuathail and the expectations of Con Moriarty added an extra spice of excitement to the day when I had breakfast in Midhurst and dinner in Killarney. The first chores, the trivial pursuits common to adventures great and small, were domestic: taking the dog for a walk, shopping, and helping to top up the local rubbish dump. Midhurst, mind you, is too consciously genteel to resist the modern preference for 'amenity sites'. This ignores the fact that an amenity must by definition be pleasing, which a rubbish dump is not. Then it was a question of working carefully down the checklist and packing the rucksack with everything needed. In fact I forgot to include footwear for indoor use. With higher things in mind, hill-walkers tend to be improvident in equipping themselves to be properly considerate towards carpeted or parqueted strata superimposed on the Earth's natural crust. One does not clump about hotels and restaurants in climbing boots, even Brasher boots, which look smarter than most. These were preferred to heavier alternatives (the difference was 12 oz). To the weight-conscious every ounce matters. But there would be shopping to do when I arrived shoeless in Killarney.

During the eighty-three-mile drive to Luton, random thoughts flitted along byways of the mind as they always do when one is alone at the wheel for an hour or two. For example, other than Luton ('The Hatters') how many football clubs acquired nicknames from traditional local trades? Certainly my childhood heroes, Yeovil ('The Glovers'), plus Northampton ('The Cobblers') and Stoke ('The Potters'). But one can read too much into nicknames. I was brought up in the era of the great Tommy Walker so my favourite Scottish club became Heart of Midlothian or 'Hearts' – known as 'The Jam Tarts' (rhyming slang) because of their maroon and white strip, not because of Edinburgh's pastry cooks.

Such trivia kept me occupied on the sunniest of October mornings, a time to be arriving in West Sussex rather than leaving it. All was green and bright and beautiful (whereas Kerry, as I learned later, was awash). Even Luton, no tourist trap, looked warm and welcoming. Two residents, an old tennis-writing chum and his wife, had kindly insisted that I leave the car with them instead of parking it at the airport. I turned up dressed for climbing – breeches and boots and all – and prepared for banter. But Bill and Marjorie did not even raise an eyebrow, thus implying that guests who looked as if they had fallen into the drawing-room off a mountain were par for the course at Luton.

The blonde at the check-in desk said the flight would be an hour late and this was confirmed by the departure board. The uncharitable thought that one could not expect anything Irish to happen on time was instantly dismissed. Flight delays had become increasingly prevalent during my thirty years of globe-trotting and had nothing to do with the Irish unless, unknown to you and me, they had conspired to shoot the world's airline schedules to pieces. I changed some pounds into punts, spent the best part of a second considering how to kill an hour, and was heading for the bar when I noticed that the departure board no longer indicated a delay. Some electrical malfunction, perhaps? Back to the blonde, who unblushingly verified the cancellation of an hour's drinking. Now this, if you like, was authentically Irish: Ryanair's delayed flight would be leaving on time...

It did, too. Flight 2539 contained eleven passengers, two cabin attendants, and presumably a driver and mate hidden up front with the steering gear. One of the latter announced over the intercom that by the time we got to Kerry it would probably be raining. This was no surprise. I had picked up a rumour that the climate was mild but no beer-drinker assumes that what is mild is necessarily dry. The afternoon was grey and gloomy as we swooped over a convention of totally unmoved Friesians and landed on the damp, glistening tarmac. By that time the rucksack had acquired half a litre of extra ballast: duty-free John Jameson. This was not for personal indulgence, though I find it more palatable than Scotch. It was to be an ingratiating gift for the mysterious Moriarty. On the phone he had sounded a considerate, good-natured chap. But the name had villainous associations (*vide* Sherlock Holmes) and mountain men are a thoughtful breed with long memories. Could it be that Con harboured dark thoughts about Cromwell's compatriots? He would have me at his mercy for a while in a remote wilderness. Yes, it definitely made sense to give him an introductory hint that here was a man worth pampering.

'This got away from the Republic,' I told him, handing over the John Jameson, 'but I caught it and brought it back.'

Con had kindly arranged for me to be picked up from the airport, thus ensuring that I would not go gadding off down the wrong peninsula. We met in his emporium, 'The Mountain Man', where I repaired the deficiency in footwear by sorting out a pair of posh German sandals while he was unwrapping himself from the telephone. The unwrapping process was impressive. There seemed to be yards and yards of Con Moriarty. He was 6 ft 5 in tall, a sparely built but well-muscled 14 st, and twenty-seven years old. I was conceding 9½ in, 2½ st and thirty-five years, and these statistical contrasts made me feel like a geriatric midget. Moreover, Con was lightly bearded and the rest of his head was encased in an abundance of untamed hair. One could imagine sheep having an identity crisis when suddenly confronted by a head like that. And it was easy to picture this athletic young giant responding to the ultimate challenges of his calling by defying gravitational forces while ascending, fly-like, wispy overhanging cracks in any crags that caught his fancy. His talk was quiet, quick, clipped. It became clear that his mind was jumping about like a box of fire-crackers. Nerve-ends were almost visible. These hyperactive types are full of beans and there is no way one can keep the lid on. They have no repose. Exhausting to live with but stimulating to meet.

In short, Con Moriarty had a wild, restless air about him. At street level, anyway (on the mountains, his natural habitat, he was at peace with himself and everything around him). He put me in mind of a bolting horse – careering about all over the place, doing its damnedest to hurtle in two directions at once, pausing to graze for a while, then taking off with a whinny of excitement as it spotted a greener patch two fields away and leapt intervening walls as if they were kerbstones and the Grand National was strictly for cissies. Two days later, while we were bouncing back down Hag's Glen in his Nissan Patrol, I told Con about this gut-reaction analogy. He roared with laughter and confessed that there was truth in it.

Those first impressions were by no means off-putting. I like a man to have a wild, restless streak in him. It means that he will open windows in the mind, that he will have a go at anything, that he will make things happen and get a job done. Not necessarily the done things, either. Such men are not shackled by conformity. They never stay with one chore for long. They take a challenge by the scruff of the neck and give it a shake, to separate the sense from the nonsense and find out whether the improbable is possible. They then move on fast to the next challenge, like dogs impatiently on the scent of some fresh *amour*. Behind them these men of ideas and initiatives leave a trail of loose ends that associates have to tidy up. Some visionaries are more practical then others.

Meantime, back in 'The Mountain Man', Con was sizing up the geriatric midget and considering where to stow me for the next two nights. He suggested a restaurant with rooms, just round the corner, so that he could easily rope me in if I strayed from the call of the hills. The Flesk is renowned for its food rather than its accommodation. Accurately, Con guessed that I was more interested in the inner man than in lolling about amid the carpeted comforts and cosmetic gloss of some up-market hotel room. I have had my fill of all that. Mind you, there are limits to one's tolerance of overnight privation. A neighbour once called during an electricity failure to ask if I could fix a refractory camping stove.

'I know you've done a lot of hill-walking and camping out,' she said. 'Perhaps you're familiar with these things'.

'You're only half-right,' I told her. 'I gave up camping when I graduated from the Boy Scouts. I don't mind a rough day's walking in wind and rain and whatever. But after that I want a pint and a hot bath, a good dinner and a comfortable bed. So I stay in decent hotels, not tents. And somebody else does the cooking.'

Whereupon power was restored and my uneasy relationship with the trickier components of camping stoves was never put to the test.

Before turning me loose on the pleasures of the Flesk, Con checked the local weather forecast and promptly asked, ominously, if I had wet-weather gear (I had). The morning would be bad news, he said, because wind would build up overnight and there would be showers to come. A late start was advisable. But we could save foot-slogging time up Hag's Glen, he added, by penetrating the fastness of the Reeks on wheels and would then be up and down Corrán Tuathail in no time. I felt a little guilty about that: it was like bedding the lady without wooing her. On the other hand one had to be single-minded. For the purpose of this book I was concerned simply with ascending four peaks, not with the usual day-long indulgences of the hill-walker.

The room was modest but the food was not: breaded mush-rooms garnished with rosemary, Killarney trout ... you get the picture? The gentle Irish muzak was familiar from the Foster and Allen tapes back home. The Flesk was evidently popular with both natives and tourists, the latter representing the cheap-rate laggards of the seasonal migration. Budweiser was on tap and from one corner of the restaurant came the relevant accent: 'We're from Dallas, Texas.' Can there be another Dallas? The place is a jumble of concrete pillars set on a vast plain and its classiest environs are populated by the kind of people who earn more in a week than most of us do in a lifetime. Dallas is too grey, too wealth-conscious, to inspire affection. On the other hand I have been lavishly entertained there by a delightfully unassuming oil baron, Lamar Hunt, who had as much to do as anyone with restructuring men's professional tennis into the thriving segment of the sporting entertainment business it is today. And it was in Dallas, in the intimacy of the Fairmont's Venetian Room, that one had the rare treat of savouring Jack Jones and Peggy Lee in concert while the likes of Charlton Heston and Ken Rosewall, taking time off from their own starring roles, sat back and enjoyed the profession-alism of others.

One's only alarming memory of Dallas concerns an

encounter with a Moriarty-sized black man who thought it would be a good idea if I gave him some money. He touched a raw nerve because I'd made the mistake of taking sterling traveller's cheques, could not find a bank willing to change them, and consequently lacked the dollars to do the shopping I had in mind. Seething with a frustration that needed just such an outlet, I risked a crick in the neck – and more – by looking up at the panhandler and rocking him back on his heels with a verbal coating based on personal finances. When I paused for breath he was visibly suffering from shock, apologized for bothering me, and wished me a good day. This was lucky. If men of any size or colour ask you for money on quiet streets in American cities, to respond as angrily as I did is to flirt with the possibility of physical damage that may be incurable. Maybe I got away with it because this was Dallas rather than New York or Miami.

The Texan group at the Flesk reminded me of an evening in Paris when I was dining with friends and our conversation was almost drowned by adjacent Americans. They were heatedly discussing their bill, which they suspected might incorporate creative accounting in favour of the patron. In order to abbreviate this discussion and reduce the noise level as quickly as possible, I went through the bill with them and agreed that they were being ripped off. 'Moreover,' I pointed out, 'you run this risk every time you wear big hats to dinner and talk loudly. In this part of the world there is a suspicion that Americans have more money than they need.' Mind you, there are diners of all nations – including my own – who converse at a volume which implies that everyone else in the place would rather listen than talk among themselves.

It was not so, at the Flesk, with a French couple who were quietly dissecting their dinners and their plans for the morrow. Cynical though the generalization may be, one inclines to the view that the difference between the Americans and the French, when busy at the trough, is the difference between gourmands and gourmets – which may explain why so many Americans

are fat and so many Parisians a mite supercilious. At dinner
with some French colleagues in Paris, years ago, I commented
on the fact that I was the only man tilting the soup-plate away
from me, as is the English way. They insisted that it was more
natural to tilt the plate towards them, and asked why the
English differed.

'Presumably,' I suggested, 'so that there is no risk of spilling
the soup on one's clothing.'

'Only the English could be so clumsy.'

'Only the French could be so bloody patronizing.'

And I once sat beside a French businessman while flying
from Paris to London. During the ebb and flow of conversation
I asked where he spent his holidays and he mentioned half a
dozen coastal or mountain resorts, all in France. Did he never
take a vacation overseas? He shrugged with his mouth and
eyebrows, the way the French do, and responded simply:
'*Pourquoi?*' Considering all that France has to offer, it was a
fair question.

An engaging feature of my two-night invasion of the Flesk
was that although May, Declan, Dermot, Josie and Mossie
made me feel at home, their family names remained as much a
mystery to me as mine did to them. Who cared? The Irish have
a saying that strangers are friends one has yet to meet and that
epigram clearly governs their unfussy attitude towards visitors.
Declan asked: 'Are you English or American?' Maybe we all
sound alike to the good folk of Killarney and there certainly
seemed to be a preponderance of American tourists, possibly
because they tended to be noisier and more amply upholstered
than the rest and, consequently, more noticeable. For example,
it took only one American and one question ('You gotta *Wall
Street Journal?*') to shatter the serenity of a Killarney bookshop. Whereupon an assistant and I, equally amused,
exchanged raised eyebrows from opposite ends of the
premises. Later she told me: 'Yesterday three of them came in
together. They sounded like a football crowd.' But this is
unkind. Americans have the edge on most European nations,

not least the British, in their uninhibited natures and warmth and frankness of manner. Even so, Declan's question was less welcome than that of an assistant in the Kilkenny shop, 'Are you French?', which was nearer the mark in terms of ancestry and cultural preferences.

The evidence of forty-eight October hours in Killarney suggested that if the place needs a coat of arms it should incorporate an umbrella and windscreen wipers. These were as omnipresent as crumbs in a bun when I took a stroll, after dinner, and peeped into the late-closing souvenir shops. Wet road surfaces glistened with the reflected glow of street and shop lighting. The only sight to enliven the imagination was that of a little old man emerging from a dark alley off Plunkett Street. With one hand he was wheeling a bicycle and in the other he held a rope attached to a carthorse. To have asked for an explanation would have ruined the pleasures of speculation. Maybe the horse had wandered. Or perhaps he had tethered it earlier in the day and forgotten to take it home with him. Maybe either horse or bicycle had been won in a bar-room bet, or collected after the equivalent of a servicing. Perhaps the old man was a jarvey and had a jaunting-car tucked away somewhere. Whatever the cause, here was a man twice blessed with forms of transport – individually useful but, in harness, incompatible.

Checking facts, getting to the truth of this and that, is a journalistic habit but it can at times be coldly clinical. We all need a little mystery in our lives, a little dreaming space for the brain cells. The old man vanished into the night with his horse and bicycle and I returned to the Flesk, arranged breakfast, had a glass of Guinness as a nightcap, fell in love with the young lady who poured it, but went to bed with sterner pleasures in mind – Corrán Tuathail. Outside, the rain was still falling softly, relentlessly, as much taken for granted as sunshine in Sydney.

In the morning there was a quantitative change in the weather. The rain was heavier. But I organized a flask of hot soup, distributed 'energy' snacks into the rucksack pockets, and ensured that the contents of the rucksack's interior bulk were protected by plastic bags. All useless. Con called to say that the Reeks were shrouded in fog, the rivers in spate – which mattered because, where we were going, rivers had to be crossed by the primitive and potentially hazardous method of boulder-hopping. No bridges. In short, Corrán Tuathail was closed for the day. This was frustrating and slightly worrying. We both had to get on with the rest of our lives. Con generously insisted that he could rearrange his plans and leave the morrow clear for our enterprise. My own deadline would be the 5.55 p.m. flight back to England. Just the one day left. Meantime twenty-four hours of extra dining and drinking threatened to reduce my vestige of fitness to a level at which it might vanish down the plug-hole.

The afternoon was not wasted. It was pertinent to this chapter's main purpose because Con found a quiet bar in which he submitted to interrogation while we made modest inroads into Killarney's reservoir of stout. His Gaelic name, he said, was Conchobar Muircheartaigh, which was exclusive to Kerry and had vague associations with the sea and piracy. For centuries his family had lived in that beautifully rugged gorge, the Gap of Dunloe. Con himself was born there and has never strayed. 'It's largely a sheep-farming community and the families of both my parents were sheep-farmers. My grandfather was a guide, to supplement his living, and in the 1920s he used to specialize in taking people up to see the dawn from the summit of Corrán Tuathail. Will you please, please, spell it properly? I've seen so many bastardizations of the words.' (After much research into the etymology, the spelling used here differs from Con's only in that he would like the elongated 'á' in Corrán to be followed by an 'i'.)

'It was a good place for climbing and I began at a very early age. There were always excuses to get out on the hills – tending sheep, herding, helping neighbours – and I got seriously hooked on mountains. My father owned a shop in the Gap of Dunloe, selling tweeds and Irish handcrafts, and on leaving school I joined forces with him and worked there for five years. Then I went out on my own and opened this climbing shop – the first in Kerry and Ireland's only exclusively mountain shop. That was in 1987. I've built it up and today it's thriving, a going concern, and I've sold shares in it to two friends, taking them in with me as partners. That gives me more time to climb. Now that the name is there and we have a really good reputation, I want to move off and do other things whilst retaining a link with the shop and a certain income.

'Nowadays I make my living largely as a guide and tour operator for a quite discerning clientele – mostly wealthy! I pride myself on taking travellers into the hidden parts of Ireland and showing them the way the Irish live and play, especially on the west coast. The tours, usually week-long, are small and intimate: between two and eight people staying in the best hotels, eating the best food, and seeing parts of Ireland that other travellers never see. I've just finished with eight golfers and on Friday I'm taking three guys fishing for a week. Golf, fishing, walking, climbing, natural history, bird-watching ... And the tours include alternative itineraries for spouses. In a nutshell, my shop is up and running and I've extended myself into setting up my own company: this exclusive, specialized tour business. It's called "The Hidden Ireland, with Con Moriarty". If Rex Bellamy and his wife want to go to Ireland and don't want to go in a shamrock-festooned coach, I'll organize it and take them around. I've been doing this for the past two years. I like it because I can spend twelve or fifteen weeks working in my shop and twelve or fifteen weeks working on tours. And sometimes I get a lot of instructional work in industry or other private companies: industrial safety and rescue, teaching guys the requirements of rope-work and how to execute rescues. I'm the leader of the local mountain rescue team. We cover the most mountainous areas of Kerry: the three peninsulas.'

Our glasses replenished, I spared Con the embarrassment of any further questions about himself. 'This morning,' I said, 'you referred to "this greasy mountain". What do Corrán Tuathail and the Reeks in general mean to you, apart from a source of income?'

Con laughed. 'They're not a source of income. If they are, it must be very indirect. I rarely see it ... First and foremost, they are my beloved hills. In the same way, I'm sure, as you like the Peak District, the Reeks are very, very dear to me. They're a lofty range of hills. Like the hills on the west coast of Scotland: narrow and rugged, with deep, steep valleys. And because of their proximity to the ocean the weather is ever changing – rapidly. All the prevailing winds and weather come in here from the south-west and the first really high land mass that the incoming winds and fronts hit are the Reeks. So we get a lot of rain. No more and no less than Skye. The midges aren't as big as they are on Skye...

'The single most beautiful aspect of Kerry, in general, is the light. It must be one of the most fascinating light shows in the world – the west coast of Ireland, particularly the west coast of Kerry. I try and recall colours I've just seen on the hills, to friends of mine in the pub, and I can't. It's so fascinating: such a tremendous variety of colour and shade. That's why I want to get you up in clear weather. We're going to get it tomorrow. Another thing about this, what we all love about the Kerry hills is their remoteness and the fact that they are so quiet. We don't have footpaths. You can go out on the hills any day of the year in Kerry and not see anybody. That's an aspect of walking that has been long lost, certainly in England. And the other really nice point is that the foothills of these high mountains are inhabited by a superb race of people, absolute experts at having fun. It's their single greatest skill. They've had so much of a struggle trying to make something of very weak land that the most logical thing left to do is laugh. Very light-hearted. Often moody, in the same way as their natural environment is moody: the people reflect that. They're mostly sheep-farmers, with a few cows and so on. In my own area this would be supplemented by an involvement in tourism.'

By this time I was more at ease with the unfamiliar rhythms and inflections of Con's 'Irish English'. Weighing his words, he had talked in a sensitive way about what his native hills meant to him: his childhood in a sheep-farming community, the light and colour of the Reeks, their remote quietness, and the engaging nature of the farming families scattered about the foothills. He had one more point to make. It concerned the human history of the now desolate valleys and reminded me of a friend's satirical comment: 'The Irish live in the past. They're always talking about Cromwell, and the potato.' That was wittily put, but unfair. Nobody can walk the hills, anywhere on our offshore islands, without walking with ghosts. They bring with them reminders that we are but links in an interminable chain of people and events. Those ghosts, those reminders, are exciting components of my affection for the Peak District. But the Irish have more cause than most to look back – with sadness.

To boil it down, Ireland was gradually brought under English control during the Tudor and Stuart eras in the sixteenth and seventeenth centuries. Three consecutive monarchs, Mary I, Elizabeth I and James I (James VI of Scotland), were closely associated with the plantations: a system of colonization that consisted, essentially, of kicking out the Irish landowners and replacing them with English and Scottish gentry loyal to the crown. This worked most effectively in Ulster and the legacy is with us today. In 1641 the Irish rebelled. Thousands of settlers were massacred or died from privation as the original landowners fought to regain their patrimony. Ireland again became, *de facto*, an independent Catholic nation. But in 1649 the avenging Oliver Cromwell turned up. It is estimated that almost 3,000 people were slaughtered when he devastated the garrison at Drogheda. Wexford suffered a similar fate. Cromwell's men laid waste to the country with a ruthless brutality that smacked of genocide, and the plantation system was reinforced. Some Catholic landlords abandoned their religion. The natives as a whole could stay on as labourers or, if they refused allegiance to the crown, move to inferior land west of the Shannon. 'They can go to hell to Connacht,' Cromwell decreed.

There were three doorways to hell: death (via killing, starvation or disease); emigration; or hovels in such remote valleys as those around the Reeks, which provided a squalid security from persecution until rent-hungry landlords decided that even the destitute might be a source of income. All this was packaged with penal laws against the Catholic majority. Thus were the Irish aristocracy and the clans crushed and the populace reduced to second or third class citizens working on land stolen from their ancestors. There were more rebellions to come but it was not until 1903 that the last vestiges of the Cromwellian plantations were wiped out. Many tenants who bought land in 1903 had the same names as the owners dispossessed 250 years earlier.

So much for the plantation system and its effects. The other influence on the human history of Ireland's secluded valleys – for our purposes, those tucked into the Reeks – was the cultivation of the potato during the eighteenth century. This increased the worth of the land, provided more farmers with a living, and encouraged landlords to demand more rent. The population, more than decimated thanks to Cromwell, almost doubled. But most of the rural communities depended on the potato and, consequently, were ruinously impoverished by the blight and awful famine ('The Great Hunger') of the late 1840s. It has been estimated that getting on for a million people starved to death or died from the feverish afflictions encouraged by malnutrition, and that maybe two million emigrated – founding Irish communities in Britain (notably Liverpool and Glasgow), North America and Australia. Many emigrants died from dysentery or scurvy in what became known as 'coffin ships'. Tenant farmers who could no longer show a profit were evicted and – like Cromwell's victims before them – fled to the deprivation of cabins in what Australians would call the outback.

The tide of emigration ran strongly until the 1920s. The immediate effect of the famine was to reduce the population from more than eight million to about six and a half million. By the 1890s it was down to about three and a half million and that figure has since risen to roughly five million in the Republic and Northern Ireland combined – which works out at the uncommonly sparse average of approximately 60 people to the square kilometre or 156 to the square mile.

Most of this I had either forgotten or had never learned and therefore had to swot up. A headmaster of my acquaintance thought it fair comment when I suggested that no more than one in ten of British school-leavers (even teachers, he suspected) could adequately discuss the plantation system of conquest and the effect of Cromwell and the potato on the history of our western neighbours. Con Moriarty skated through it, with feeling, because the past enhanced his appreciation of the Reeks and the valleys around them. With heavy irony he talked of Elizabeth I ('very wise, very shrewd') and Cromwell ('that very likeable Englishman, who chopped the heads and wiped out the town of Drogheda in an afternoon'). That led us to the subject of Connacht, a province that had little to attract the invaders and consequently remained essentially Irish and assumed historic importance because of its contribution to the survival of the Gaelic language and culture. This has parallels in Scotland and Wales and, to stretch a point, in the nineteenth-century Indian reservations of North America.

'Cromwell came over to knock the Irish into shape and pave the way for the plantations,' Con said. 'He issued this decree that the Catholics should go to hell or to Connacht – a beautiful land but, by and large, the crappiest. Real rubbish. A hard, poor land. My father has always said that it was largely during this period that the remote valleys of Kerry, the Reeks, were inhabited *en masse*. The Moriartys, the O'Sullivans, the O'Connors, who lived in the lowlands around Killarney, fled from this tyrant. They didn't have the energy or maybe the means of getting to Connacht, so they fled into these valleys, in which the English had no interest. Today the valleys are totally uninhabited but you can see the ruins, the stone walls, where maybe ten or twelve families once lived.

'The reason they're now empty is that, later, the landlord realized there were families living in hovels in places like the Black Valley. So he said, "Hang on a second – we can get some rent out of these guys." He went up into the valleys, counted all the houses, and levied a pretty exorbitant rent. The population became almost totally dependent on the potato as a foodstuff – and there was this exorbitant rent. Then we were struck by the famous potato famine of 1845. The crop was hit by blight. It happened for three consecutive years. "The Black Forties". People would have gone out and dug the same plot of land ten, twenty times to see what might be in the ground. They just died of starvation – as people did in Ethiopia and the Sudan in the past few years – or they emigrated.

'So when I take people to the hills, which are beautiful in themselves, what makes it all the more enriching for me – a modern-day walker and climber who goes to play with technical equipment on the cliffs and crags – is to realize the vast amount of human history that lies in the valleys.'

That wrapped it up. I knew enough about Con Moriarty and the sources of his affection for the Reeks and, like a restless dog on a leash, was fairly panting to be up and doing. Eating beats the hell out of studying the menu. First, though, a brief aside . . .

Apropos the potato, I was browsing through the *Irish Independent* that evening and, while glancing at a twelve-page supplement concerning the national ploughing championships, focused with growing disbelief (I read it three or four times) on a short item that read like the fantasy of a bar-room raconteur whose imagination had been over-Guinnessed. It seemed that someone had invented coloured, dummy potatoes – much like the real thing in shape, weight and texture – containing electronic devices that recorded the damage done during

harvesting, grading and handling. Would you like me to run
that by you again? Perhaps not. Ask your own questions and
make up your own answers. My only conclusion was that the
potato remained a powerful influence on Irish thinking.

At eight o'clock next morning I combined the chore of
shaving with periodic peeps out of the window to admire a
rainbow. It was still raining. There was a knock on the door
and Con appeared, looking quizzical. It seemed that another
front had come in, he explained. The decision was up to me.

'My plane goes at 5.55 pm,' I said. 'Meantime, let's go for
it. At worst, I'd like to rub my nose in it.'

'I'll do that all right,' he responded, with just a hint of the
smile sadists switch on at the sight of masochists.

We were lucky. The leg-work began and ended in light rain
but, in between, the only water we came across was that
already nourishing the greenstuff, plus the vapour of a mist
that – except on the summit – was never bad enough to
assume the status of fog. We were up and down in five leisurely
hours and they were the best hours of the day.

The drive up Hag's Glen was more startling than any of the
more familiar little adventures that succeeded it. Imagine, if
you will, that an avalanche of rocks has poured down the floor
of a long valley and that this disordered debris has formed a
narrow embankment poised – hazardously, in places – above
flanking brooks and tufted vegetation. That was how our route
looked, anyway. It must have been tidied up in a cursory way
but evidently the tidiers soon realized that they were on a
hiding to nothing and dropped the idea. This broken, jagged
nightmare of rocky wreckage serves as a causeway but must be
like a bed of nails for walkers. No self-respecting mountain
goat would give it the time of day. To describe it as unsuitable
for vehicles would be to describe the Olympic sprint
programme as unsuitable for sumo wrestlers wearing suits of
armour. Yet, *faute de mieux*, that causeway suffices as a means
of access to the foot of Corrán Tuathail – and I was driven
along it at speed, with much metallic clattering as we bounced

upwards and downwards and sideways. Con Moriarty was
justifying the best and worst of my first impressions: that the
wild streak in him could make for exciting but alarming
company.

I should have known what to expect because, before we
charged out of Killarney, he explained that the passenger door
could only be properly closed from the outside. No wonder. As
we raced across those sharp fragments of basic Kerry, logic
insisted that the entire vehicle must collapse into a scrap-heap
of battered assembly units and shredded tyres. But nothing of
the sort happened. Our conveyance, Con told me, as he
casually swung the steering wheel this way and that, was a
Nissan Patrol equipped with special heavy-duty suspension
and shock-absorbers. I had never realized what a wealth of
meaning could attach to such dull compounds as 'heavy-duty'
and 'shock-absorbers', and was grateful for the astonishing
resilience with which Con's brave Nissan penetrated the heart
and lungs of Hag's Glen and lifted us to about 800 ft (244 m)
before we got our boots mucky. Mind you, a hovercraft would
have been preferable.

Jokes aside, the drive was an exhilarating introduction to
the prospect that, ever more impressively, loomed before us: a
prospect to warm the vitals of any hill-walker who has not left
his soul with the toast and marmalade. Nowadays the floor of
Hag's Glen and the environs of its two lakes, Callee ('Hag's')
and Gouragh ('Goat's'), are too treelessly bare to tickle the
aesthetic palate. But six people lived up here little more than a
century ago and as we began our ascent Con turned and,
looking down, pointed out the dark, sad remnants of what had
once been a pine forest. Via contrast, the barren nature of the
glen enhances the visual impact of the mighty, magnificent
Reeks at its head. The heights look awesomely terminal and
the overall effect is breathtaking. Corrán Tuathail is such a
neat pyramid that it might have been sculpted. A child, asked
to draw a mountain, would produce a reasonable facsimile of
Ireland's summit. Left of it, to the south-east, is a saddle

approached by an obvious scar on the hillside, the greasy, rocky chute known as the Devil's Ladder.

'Hag's Glen is a beautiful valley,' Con said, 'and definitely the best approach for the first ascent, because the peak looks stunning. It often reminds me of a picture of K2. The other approach is the Coomlothair Glen horseshoe, which covers the three highest peaks in Ireland. There are three beautiful lakes in the Coomlothair Glen. Follow the river that drains the valley, go along by the lakes, and strike for the lowest point on the ridge between Caher and Corrán Tuathail. The going here is a very easy scramble up a gully that leads to the ridge. Then attain the summit of Corrán Tuathail, which is five minutes from the head of the gully. You can head over to the "hill of the sheep", Beanncaorach. Now, you may want to advise people that this is quite a narrow ridge. But all the difficulties can be turned by an obvious track on the western side of the ridge. Some of my colleagues spend a lot of time in the driving rain and wind on very high ground. I prefer to go into the valleys and gain the ridges up the back. The beauty of a lot of these mountain ranges lies very much in the valleys.'

Bases? We know about Killarney and Killorglin. 'My suggestion,' Con volunteered, 'would be to base yourself in a good bed and breakfast place in the Beaufort–Gap of Dunloe area. People who stay there pull back their blinds in the morning and see the hills, which is nice.'

Transport? 'Public transport doesn't exist. You want your own car. But it's a good country to hitch in and there may be a summer mini-bus service in the pipeline.'

The only transport we had now was that with which we were born. Legs. And I soon began to envy Con because his were a lot longer than mine. In the 1960s and 1970s there was a prominent and personable tennis professional called Cliff Drysdale, a charming man but vain enough to invite the teasing I sometimes inflicted on him. My come-uppance came at some tournament in Florida when, having thoughtfully inspected my sartorial compromise with the heat and humidity, Cliff concluded: 'Rex, if I had legs like yours I'm not sure I'd wear shorts.' For a decade or so I was a giant but somewhere in my early teens I stopped growing – while others carried on – and, hitting a lifetime peak of fractionally more than 5 ft 7 in, became Mr Below Average. As a cub reporter I covered an athletics meeting at which a blond superman (I looked him in the neck rather than the eyes) came over and introduced himself. At junior school, he reminded me, he had been a pallid, frail little target for bullying until I became his self-appointed minder and thumped anyone who bothered him. Ray Goddard was one of the lads who kept on growing when I stopped.

The serrated crests of Macgillycuddy's Reeks were mostly lost to view as ill-assorted Irish and English legs took us onwards and upwards. Essentially, we were no longer looking at hills. We were at grips with them. At least, our boots were. But there was an enchanting backward panorama of the glen, the lakes and the eastern heights of the Reeks. Our winding, westward ascent towards the ridge between Corrán Tuathail and Beanncaorach was no easy stroll. One seldom enjoyed the luxury of putting one foot in front of the other. Above the other, yes. Because that climb was more consistently steep and strenuous than the subsequent challenges of Ben Nevis, Snowdon and Scafell Pike. True, I was better prepared for those. But a clinometer, or the contour lines on a decent map, would confirm that Corrán Tuathail was the most arduous task. Con was patient and caring in adjusting his pace to mine. He also took charge of the camera and sporadically, while waiting, pressed the button to ensure that there would be a pictorial record of my travail. Too old to be embarrassed, I sent some of the prints to my brother, my hill-walking companion of forty-odd years earlier. Don's response from Toronto included this comment:

'It looked as though the little legs were getting a bit of a hammering on the way up. You appeared to be doing a sort of all-fours scramble, with hat askew and an "Oh, bloody hell!"

expression. A lot different from the debonair "nothing-to-it" shots on the way down.'

That was fair comment. The joke about rubbing my nose in it recoiled on me, particularly when Con gently introduced a little rock-climbing (There won't be any more, I promise you'). It was a trivial pitch, no more than 12 ft, and would be classified as 'easy' only because there is no more shamefully frivolous classification. Any reasonably active old lady would take it in her stride. Well, maybe two or three strides. So I was careless and, in yanking myself up, tweaked a muscle in the drinking arm. No matter. That muscle was engaged in the lightest of duties for the rest of the day. But it had a ruinous effect on my golf for a week or two. Would you believe a Stableford round of fifteen points?

That little incident was too trifling to merit comment at the time but, nevertheless, was instructive. Out of condition and getting on in years (though flaccid muscles can afflict us at any age), I had prepared the legs for Corrán Tuathail but had forgotten about the arms; and any hill-walker who goes high must expect some rock-scrambling, an exercise in which the arms and hands not only serve as support and as aids to balance, but may modestly reinforce the cause of upward propulsion. So the relevant muscles and sinews need to be in moderately good trim.

When toning up for any kind of physical challenge one should never forget fundamentals. One of Cliff Drysdale's most popular contemporaries was Bob Carmichael. 'Nails' (he had formerly been a carpenter) was a burly man with a doom-laden voice. Words rumbled a long way through hidden hollows before they emerged from the uppermost caverns. You could hear them coming. 'Nails' was good enough to reach the 1970 Wimbledon quarter-finals but the tournament on which he set his heart was the 1967 French championships. For two weeks he trained with Roy Emerson, an experience that would have put most men into intensive care for a while. 'Nails' ran, exercised, practised – but was beaten in straight sets in the first round by a Japanese whose name was hardly a rumour. 'I'd never been so fit and I had a good draw,' the dejected Australian told me later, 'but I couldn't play . . .'

In other words his otherwise diligent preparation had missed out on the fundamentals: a sharpening programme of match-play. Between us, you and I could recount a host of other examples illustrating the importance of attention to detail.

Light conversation and, in my case, heavy breathing punctuated our advance into the first of those 'three interesting hanging corries' to which Con had referred in our original phone call. He pointed out a rock-climbing route he had pioneered: a slanting, overhanging crack in a crag known as 'The Black Stacks'. Gouragh, the lake at the foot of these western Reeks, became a smaller component of the expanding panorama as we gained height via damp herbage and scattered slabs and outcrops. 'The rock is Old Red Sandstone,' Con explained, 'of the same period as the Torridon range in Scotland. The foldings in that period were all east-west. These were individually carved ice coombs which joined in the main valley.' We scrambled up wet rock between a waterfall and a massively intimidating pillar of stone which Con identified as Stumpīndubh, 'The Black Stump'. Hereabouts we were picking our way through a geological jungle.

'This is an accident zone,' Con said. 'In my role as leader of the rescue team I come across a lot of accidents.' He nodded towards the depths left of us, to the south: 'An English climber was lost down there. It was months before he was found. These are the best hills in Ireland but Corrán Tuathail can be more serious, more dangerous, than any of the three peaks in the UK when they are climbed by the tourist routes. It's so remote, isolated. There are no clearly defined footpaths or way-markings, no footbridges. The rivers are not deep but they're prone to flash flooding – like yesterday morning. On the other hand the Devil's Ladder, a scramble up an eroded scree gully, is the only steep bit of the easy route.'

He indicated a huge buttress rising sharply on our left, towards the summit. This, decidedly, was anything but easy. It accommodated what Con described as 'three classic climbing routes – from "difficult" to "very severe"'. I had never before seen any recognized climbs on which rock pitches were so abundantly interspersed with greasy greenstuff: a side-salad, so to speak.

The morning was grey but clear. One felt, accurately as it turned out, that the rain had not really stopped but had merely paused for a few hours. High above us, on the confining walls of those deep coombs, black-faced sheep were wandering about in places where many a man would fear to tread. Tilting his head back, Con had his eyes on them, watchful for those tending to stray from grass to crags. From time to time he cupped his hands to his mouth and, as if directing a sheepdog to urgent duties, gave voice to echoing bellows that rang round the hills. It seemed to work, too. The sheep mostly turned back towards the grass. The mountain rescue team and the sheep-farmers had much in common, he said, in their attachment to the Reeks and their intimate knowledge of the devilishly awkward terrain. They sometimes worked together and he had often been amazed by the surefooted ease with which wellington-booted farmers strolled about on dodgy slabs.

'Up to forty sheep a year can be lost on the rocks, through falling.'

What was the form, I asked, if sheep lounging about in dangerously tight spots could not or would not respond to his calls?

'I'll tell the farmer when I get back and he'll come up with a dog. Or it may be me, with a rope.'

Later, after our descent to the valley, Con identified two slowly moving dots high on the skyline as farmer and dog, and his mind was at rest. At heart he had never left the sheep-farming community of his childhood. He knew the value of sheep and the need to care for them.

The hanging corries, he said, were Coimin Iochtar (lower),

Coimin Lár (middle) and Coimin Uachtar (upper). A coimin is
a common pasturage. I did the translations later, with the help
of an Irish dictionary. At the time I did not want to bother Con
with too many questions and, in any case, was too heavily
engaged to mess about with notebook or tape recorder any
more than was necessary. Those corries, each self-contained,
were delightful in their variety but the first two made no
distinctive impression on the memory except for such striking
features as 'The Black Stacks', 'The Black Stump', and what
looked like man-made arches embedded in a cliff: an extraordinary example of rock folding under pressure. Otherwise I
was preoccupied with lifting 11 st 6 lb – plus boots, clothing
and rucksack – up that wet, relentlessly steep jumble of stone
and grass. This had to be done with care, to avoid undue stress
on the assorted elements of ageing legs. It would have been
damned annoying had the mission been aborted because of a
ricked ankle, or whatever.

Our oblique ascent towards the ridge that links Corrán
Tuathail to Beanncaorach, a ridge tantalizingly hidden beyond
a series of high corners, was slow but steady. On a gigantic
scale it was rather like climbing the crumbling, winding steps
of some ruined, weed-infested church tower. There was a
growing sense of being walled into a silent seclusion, always
benign, by the green and grey heights that soared around us.
That sense of benign seclusion culminated in the third hanging
corrie, Uachtar, a deeply intimate, enchanted hollow. The
original Landscape Architect decided that any man who got up
there deserved repose and refreshment for the soul. Local
mountain men know Coimin Uachtar as 'the inner sanctuary'.
Imagine an immense cavity – a much magnified compromise
between cup, bowl and funnel – in the crust of Kerry. Except
for the narrow entrance from below (which might well have
borne some such sign as 'Private – Staff Only'), steep banks
and crags rose all around us for maybe 600 ft (183 m). There
was no sound except for the softly reverberating calls of ravens
and choughs; no movement except for the lazily grazing sheep

scattered about the heights. And resting blissfully at the bottom of this massive hole in the hill was a charming pool that in the Lake District would be classified as a tarn. 'It's the highest corrie lake in Ireland: 2,300 ft,' said Con. The latest map suggests that the figure may be 2,400 ft (732 m) but in the presence of bewitchment one cannot be bothered with the small change of statistics.

This was a place where one could be alone without being lonely. In different circumstances I might contentedly have taken a leaf out of the Rip Van Winkle story and dreamed away the afternoon. But Con, ever mindful of my appointment at the airport and the stern leg-work to be done in the mean-time, directed my attention to the exit. This was a fork to the left up the equivalent of a huge escalator which had been out of action for so long that Nature had reclaimed it, clothing the grating with grass and scattered rocks. That seemingly inter-minable climb was not what I needed at the time and knocked out most of the stuffing left in me. Aware that I was just about knackered, Con called on the familiar stick-and-carrot routine ('Let 'em catch up but don't let 'em stop'). It had been used on me before and in youth I had used it on others. The routine consists of the leader moving well ahead, then waiting until the led joins him – at which point the leader instantly resumes the advance and thus frustrates desperate hopes for a breather.

Conversation was now minimal but from time to time I plaintively asked Con a jocular question that used to be a stock jest in the pre-computer days when journalists dictated long articles by phone. In full flow, an imminently off-duty copy-taker with a train to catch sometimes interjected: 'Is there much more of this?' The enquiry became a popular catchphrase and put-down, particularly when some long-winded raconteur was exceeding the limits of reasonable tolerance. Physically, that long haul out of Coimin Uachtar was certainly exceeding the limits of reasonable tolerance.

All bad things come to an end one way or another, and we finally set foot on the ridge. At which point my dashing young captain, who did not want the geriatric midget to die on him, decided that we could pause for a minute or two. Possibly he wanted to find out if, having finally assumed an upright position, I would maintain it or buckle at the knees. Turning for a last look at the plunging depths behind us, I asked:

'Does that bloody nightmare have a name? If not, I have a few suggestions...'

Con grinned. He knew the kind of suggestions I had in mind.

'O'Shea's Gully,' he said.

Now, until that moment I had good feelings about the O'Sheas, having been married to one for almost forty years. Maybe the clan had been saving up some suffering for me, concentrating all of it into the climb out of Coimín Uachtar on that memorable October day. The gully is believed to have taken its name from some sandal-shod religious, a Brother O'Shea, who used to clamber up and down it in an age long gone. Goodness knows why, unless it was a penance. Or it may be that whenever he had a lot on his mind he craved a few hours of peaceful contemplation amid the serenity of 'the inner sanctuary', a prize that would just about have justified the hard labour of winning it. Perhaps I exaggerate. If so, put it down to the fact that the position of O'Shea's Gully exaggerates its severity. This grassier, lumpier equivalent of Brown Tongue (the direct route from Wasdale Head to the Scafells) occurs not at the beginning of a stiff climb, when the batteries are fully charged, but towards the end of it, when the legs and lungs have already taken a beating. In boxing, the punch that puts a man down for the count is not always the hardest that has hit him. Often, it just happens to be one punch more than he can take.

What was left of Corrán Tuathail was powdered with snow. 'The first showing of winter,' Con said, as we lingered on the ridge. 'Six weeks earlier than last year. I feel good when I see that. The mountains look best dressed in white.'

Now, one would not dispute mountain craft with a man

who has spent his life on the hills, but this was an aesthetic judgement and I could not agree with it. True, there is a lovely elegance of line about mountains clothed in the purity of fresh snow, just as there was about those legendary Grecian ladies in flowing white chitons. True, snow enhances the challenge confronting winter mountaineers and gives them a thrill. But all that is, for me, outweighed by what is missing: the diversity of the landscape's detail, the delicate variations of colour and shade. One should go to the mountains when such visual pleasures are naked, not when they are covered up. Do beautiful women look best when veiled?

Skiers are a breed apart and can be discounted. Skiing is more of a sport than a recreation. Its devotees go up slowly for the exhilaration of going down fast and need mechanical assistance in both directions. That is an alien concept to hill-walkers. Equally, it would probably be a waste of time trying to convince a skier that one should go to the Alps when the flowers are in bloom, the birds are singing, and the mountain streams are dancing in the sunlight and making music as they chuckle towards the lowlands.

But life would be much less interesting if we all had the same preferences. Divergent opinions are stimulating, educational. They encourage tolerance. Stubbornness should not be confused with determination, any more than an open mind should be mistaken for infirmity of will. The closed mind indicates a retreat from reason and an advance towards bigotry. The former German Chancellor, Konrad Adenauer, put it neatly: 'If two people are always of the same opinion, they are generally not much good.'

In short, those who differ from us may be at least half-right. Every coin has two sides. There may have been people who thought Perry Como was a fidget. There may now be people who think Cilla Black and Jimmy Savile talk standard English; people who can watch Barry Humphries ('Edna Everage') without wincing on behalf of Australia; people who would like the Dimbleby brothers to take themselves more seriously; and people who regard traffic wardens and double-glazing salesmen as necessary components of civilized society. There are certainly people who think dignity comes out of a wardrobe in the form of a civilian 'uniform' and see no paradox in describing this or that as 'frightfully good', a comment best reserved for well-made horror movies.

Some of these beliefs could be harboured only by the unhinged but some could conceivably have a rational basis. And Con had a measure of logic in favouring snow-clad mountains. One could understand where he was coming from. But there are degrees of beauty; and mountains look even better without snow than with it.

Physically, the brief break did me no good. The last lap of the ascent, from the top of O'Shea's Gully to the summit, was like a wrecked staircase of stone. It seemed interminable. Weariness had shoved the brain into a neutral gear and, with sporadic stops for breathers, I was progressing in a posture some way between stoop and crouch. That was foolish. Con gently reminded me (there should have been no need) that the lungs work better if given room in which to function, that one should keep upright with the weight on the soles of the feet. Elementary. When the body feels like crumbling it is time for the mind to exercise its authority over matter: time to remember Kipling's advice about pushing on in spite of the fact that the engine room is ready for the scrapyard. All this was not the fault of Corrán Tuathail, steep though it is. The stress, almost distress, arose from the fact that a sexagenarian was inadequately prepared for such a tough climb. Most of you are younger and fitter. A more suitable challenge for me, taking to the hills again after a long lay-off, would have been some eminence in the Peak District or the Ochil Hills. But one benefit of tackling Corrán Tuathail first was that it knocked me into shape for the other ascents.

Suddenly there was nowhere to go but down. We had reached the summit of Ireland – and gravely shook hands as if something wonderful had happened. Maybe it had. There must have been moments when Con doubted whether I would make it to the top without a tow. The only gratifying feature of an otherwise feeble performance was that the idea of quitting had never occurred to me. Put that down to a bloody-minded streak that comes from the Yorkshire half of the family.

It is common enough to find the renowned peaks of our offshore islands furnished with a crude rock shelter and a trig point. But Corrán Tuathail is unique in my experience in that it is crowned by a huge cross, a reminder of Brother O'Shea and his kind and the faith they embraced. This is as it should be, because however vague one's religious perceptions may be it is impossible to feel closer to the Boss than when standing on the tip of a mountain after hours of slogging endeavour. It is at this point, too, that the authors of serious mountaineering books give us detailed descriptions of the vast panoramas spread before them. In our case the plain truth was that, except for each other and the cross and a mass of wet rock, we could see bugger all. At that height, on that day, the hill-fog was impenetrable. I recalled Con's comment that 'The beauty of a lot of these mountain ranges lies very much in the valleys'. There are many days when one sees more from the valleys than one does from the hills – from the misty summits, anyway. On such days, on such ascents to high altitudes, there comes a point on the contours at which the blinds are drawn, the world vanishes, and we are plunged into the silence of an intimate solitude. Coming down, it works the other way. In our case, happily, that point on the contours was not far from the top. The views from the ridges north-west and south-east of the peak were breathtaking in their extent and their charming diversity. We looked down on Con's attractive alternative route, the lake-studded Coomlothair Glen, and across Dingle Bay and the Kenmare River to the adjacent peninsulas. The hills of Kerry stretched before us in softly undulating folds to the wide backdrop of the Atlantic. The stillness and beauty of mountains and sea achieved a visual harmony that no words, no photographs, can ever capture: because it was not merely seen but felt, deep down, in that mysterious concept known, for want of a better word, as the spirit. Sutherland provides similar sensations but the hills of Kerry, less stark, were even more alluring. It is because of such prospects, and their effect on us, that mountains simply have to be climbed.

Con brought up the imminently relevant subject of the Devil's Ladder and asked how my knees were. His interest in the care and maintenance of shock-absorbers was not restricted to vehicles. The knees were in great shape, I told him, as we began the easy, hands-in-pockets descent towards the saddle, 2,400 ft (732 m) in height at the top of the Ladder. Out of prudence I refrained from adding that the rest of me felt a hell of a lot better now that the uphill part of the day was behind us: it might have given the man wild ideas had I even hinted that the invalid was beginning to fancy himself as an athlete. I had read and heard enough about the 500 ft (152 m) Devil's Ladder to assume that it was no place for softies (true enough) and might be sufficiently exposed (untrue) to test the nerves. 'Treacherous screes,' wrote Irvine Butterfield in *The High Mountains of Britain and Ireland*. This was reinforced in Harry Mulholland's *Guide to Ireland's 3000-foot Mountains*: 'Very steep and stony with a loose surface, especially after rain, and needs great care ... The climb down can be more trying than the climb up.' And Con, as you know, had described it as 'the only steep bit of the easy route', though this provided no comparative enlightenment because – without exerting the slightest stress on the muscle between the ears – I had tumbled to the fact that, so far, our itinerary had not impinged on anything that could be construed as an easy route.

Mistakenly, I was expecting a strenuously steep scramble down a big-rock scree slope. It would just be a question of how well the legs would take it – and how much one might have to demand from a dodgy forearm. But the legs were fine and the arms were never needed except in the cause of balance. Moreover, the gradient was moderate. I was grateful for that but at the same time a little disappointed. Mentally, I was geared for something much closer to the precipitous, which would have been exciting rather than worrying. Unless one is poised over a few hundred feet of air, the downhill stuff is not intimidating as long as one has a perch for a boot and a fistful of rock to hang on to. Anyway, the descent through a watery jumble of rocks and greenstuff was so simple, technically, that there was time to enjoy the lulling music of infant cascades streaming into the Ladder. And I had enough experience to know that such tasks are less jarring, less tiring, if treated with respectful patience. Be warned that patience is needed: the Devil's Ladder has a mischievous knack of suggesting that the bottom (or, if you are going the other way, the top) is closer than it actually is.

The only challenge left consisted of crossing a rushing torrent by the boulder-hopping method. Con's long legs were better designed for this than mine were and had a lot more spring in them. I needed a supportive hand. After that we had a gentle splosh back to the Nissan Patrol in light rain. It was as if somebody looking after the celestial drainage system was telling us: 'You've had your fun. Now I can get back to business.' We paused for what, in my case, may have been a last look at the spectacular pyramid of Corrán Tuathail. Con gave my morale a boost by suggesting that five hours was not a bad time for the trip, that in different company it had sometimes taken as much as eight hours. But he earnestly recommended that, as this was October, I should tackle the next assignment, Ben Nevis, as soon as possible. Fair enough. One had no intention of hanging about until the weather turned thoroughly nasty. All had conspired in our favour on Corrán Tuathail but note that without Con's guidance it would have been tricky to plot that confusing route from Lough Gouragh to 'the inner sanctuary' of Coimín Uachtar.

Back at the airport, I was panting for a beer but had no time for anything except the necessary chores of cleaning up and repacking the rucksack. Well, such sacrifices must be expected by those who climb Corrán Tuathail between breakfast in Killarney and supper in Midhurst. The long overdue beer slipped down during the crowded flight back. My companion turned out to be a nurse, by name O'Shea. 'Really?' I said. 'I married one. And did you know that on the highest mountain in Ireland there's this gully...'

One down. Three to go.

GLOSSARY

Irish maps are not yet as detailed as those of England, Scotland and Wales. Moreover, the language of Irish topography is confusing, with many variations in spelling. The Gaelic and English alphabets differ and the original cartographers were Englishmen translating and often corrupting an alien tongue. That is why Irish place names remain perplexing, though the muddle is gradually being sorted out. An additional problem is that the Irish tend to change the first one or two letters of a word according to the context. For all these reasons the following must be considered no more than a rough guide. In the text of this chapter I preferred the Irish version to the English wherever it made sense: a practice that will become increasingly prevalent.

Abhainn	River
Ard	High place
Barr	Top; point
Beag, Beaganna	Small
Binn, Beanna, Beann	Peak(s); cliff(s)
Buaic, Buaiceanna	Highest point(s)
Caher, Cahir, Cathair	Stone fort
Carracan or Creagan	Rocky eminence
Carraig	Rock
Cill, Kill	Church; monastic cell
Clais	Gully

Cnoc or Knock	Hill
Creig or Sceilg	Crag
Coire or Corrie	Deep, steep-sided hollow
Cruach	Stack; pile
Cuas	Cavity; recess
Dearg	Red
Droim or Iomaire	Ridge
Dubh	Black
Dun	Fort
Gleann	Glen; hollow
Lochan	Small lake
Lough, Loch, Linn	Lake
Mhor or Mor	Big
Mullach	Summit; high ground
Screathan	Scree
Sliabh	Mountain
Sruth	Stream
Tulach	Low hill

Scotland: Ben Nevis

4,406 ft (1,344 m)

Con Moriarty's plans for the winter included an Irish invasion of Nepal, which is well off for mountains that would make Corrán Tuathail look like a foothill and a tiddly one at that. His concern that I should tackle Ben Nevis quickly, in October rather than November, reinforced the obvious. It is no mind-bending exercise to work out that although hard-nosed mountaineers get a mad gleam in their eyes at the prospect of snow and ice and associated meteorological purgatory, hill-walkers should have the sense to stay away from all that. So I monitored the three-day weather forecast for 'The Ben' and its environs, waiting for a hint that the chore of driving there in a day might be rewarded by tolerable conditions for an ascent to the highest point on our offshore islands.

What was needed, in addition to an encouraging forecast, was a method of coping with such a long drive without falling asleep at the wheel or, at least, tiring to the point at which one would become a traffic hazard; not least, to the 18 cwt (915 kg) of traffic containing me. Driving to Rome and back, plus an assortment of other long-distance motoring excursions on the European mainland, had been all very well for leisurely holiday jaunts. Midhurst to Fort William in a day was something else. The prospect was more daunting than the slog up

69

Ben Nevis, which would be quicker in one sense if slower in another. So the brain cells were activated. It may be that so far you have been smart enough to avoid so many hours at the wheel. But circumstances, or some flight of fancy, can confront anyone with just such a task at any time. Because my findings were to be justified, you may want to know what they were.

The route itself was straightforward. The problem was the distance between each end of it, which I estimated to be 550 miles. A stress-free average speed – including regular breaks to refresh eyes, mind and body – would be 40 m.p.h. At that rate the drive should take thirteen hours and three-quarters: tough, but not ridiculously so. The mileage was in fact 565 and the time thirteen and a half hours. These figures were close enough to the estimates to be gratifying, but the timing would not have been so accurate but for the self-imposed disciplines diligently observed *en route*. Point one: this was a long-distance run, not a sprint, so it would be silly to sap nerves and concentration by rushing. Point two: as a further means of averting tiredness I would drive for no more than two and a half hours without a break and would adjust the length of a break according to that 40 m.p.h. average. For example, having covered 80 miles in an hour and thirty-five minutes one would have twenty-five minutes to spare for a rest. Point three: as further precautions against the risk of drowsiness, there would be no alcohol and no more than light refreshments (a vegetable or fruit salad rather than a cooked meal). Point four: as a last aid to alertness, one would sporadically indulge in such sedentary exercises as turning eyes and neck from side to side and flexing the shoulders and toes.

That was the programme, and it worked.

How odd it was that one should go to so much trouble, driving almost the full length of Britain, to climb a mountain previously ignored. In addition to a solo hill-walking trip to Sutherland, we must have passed Ben Nevis more than a dozen times without giving it much thought. That was in the course of family holidays: at Inveraray, where the hotel's wine waiter took the tables in strict rotation and tended to reach ours at the same time as the dessert; at Perth, where our Sheltie, at full speed in pursuit of an Afghan hound loping along in first gear, lost ground so quickly that he seemed to be going backwards; and at Glenfinnan, where Charlie Macfarlane, in full highland gear, kept us waiting for breakfast and dinner while he played the bagpipes and did a slow march up and down the panelled hall. Such engaging trivia occupied our minds far more than Ben Nevis did. It was simply an intermittent, looming presence, imagined rather than seen: because its vast bulk was hidden behind the subsidiary heights of Meall an t-Suidhe, 2,322 ft (708 m) high, which many casual tourists mistake for 'The Ben' itself. We had made only one brief stop in Fort William, but that was of lasting benefit. In replenishing the provisions we were introduced to the bridie, which is less outrageous and more palatable than the haggis and, even in its anglicized forms, has remained a family favourite.

You may reasonably wonder how any enthusiastic hill-walker could have a mental block concerning Ben Nevis. The deficiency arose from ignorance of the mountain's possibilities and misconceptions about its reputation. There would be no point in dissembling. There seldom is. Honesty is the best policy, because that way one is never found out. Well, not often. Having missed a school prizegiving because of a date, I told the truth when interrogated by the 'head' next morning and was awarded a rigorous caning. But honesty, like most other principles, is not worth much unless it remains rock solid when tested. And the only reputation that matters is dictated by conscience rather than the judgement of others. This very subject cropped up the other day in conversation with a golf chum.

'I've tried to acquire a bad reputation,' I said, 'because it must be more fun to live down to a bad reputation than live up to a good one. But I don't seem to be cut out for the role.'

'Don't worry,' he responded. 'You're making up for it on the golf course...'

To get back to Ben Nevis, one's apathy had roots of a sort. For a start (and not a good start), take its name. Alternative translations of the Gaelic provide such unwelcome hints as 'malicious' and 'head in the clouds'. Nobody disputes the fact that the upper slopes attract appalling weather. Moreover Ben Nevis is, as mountains go, a massively uninteresting lump – lacking the elegant lines of, for example, Corrán Tuathail or Snowdon. Finally, much that has been written about 'The Ben' implies that the tourist track is an interminable bore and that alternative routes to the top demand climbing skills beyond the reasonable capacity of hill-walkers. These implications are not exactly nonsense but they are misleading, merely flirting with the truth. For much of its course the winding tourist track is spiced with variety and most of it commands spectacular views. The monotonously consistent gradient is explained by the route's origins as a pony track to the observatory that functioned on the summit until 1904. As for alternative ascents, Ben Nevis lacks Snowdon's enviable wealth of intermediate, moderately demanding routes for the hill-walker. But options are available, carrying no risk of damaging consequences.

Before checking all that, one first had to get to Fort William; and a promising forecast was soon forthcoming. I put down the phone and joined wife and mackerel and Norfolk terrier in the dining-room.

'It's all systems go. I'll be off to Fort William in the morning.'

'What time?'

'About six.'

'Don't wake me up.'

At 6.03 a.m. I was on the road. The time mattered because it was relevant to the mental arithmetic that, throughout the drive, would keep one's average speed hovering at or above 40 m.p.h. Darkness and mist eventually gave way to a grey, reluctant dawn – and the congenial company of the 'Today' team on Radio Four. Nowadays the BBC's liaison with the

English language is often uneasy, even when programmes are scripted. A typically amusing example was a weather forecast that referred to 'a depression over the north of Scotland, which is moving slowly to the north-east.' This raised visions of colliding land masses, with panic spreading all the way from Bergen to the Lofoten Islands as Norwegians digested the news that a chunk of Scotland was coming their way. But declining standards of literacy, grammar and pronunciation are not peculiar to the BBC, and such programmes as 'Today' do cast a little light into the gathering linguistic dusk. There is just one complaint to be made about these good companions. They have an infuriating habit of prefacing long questions to inter- viewees with the words 'Very briefly ...' That could be remedied in a week if those afflicted with the 'very briefly' virus had to pop a pound into a charity box every time they allowed a symptom of the virus to become audible.

After two hours and 102 miles I was feeling perky but, with an effort of will, took a break anyway. It would become increasingly important to stop before rather than after the onset of tiredness: to avoid the condition rather than feel a pressing need to recover from it. Rain washed the car as the A272 was succeeded by the A34 and the M6 in turn. At 200 miles came a second coffee break and, via the voice of the waitress, a memory. Almost half a century earlier our family of four often cycled from Sheffield to Wincanton and back, renewing bonds with the Somerset half of the clan, and the changing accents *en route* were fascinating. What a wonderful range of accents and dialects there is on this island of ours, even the English bit of it. My father could never quite come to terms with the Somerset tongue and, many years on, Bruton relatives playfully teased my wife with a reference to 'tiddies' (potatoes) and the question 'Where be it to?'. An advantage of a childhood split between Somerset and Yorkshire was that it left one attuned to both accents and capable of telling a favourite after-dinner story. This concerns a lady, a city type, who stopped her car when driving down a Somerset lane and addressed a farm labourer who, pipe in mouth, was leaning on a gate and looking at the day.

'Excuse me,' she said. 'Can you tell me why that cow over there has no horns?'

The labourer examined his interrogator and the animal in question, drew meditatively on his pipe, and decided to have some fun. You'll have to imagine the accent...

'Well, ma'am,' he responded, 'some cows have the buds taken out when they're babies, because 'orns can do a lot of 'arm with just a flick of the 'ead or when the cows are just shovin' each other. Some cows don't get no 'orns until they're seven years old and some don't get no 'orns until they've calved. But that beast over there ain't got no 'orns because it's a bloody 'orse.'

The halfway mark was estimated to be 275 miles. That figure was passed at 12.10 p.m. and celebrated with a salad and apple juice at Forton, which was little more than a rumour (even in Lancashire) until its name was applied to a service station on the M6. A beer, maybe two, would have slipped down easily. But there were compensations for abstinence: the 40 m.p.h. average remained intact, even after that leisurely lunch break; the weather was brightening; and the landscape was acquiring some interesting bumps, hints of the Cumbrian scenery to come. On the eastern flank of the Lake District the sky was a tantalising contrast between sunshine and low clouds – except in the vicinity of Shap, where mist and rain are so prevalent that one takes them for granted. This lofty and lonely one-street village has been inhabited since prehistoric times, so we must assume that either the climate has changed or our remote ancestors were barmy. A few years earlier I turned off here to join some chums for a day's hill-walking around Haweswater, which swallowed the village of Mardale during a transformation from lake into reservoir. We did Striding Edge and Helvellyn, too, and in the process collected a couple of strays who had got up but were uncertain how to get down.

Diversions to Gretna and Lockerbie failed in their optimistic purpose. Tracking down a filter to fit a compact camera is no easy task. But it was good to be back among the rolling hills of the Border country and the relentless drive towards Iceland was illuminated by a spectacular late-afternoon cloudscape as sunshine and clouds played games together and kept changing the look of the landscape like a couple of scene-shifters. The Glasgow ring road provided no food for the soul, merely a menu, a promise of the aesthetic feast that is Loch Lomond – especially at such times as late October, when the narrow, winding road along the western shore is not cluttered with distracting tourist traffic. Much of this tends to gather in the vicinity of Luss, a pretty village with rose-heavy cottages. No matter how gregarious we may be, people *en masse* blunt our sensuous appreciation of such environments as Loch Lomond. But I was lucky in my timing: there was hardly a soul about and conditions were perfect for what Con Moriarty had described, in the context of Kerry, as the 'light show'. The scenery was already familiar but had never looked as charming.

The marriage of mountains and water is most harmonious in the hour or so before sunset. The visual impact of that clear, sunny autumn evening (raising hopes for the morrow) was breathtaking, exploring every nuance of lighting and colour – greens and blues and browns, even a few touches of pink. All that, plus the diversity of curving lines in the immense land-scape, was softly illuminated by the imminent gloaming. The beauty was so subtle yet so striking that it challenged belief, vividly though it lingers in the memory, the eyes of the mind. Mind you, the highland cattle – munching, eyes down – were too familiar with the art gallery to be interested in buying tickets. All they wanted to do was eat.

The loch is dominated by Ben Lomond at 3,192 ft (974 m) and the rugged profiles of a formidably heavyweight supporting cast. Loch Lomond has thirty islands and is Britain's biggest freshwater lake. It is about 23 miles (37 km)

long and, at its widest, measures 5 miles (8 km). The surface
covers some 25 square miles (65 square kilometres). The loch's
ambience is so evocative that one can easily picture early
missionaries pottering about, clans sorting one another out,
troops on the march, cattle drovers and, more recently, starry-
eyed poets and hard-eyed mountaineers. The place abounds in
history and legend. There is a good tale about the Norwegian
king who, in 1263, cruised up the Clyde and Loch Long and –
eager to invade Scotland more deeply – somehow had his longships hauled over the hill from Arrochar into Loch Lomond.
He was to come unstuck at the battle of Largs but give the man
ten out of ten for initiative. Norwegian longships in Loch
Lomond. Now there's a thought ... A more enduring
inhabitant of the loch is a rare sub-species of whitefish, the
herring-like powan: closely related to the pollan found in
Lough Neagh (Northern Ireland), which is six times the size of
Loch Lomond. It could be that as the glaciers on our offshore
islands receded a few freshwater lakes, accommodating remote
ancestors of the powan or pollan, were a connected series
stretching from Loch Lomond to Lough Neagh. The geography
has changed but the fish remain: bizarre reminders of a long-
ago age that can only be imagined or deduced, because it left
no written records.

You will have gathered that the drive up Loch Lomond was
both pleasing and stimulating. But by this time one was
becoming impatient to see the words 'Fort William' on a road
sign. That happened at Crianlarich, a former Roman outpost
that matured into a road and rail junction and, in season, a
tourist centre for those with the sense to walk or climb in high
places. On Rannoch Moor the mountains looked awfully
threatening, partly because dusk exaggerated the darker
possibilities of the black bulks to the west. This is Munro
country. The name has immortalized Sir Hugh Munro, who
tabulated every Scottish peak that exceeds 3,000 ft (914 m)
and thus kindled fires in generations of climbers who wanted
to get up the lot. As there are 277 Munros (plus 240 subsidiary

'tops' that qualify in terms of height but are not regarded as genuine Munros) this is not the kind of ambition that can be satisfied in one mad flurry of activity.

Rannoch Moor is no place to run out of petrol or to be afflicted by a mechanical breakdown, especially at night. True, it is crossed by a road and by the Glasgow to Fort William railway – built on massed tree trunks so that the line would not sink into the bog. The moor is not the most isolated wilderness in Scotland but has a dreadful air of desolation. Studded with lochans (mini-lochs), Rannoch Moor is essentially a peaty marsh on a granite base. It used to be a heavily wooded segment of the ancient Caledonian Forest. Now it is totally bad news except for the likes of geologists, botanists and those toying with a death wish. You can guess how I felt – having spent thirteen hours on the road and traversed Rannoch Moor in advancing dusk – when a shadow darker than the rest leapt from the gloom onto the road immediately ahead, at the top of Glen Coe. Did I brake? You bet I did. Was the imagination working overtime? You bet it was. But this was no ghost of a Macdonald fleeing from that horrendous 1692 massacre: merely a magnificently antlered deer hastening to some urgent appointment in the night.

The deep defile of Glen Coe is awesome in daylight and even more so when the headlights, on full beam, are piercing a blackness that suggests an almost human capacity for malevolence. The flanking heights are renowned among climbers but 'the glen of weeping' (or 'tears') has a wider notoriety because of the late seventeenth century's politics and feuds and their bloody consequences. Jacobites were at grips with Hanoverians, highlanders with lowlanders, and clans with clans. The overall scene was thoroughly nasty. The pertinent Glen Coe story is best told by Scots, especially by those Macdonald raconteurs with a gift for doom-laden thespian drama.

Highlanders were reluctant to accept the joint rule of William and Mary in place of that exercised by James II (James VII of Scotland). The rebellious clans were ordered to take an

oath of allegiance to the crown by the last day of 1691.
Macdonald of Glen Coe was the most tardy of the chiefs but
when he heard that everybody else had toed the line he decided
that the better part of valour was discretion. Unfortunately he
left it late and neglected to do his homework. In what he
thought was the nick of time, on 31 December, he turned up at
Fort William – where nobody was empowered to accept his
oath of allegiance. The right place for that was Inveraray, the
seat of the Campbell clan. But roaming about Scotland in mid-
winter was an arduously slow task, particularly for the elderly,
and Macdonald did not get to Inveraray until 6 January. His
oath was officially accepted but chicanery ensued, down in
Edinburgh. The middle layers of Scottish government were
heavily influenced by Campbells and their adherents, who had
nothing but bad thoughts about Macdonalds. Instead of
letting the Macdonalds off the hook, why not make an
example of them, to quell the simmering resentment of clans
still in sympathy with the Stuart cause? Consequently
documentary evidence of Macdonald's oath of allegiance was
cunningly mislaid – and a treacherous scheme of slaughter
malignantly took shape.

On 1 February some 120 to 130 Campbell soldiers turned
up in Glen Coe, seeking billets on the grounds that the Fort
William barracks were full. The highland code imposed the
duty of hospitality and for twelve nights and days the
Macdonalds entertained the redcoats. Meantime the
Campbells surreptitiously reconnoitred the glen so that
soldiers could be posted to cover every escape route. Before
dawn on 13 February, at about four o'clock, the sleeping
Macdonalds were brutally killed – shot or butchered. The
carnage was merciless. Men, women and children, octoge-
narians and babies: all were indiscriminately murdered. Those
who tried to flee through the darkness and the snow were slain
on the passes or died of exposure. That noble valley became an
abattoir, with getting on for forty corpses. Glen Coe, by no
means a built-up area, was depopulated. Then the Campbells

burned the cottages and made off with the cattle and sheep the dead had so recently been tending.

The callous savagery of that winter morning's massacre inevitably had repercussions. The king and the Scottish parliament passed the buck among themselves. Nobody would accept responsibility and it was difficult to nail down the guilty. Three years later parliament ruled that the killings were unlawful and the secretary of state was sacked. And half a century after that, the clans were still so militant in their support for the Stuarts that Bonnie Prince Charlie's invading army got as far as Derby. In 1747 the clan system was stripped of its legal status. The associated social structure and cultural traditions declined but were revived in a romantic if diluted form by the increasing popularity – from the nineteenth century onwards – of those flamboyant genuflexions to a proud past, the tartan kilt and plaid. The tartans, the pipes, and the terrible details of what happened on 13 February 1692, have done no harm to Glen Coe's tourist business. But even now, three hundred years on (just nine or ten generations), it remains a social *faux pas* to introduce a Campbell to a Macdonald. Scots have long memories and, often, short fuses.

All that remained of the drive was an easy last lap along the shore of Loch Linnhe to the largest town left on Britain's north-western coast, Fort William. This was formerly known as Maryburgh but was renamed to honour king rather than queen. The original earthen fort, built to suit Cromwell's purposes, remained vulnerable to rebellious highlanders and was reconstructed in stone. A link in a chain of garrisons, it resisted Jacobite attacks in 1715 and 1746 but was demolished in 1884 to make room for the West Highland Railway. Fort William and its environs were later to acquire an aluminium factory, a whisky distillery, a pulp mill, and an enviable reputation as a tourist and shopping centre and the hub of a variety of transport routes. When approaching the town from Midhurst or anywhere else in England one has to drive the length of Fort William on the A82 (the road to Inverness) before turning right, into Glen Nevis, at Nevis Bridge. As you do so, note the proximity of the Nevis Bank Hotel, a popular watering-hole among walkers and climbers, and the Glenlochy Guest House, which is modern and well run but a little too neat and antiseptic to suit my predilection for the informal. One can easily slot into first-class hotels or inns full of noise and smoke and dogs, but the in-between places tend to be too suburban in character. *Chacun à son goût.*

Fort William was a welcome sight, especially at the reasonable hour of 7.30 p.m. Before checking in at the guest house and testing the resources of the bar at the Nevis Bank, it was necessary to touch base and make arrangements for the morrow. Base was the Glen Nevis Centre, next door to the youth hostel. Red Indians have (or had) a tradition that the gods, compensating for hereditary deficiencies, are kind to the sick in mind. That could explain why my preliminary planning for this first close look at 'The Ben', the telephoned enquiries about this and that, had somehow focused on Heather and Scot Gunn. This charming couple built up the Glen Nevis Centre from scratch and, quietly and without fuss, have a knack of making every visitor feel special. For them, a fresh face at the door is not so much a customer as a welcome new acquaintance. They have a dream: paying their way in the world by helping others, mainly like-minded enthusiasts for the diverse pleasures of ben and glen. So they are happy living where they want to live, doing what they want to do, and raising two sons who – given such a domestic and geographic environment – need no formal tuition in the necessary components of a good life.

The Gunns are the kind who would rather listen than talk, who would rather give than receive. They are not concerned with making a fortune but nor are they running a charity, though the ambience around them sometimes suggests that the Glen Nevis Centre is a Citizens' Advice Bureau for the mountain-minded. There has to be a delicate balance between principle and practice – between, on the one hand, the Gunns' kindness and their distaste for overt merchandizing and, on the other, the need to sell a product. That product covers a range of equipment and goods which are either hired out or sold. The equipment on hire is mainly rucksacks, boots and water-proofs but extends to bicycles, maps, crampons, ice axes and even slings – those baby-carriers that are slung round the neck (the mother's, not the baby's). The sales side includes packed lunches, meals on the spot, and arts and crafts: exclusively local, as distinct from the commercial souvenirs displayed in gift shops.

Scot first saw the light of day on the northern edge of Sheffield, at Ecclesfield (four miles from my own birthplace at what in those days might reasonably have been described as the roughest bit of the roughest end of the city). When he was seven the family moved to Wales and later the Gunns settled in Liverpool. 'At seventeen I came to Glen Nevis with my parents – who ran the youth hostel – and my brother. I worked with them for thirteen summers and got ideas for this business, through people asking for things that were not available. The Ben's my bread and butter. People wanting to hire equipment. We do the whole deal. They can come and hire boots and waterproofs and buy a packed lunch. Then they come back and want a cup of tea and a snack. There's real continuity in that you warn them what to expect and get a nice feedback later. We're both avid listeners...'

The Gunns were married in 1972. 'Heather's from Ottawa. She stayed at the youth hostel while travelling, climbed the Ben with my advice, took me out for a beer in Fort William that night, and never went back to Ottawa. She's been home since, to see the folks. I was a forestry contractor for about a dozen years. My brother, Heather and myself planted trees for private forestry companies. All over Scotland. We planted 250 acres a season, about 250,000 trees. That's where the money came from to start this business. Summer at the hostel, winter and spring planting trees ... The rest of the time I just enjoyed myself on the hills. I'm not a technical man and don't always feel the need to go to the top of the hill. But I like ridge-walking, easy gullies, a little bit of snow.'

There was no Glen Nevis Centre until the Gunns had it built ('You should have seen us in 1987 in our little tin shed, with a tiny sign outside: Cycle Hire'). The Centre was opened at Easter 1989. Its facilities have already been detailed. The arts and crafts section is intensely personal. 'My brother does the oil paintings, the tee-shirts, and the black and white sketches for the postcards. Heather and I do the leather work and Heather makes leather jewellery and accessories. Our main source of income is the food. The first year we did no food and were not going to make it. But as soon as I saw that side of the market ... Now, it supports the rest. We serve hot and cold food twelve hours a day, seven days a week. On holiday, every way you turn you have to spend something and mostly all you get back is the raw product. But the West Highlands are famous for hospitality. We're offering a service and genuine friendliness. I don't want to lose the personal contact. Every person coming through the door should feel that they've been noticed and acknowledged. There's no reason why we can't make a living here and still maintain our standards. It's just a matter of balance – and hard work.'

All that is, if you like, the continuing love story of a lad from Sheffield and a lass from Ottawa who had a dream – and made it happen. And Heather went up Glen Nevis as just another overseas tourist...

The proximity of Ben and Glen is a mixed blessing. Each distracts attention from the other, though the allure of the highest mountain in the British Isles gives it an edge over one of the longest, loveliest, most fascinating glens in Scotland. Granted enough time and energy one can, of course, explore both – most sensibly, the glen first, as a physical warm-up for the icing on the cake, the steeper challenge of an ascent to the summit. Because of age or infirmity or the company of young children, many must make do without the icing. But the glories of the glen, a deep glacial valley, are enough in themselves: for picnickers, botanists, ornithologists, students of human and natural history, and those nature-lovers who simply appreciate beauty in all its diversity of scale and detail without feeling any pressing need to classify and analyse what they see. The glen cuts round the western and southern flanks of the Ben Nevis massif but its gradient is moderate. The uppermost car park (by no means the end of the glen, which can and should be penetrated more deeply via footpaths) is less than 500 ft (152 m) above sea level. This is not a lot for a drive that, from the creature comforts of Nevis Bridge, covers more than six miles (roughly ten kilometres). It follows that, whether one is on foot or at the wheel, reaching the heart of Glen Nevis is no big deal.

The lower section has to some extent been developed for the benefit of visitors, without being ruined. The immense span of the glen's human history is probably best exemplified, if you put your imagination to work, by the remnants of Dun Deardail, up in Nevis Forest about a mile due south of the Glen Nevis Centre and youth hostel. Built about two thousand years ago, Dun Deardail was originally a fort made of stone, wood and peat – fused together when the place was burnt. The consequence was a glassy appearance that induced cartographers to label the relic 'vitrified fort'. The glen became home to a branch of the Cameron clan and the chief had his headquarters at Dun Dige, behind the youth hostel and the Gunns' enterprise. If you have a taste for that sort of thing there is an ancient graveyard at Ach nan Con ('dogs' field'), east of Dun Deardail on the opposite side of the river. And tucked among crags across the water from the top car park is the small, well-concealed Samuel's Cave, where a few women and a child hid from government redcoats during the 1745 rebellion. But the hunters had more luck than the hunted, who were robbed and raped. Farther up the glen is the old Steall Cottage, now a Lochaber Mountaineering Club hut, and other vestiges of little, long-gone farming communities.

There is no danger of drought in this area and Nature's generous irrigation arrangements splash out in a big way at three spots along the Nevis. The first, just after the river swings to the east, is a double cataract known as the Lower Falls. The adjacent Polldubh ('Black Pool') Crags, popular among rock-climbers, are a contrasting visual bonus: especially when the finger-and-toe brigade are at grips with the enemy. The second, north of the car park at the top of the road, is the 1,150 ft (350 m) Water-Slide which crashes down a series of slabs from Allt Coire Eoghainn. Keep your distance. This is not to be confused with the children's water-slides in theme parks. As the crow flies, the summit of Ben Nevis is less than a mile and a half from the car park via the Water-Slide. But we are not crows. This relentlessly steep and awkward ascent is fraught with hazards and should be attempted only by those who know their stuff – and the details of the route. The third big splash demands a walk from the car park through the magnificent Nevis Gorge. Beyond the southern end of that roaring tumult of water, An Steall ('The Spout') crashes down a 330 ft (100 m) wall into the Nevis. An Steall is the drainage outlet for the inner ring of The Mamores, a renowned range that includes eleven Munros and provides the hardiest of mountaineers with everything they need in the way of exercise and fresh air.

As for the flora and fauna of Glen Nevis, there are plant-ations of conifers on the western flank of the lower section, birch-woods to the east (and near Achriabhach), alder lining the river, and Scots pines in the upper section. Botanists can have fun in more ways than one by discreetly mingling with rock-climbers on the craggy flanks of Meall Cumhann, north-east of Nevis Gorge, and rummaging about on the stretches of greenstuff. The terrain is steep enough to deter the fauna from making a meal of the flora. The wildlife, a category from which sheep and cattle must be excluded, includes – if you are lucky – buzzards, deer and pine-martens. But one needs to be out early or late to catch the deer at the buffet. At such times –

and in calm weather after rain – beware of the maddeningly familiar midge, which can make the outdoor life intolerable. Midges have a special affection for the highlands in summer and some species drink blood, which is particularly unpleasant if the blood is yours. There is a theory that only the females do this, but who cares? The bitten are not concerned with the sex of the biter, any more than the biter is concerned with the sex of the bitten. In any case, how can we tell? In the presence of a crowd of midges, communication problems would make it futile to utter some such comment as 'Hang on a second – and get in line for a sex test'.

In 1982 I was ensconced in a little hotel up in Sutherland, having a quiet beer while our Gordon Setter dozed at my feet after a tiring day on the tops. A young chap rushed in: wide-eyed, evidently and audibly close to the screaming habdabs. He had been blitzed by midges while bivouacking and was begging for refuge. The hotel was full but the understanding landlord let him sleep in the lounge. Mind you, when it comes to nuisance value highland midges are hotly challenged by Australian flies. In 1987 I was in Melbourne for the last Australian tennis championships to be played on grass and made some testy comment about the flies. 'No worries, mate,' said an Aussie chum. 'You should see the big buggers. They can lift you off the ground.'

Glen Nevis offers two obvious ways to the summit of the British Isles. The tourist track, no more than a prolonged slog unless the weather turns nasty, can be approached either from the village of Claggan and the road up to Achintee House (two miles from Fort William), or by crossing a bridge near the youth hostel. The Water-Slide route has already been discussed and cannot be freely recommended. A third option, providing increasingly close-up views of the mountain's spectacularly awesome north-eastern face, is the path up the wide valley of the Allt a' Mhuilinn (which sounds more interesting than 'Mill Stream') from the distillery or the golf course. This steady ascent introduces three possibilities. The easiest and safest has an intermediate target that must also be regarded as a junction: that well-known refuge, the CIC Hut. This was named in memory of a Scottish climber, Charles Inglis Clark, who was killed in the First World War. From the CIC Hut, which is 2,250 ft (686 m) up and at the foot of the cliffs, one doubles back to the north-west before swinging south to join the tourist track above Lochan Meall an t-Suidhe, often known as the Halfway Lochan. Obviously this link between the Achintee and Allt a' Mhuilinn access points can be forged the other way round. Whichever direction is chosen, note the modest transport problems between start and finish.

The other two means of ascent from the Allt a' Mhuilinn are more demanding. From the CIC Hut it is possible to go straight ahead up the Coire Leis, bear south at the head of the corrie (there's an emergency shelter above a tiny lochan), and then clamber steeply up boulder scree – no easy task – to the lowest stretch of the famous Carn Mor Dearg arête. This is rough going, in an accident area. There is hard, dodgy work to be done in the half-mile or so (getting on for a kilometre) between the exit from the Coire Leis and the summit of Ben Nevis. I'm told that the other line of attack from the Allt a' Mhuilinn, via that same saddle on the Carn Mor Dearg arête, is the best route for competent hill-walkers. It involves getting out of the valley much earlier by climbing onto Carn Beag Dearg, 'Little Red Mountain', and following the ridge to the top of Carn Mor Dearg, 'Big Red Mountain'. That earns you a bonus point for reaching 4,012 ft (1,223 m) and just leaves you to deal with the arête at the head of the Coire Leis and the final pull to the bull's-eye. But I have no more than visual and second-hand knowledge of the Coire Leis and Carn Beag Dearg approaches and strongly suggest that, if interested, you should wait for decent weather and acquire detailed information and the company of somebody aware of the snags. Such reservations also apply to the Ben's back-door entrance: upstream from the Steall ruins, which are about a mile (1.6 km) east of Nevis Gorge, before a steepish clamber up to the Carn

Mor Dearg arête. Two Munroists (which means that they have climbed every Munro) tell me that this last route is their favourite and that even their dog found it tolerable.

Whether one climbs Ben Nevis or not the important thing is to explore its craggy flanks, particularly from Glen Nevis and from the vicinity of Torlundy on the A82 – a location with a striking view of the mountain's second best claim to fame (the first is its height), the 2,000 ft (610 m) precipices of the north-eastern face. That face is all cliffs and buttresses, ridges and gullies; and strictly for the hard men of the rock-climbing and mountaineering school. The western slopes are wide open to the public as a whole. The vast arc of the Ben's south-western, southern and south-eastern ribcage is comparatively modest in reputation. 'It's beautiful,' said Scot Gunn, 'but almost ignored. Every burn is a gorge. But there are hardly any people. Geographically, the Ben is fascinating – a huge mountain with four sides. It's a very interesting hill but most people don't know anything about it until they get on it, except that it's the biggest in Britain.' Oddly, Scott never referred to Ben Nevis by name. It was always 'The Ben' or 'The Hill'. He was on such familiar terms with it that he used the French *tutoyer* method of reference.

Having touched base with Heather and Scot at their Glen Nevis Centre I checked in at the guest house and surged to the bar of the Nevis Bank Hotel on a wave of anticipatory pleasure. Driving is a sedentary occupation and does nothing to sharpen the appetite (I made do with soup and dessert) but, on the other hand, can work up one hell of a thirst. In prospect, the first pint had been teasing the palate of the mind for about eight long hours at the wheel. It slipped down with no trouble at all. The second pint was savoured at leisure. The beverage was cider: the nation-wide commercial stuff rather than the 'rough' one prefers. But when a man with Somerset roots finds cider on tap in Fort William, good memories permit no nit-picking. At breakfast next morning an inimitably vibrant Piaf record, on the radio, put me more at ease with the rather strait-laced ambience of the guest house (Piaf attracted a lot of adjectives but there was never a remote possibiiity that strait-laced would be one of them). The weather was even more heartening and it was in a dashing mood that, as arranged, I turned up at the Glen Nevis Centre as the clock struck nine. Was this to be a solo or would the geriatric midget have company up the tourist track? Repress your disdain. I had no high-falutin ideas about fancy routes and was simply zeroing in on the business of getting to the top.

One of Scot's chums, Philip Morgan, was available and willing. He had a hangover and needed some exercise and fresh air. But we were turned down flat by the resident Sheltie, Shadow, who was clearly what we knew in the tennis-writing trade as a 'main-chancer'. Dogs are smart and Shadow instantly decided that Heather and Scot would give her an easier day than Philip and Rex would during a rocky walk up a 4,406 ft (1,344 m) mountain. Ben Nevis, incidentally, owes its supreme status to the invention of clinometers, which enabled surveyors to verify heights and thus convince themselves and everybody else that at 4,296 ft (1,309 m) Ben Macdui in the Cairngorms was merely the runner-up rather than the winner. Science was also responsible for the popular but much denigrated tourist track, which was originally hacked out of the landscape as a bridle path to the observatory on the summit. This track was five miles long and took the lines of least resistance. It has since been eroded but remains a convenient route to the top. Why disdain the legacy of a proud history? Moreover, I was soon to discover that preconceptions about the nature of the old packhorse trail had been no more than half-right, as most preconceptions are. The imagination had suggested a seemingly interminable trudge up a gloomy, winding path along shadowed ledges tucked into steep slopes. Trudge it is. Interminable it seems. But the track zigzags rather than winds – and there is no gloom, no shadow, and hardly a hint of a ledge. Just open terrain, a vast expanse of sky, and an enchanting panorama to west and south across the heavily

Con Moriarty and his four-wheel drive at the head of Hag's Glen. The Devil's Ladder falls from the depression at the right-hand extremity of the skyline.

are luxury, level terrain, during the first phase of the ascent.
e gentle eastern heights of Macgillycuddy's Reeks are pictured across Lough Gouragh.

An example of the relentless, lung-searching going presented by the three hanging corries that lead to the ridge between Corrán Tuathail and Beanncaorach.

An Irishman on the cross-crowned summit of Ireland.

en the restless Con Moriarty can take time off to admire an ever-fresh scene
niliar since childhood.

Taken from below, this photograph distorts and moderates the gradient of the Devil's Ladder, which is steeper than it looks. But the nature of this wet and grassy scree slope evident.

'The Mountain Man' and the mountain. From this direction Corrán Tuathail approaches pyramidal perfection.

Pip Morgan, enjoying a break from abseiling down oil-rigs, looks west over Ballachulish and Loch Linnhe towards the hills of Ardgour.

A higher view over Glen Nevis and Loch Linnhe, from the vicinity of the Red Burn.

The trig pillar on Ben Nevis's summit cairn is the highest point in the British Isles.

The rocky summit 'plateau' and the shelter built on the ruins of a former observatory.

e descent towards Glen Nevis and the bar of the Nevis Bank Hotel.

Heather and Scot Gunn, 'paying the way in the world by helping others', at the Glen Nevis Centre.

Misty, the spaniel who lives on 'The Hill', cannot be photographed at home - Achintee - without the help of retaining hands.

wooded Glen Nevis. Philip was to inspect the Mamores with an affection born in other, more challenging days.

We set off at 9.10 a.m., crossed the river bridge outside the youth hostel, and clambered up a man-made staircase of boulders to join the historic pony track from Achintee. Aluminium footbridges over a couple of burns confirmed that Ben Nevis had been partly tamed, had lost a little dignity, while retaining (higher up) its capacity to kill, maim or at least humiliate. The previous evening the committee of the mountain rescue team had gathered at the Nevis Bank and Philip had joined his chums for an occasion that had clearly been no temperance meeting. Now dehydrated, he made periodic stops to imbibe gulps of water from this or that mini-fall ('They sell the stuff in bottles and this is a good year ...'). He was careful, though, recalling the day when a huge slug had been within a split-second of going down his throat with the spring water.

Scot and I came into the world in Sheffield and Philip was born and raised in Leeds. So we spoke the same language and were all qualified to play cricket for Yorkshire, which two of my schoolmates subsequently did. Philip had worked for British Rail and he had worked in a pub. The latter environment was more congenial than the former but he decided that, job-wise, life's orchard had tastier fruits to offer. Moreover, he reasoned that although Leeds was not the worst of bases for a climbing enthusiast, nor was it the best. In 1987 he became assistant warden at the Glen Nevis youth hostel and two years later he joined the construction team installing ski lifts on the Aonach Mor development, just round the corner from Ben Nevis. Aonach Mor ('Big Hill Plateau') rises to 4,006 ft (1221 m) and its skiing resort – known as the Nevis Range – was a remarkable engineering feat that cost about £8.25 million. A special feature, unique in Scotland, is a gondola (cable-car) lift that rises more than halfway up the mountain and terminates at a restaurant commanding an impressive panorama: an inevitable bonus unless they had built the place without windows. There are plenty of other mechanical aids to elevation, one of which goes all the way to the top, for those who consider that going up mountains is a waste of time and energy, but a price that has to be paid for the fun of racing back down in outfits that make them look like moon-walkers with appendages. This kind of skiing, as distinct from the cross-country stuff, is an animated, sophisticated form of snakes and ladders.

In 1990 the Nevis Range was more or less finished and Philip became an 'access technician'. That could have meant all sorts of things. Was he, perhaps, a locksmith? Far from it, he explained. The job involved pottering about the North Sea and abseiling down offshore oil-rigs to do repair work. Rock-climbers and mountaineers are renowned for devising imaginative and often sensational means of keeping in trim for their recreational pleasures, but this was something new – and Philip was getting paid for it. He was a member of the Lochaber Mountaineering Club and was on the rescue team's reserve list: their apprentices, so to speak. Other than salary and scenery, the main difference between work and play was that at work he had to go down before going up and at play he had to go up before going down. He was often away for two weeks at a stretch, he said, but then had a week or two at home in Fort William. It was during one such break from paid labour that I was lucky enough to cross his path.

It will be interesting to find out what Philip gets up to next, not least in his domestic arrangements. These, I discovered, were as unconventional as his professional curriculum vitae. His girlfriend came from Aberdeen but did a midwifery course in Leeds and then settled down to work in Inverness. The mind boggles at the uncertain progress of true love as pursued by an Aberdonian midwife based at Inverness and a Yorkshire-born mountaineer and oil-rig technician sporadically based at Fort William. Not the obvious woosome twosome. Apart from all else, they must have been getting through countless hours and countless gallons of petrol as one or the other hustled along the

A82 so that, occasionally, they might fetch up at the same place at the same time.

The track was stony, the slope gentle, the adjacent terrain a mixture of grass and heather, peat and rock. The only risk of straying occurs shortly before the bog-framed Halfway Lochan, when the path doubles back on itself and the unwary may be tempted to climb east with difficulty rather than west with ease. It was a lovely morning and whenever we paused, or whenever zag succeeded zig, there were enchanting westward views: all the way from the hills above the bridge at Ballachulish round to the head of Loch Linnhe, the pointing finger of Loch Eil, and such distant islands as Rhum and Eigg. And at one point Philip directed my attention southward to the 'White Peak', Stob Ban, 3,274 ft (999 m) high, an outlier of the Mamores. From the way he looked at it and talked about it, Philip was briefly in communion with the poetic Muse, Calliope, one of the nine daughters of Zeus and Mnemosyne. I doubt if Philip's interest in mythology extended much beyond Bacchus but the sight of Stob Ban that morning would have touched any man's soul. It was quite a spectacle: steep and dark, with glistening ridges and, just to add an air of mystery, low cloud drifting lazily over its peak like an uneasy halo.

We crossed the tumbling Red Burn – with which the tourist track carries on an irregular flirtation – and became engaged with the bare grey scree slopes that cover the upper 2,000 ft (610 m) of the route. It is on this stony wasteland that, unless fanatical about mosses and lichens, the botanist tends to remember pressing appointments elsewhere. Given the fact that nothing interesting is happening, even the simple hill-walker can be afflicted by a wandering mind. Mine wandered to the nineteenth at Cowdray Park, where the rest of the veterans would at that very moment have their fists wrapped around refreshing pints after the monthly Stableford. Thomas and Barney and a host of other good companions would all be at the trough. I hope they thought about me ('Where's Rex?' ... 'Probably climbing some bloody mountain...') because when trudging up the screes I certainly thought about them. Philip Thomas's labrador cross, Spark, would be tethered by a tree outside the clubhouse, contemplating his love life. Spark is a good lad, but lusty. Philip T. got home one day – he had been playing at some uncivilized course where dogs are barred – to find that a neighbour had pinned a note to his front door: 'Your dog is at Petworth police station. The charge is rape.' That sort of story is a fertile source of conversation at the nineteenth: and also in the lower bar of the Noah's Ark in Philip's home village of Lurgashall, where Kathie and Ted Swannell cheerfully supervise such a fifty-fifty assortment of people and dogs that the ambience is akin to having a bar supper in a small corner of Cruft's. Spark always joins us – unless recent sexual activities have reduced him to a condition in which he can't even walk the hundred yards across the green.

The tourist track is that used for the annual Ben Nevis race and its little brother, the 'Half-Ben'. It must be distractingly crowded during the holiday season but in late October was no more than agreeably busy. Scot Gunn had given me the picture: 'The Ben's a great leveller, a social event. When you're freezing cold, and tired, you speak to people you might normally be reserved with. Everybody is looking for information from everybody else. "What's it like?" People coming up ask people coming down.' With the proviso that we were neither cold nor tired, that was how it was. The camaraderie with other hill-walkers, met and re-met, had the flavour of a family gathering. Which to some extent it was – the family of hill-walkers. Mind you, one would not expect that tourist track to be quite so congenial during the summer swarm. The pleasures of intimacy demand small numbers. In our case the small numbers audibly included a few Australians, whose compatriots had enlivened almost half a lifetime on the tennis circuit. The occasionally bacchanalian company of 'Emmo', 'Newk', 'Philby' and the rest had cost me a lot of sleep. But to hear the accent again, on Ben Nevis, brought back nothing but good memories – except for the hangovers.

The fresh air and exercise were healthy, the distant scenery attractive. But it has to be said that ascending a huge pile of lava resting on granite was about as exciting as watching the Boat Race or climbing a crumbling staircase with no conspicuous terminus. Philip, attentive to his tutorial responsibilities, explained that a colourful blob on the Carn Dearg screes to the north was an emergency shelter. The last rise to the summit is the only hazardous stretch of the entire tourist track. Watch your step, especially when there is snow or fog about. We had a good day and the hazards were obvious: just to the left of the track were two awesomely steep drops down gullies cut into the top of the mountain. Even in October there was still snow in them, left over from the spring. Their names, Philip told me, were Tower Gully and Gardy Loo Gully. The latter took its name (a corruption of the French *Gare de l'eau* – 'Look out for the water') from the yell of warning uttered by Edinburgh folk when they were about to empty the slop-pail out of the window into the street below. Whether the slop-pail contained nothing but water – used water – is a moot point, but in those days people certainly had to be nimble. Thank goodness for modern plumbing and drainage.

The main difference between the top of Ben Nevis and the screes approaching it is that there is no longer a slope, because the mountain has run out of material for elevation. I hesitate to use the word plateau, though one definition ('a stable state reached in the course of upward progress') is near the mark. It is a huge area, comparatively level if one had a tape measure long enough to run from one flank to another. But its surface, frost-shattered chunks of lava, has qualities that could be associated with the bottom of a quarry after an explosion or a built-up area after a bombing raid. A redeeming feature is that this repository of rocks on the roof of Britain must be about the same size as a football pitch and, consequently, can accommodate everybody who takes the trouble to get there. I assume so, anyway. It may be that at the height of the season those wanting to tread that spacious summit have to wait until others get off it. Even on 19 October there were thirty people up there, plus a white dog of indeterminate breed but inexhaustible energy. The dog was so frisky, so eager for more action, that its favourite record could only be the Peggy Lee classic 'Is That All There Is?'. Maybe it was just restlessly wondering what had happened to such essential components of a dog's life as trees and scented greenstuff.

It was 12.35 p.m., which meant that a leisurely ascent had taken three hours and twenty-five minutes. This is a respectable average time for the general run of hill-walkers. We passed the time of day with those in residence and those coming over the brow to join the sociable summit conference. Many were already faintly familiar because we had met them *en route*. It took a few minutes to sort out a couple of vacant perches that carried no risk of impalement, but having done so we shared my soup and Philip's coffee and, thus refreshed, examined the premises in more detail. Nobody on top of Ben Nevis can be unaware of its human history. Structurally, the place looked like the remnants of a stone-age village and a good deal of it reminded both of us of the dry-stone walls familiar in the Peak District and Yorkshire Dales. The clutter included the inevitable cairn, surmounted by a trig pillar that increases the mountain's natural height to an unnatural 4,418 ft (1,347 m); a battered viewfinder; the residue of what used to serve as a 'hotel'; a war memorial; and, most prominent of all, the sadly evocative pile of the once-proud observatory. This last was incongruously surmounted by the faded orange corrugations of a ramshackle shelter.

The history of the observatory era was recounted, in prose quaintly reminiscent of its time, in a book that is not easy to track down: William T. Kilgour's *20 Years on Ben Nevis*. We will make do with a selective abstract. The first, tentative meteorological observatory on the summit, in 1881, was the brainchild of one Clement L. Wragge, who little knew what he was starting. His initiative was the basis for building work carried on during the next two years. There was plenty of granite available and at ground level the walls were more than 10 ft (3 m) thick. One room was about 13 ft square. The observatory was formally opened in October 1883, and was to record, analyse and forecast the weather every day for twenty-one years. It worked in harness with a sister station at Fort William. Teams of four did two-month stints on top. A couple of packhorses, each burdened with two panniers full of provisions and fuel, went up the mountain daily whenever conditions permitted. Then came the tourists; and a makeshift 'hotel' was built, about fifty yards from the observatory, to provide refreshments and sleeping accommodation from June until September. The foot race from Fort William to the top and back dates from 1895; and Kilgour, ever attentive to detail, asked us to believe that the observatory team smoothed out a frozen block of snow and played ping-pong on it. The lengths men go to in the cause of sport...

That brave enterprise (the observatory, not the ping-pong) ultimately foundered because it became too expensive to maintain the summit venture and the complementary station at Fort William. Closure was scheduled for October 1902, but in fact the place functioned for two more years before it was dismantled and, on 8 October 1904, locked up. One has no wish to disparage the devotion to duty of those hardy men who lived and worked in such a hostile environment, but no doubt they had to tolerate the obvious, simplistic joke. There is no secret about Ben Nevis weather. It's bad. Research, largely based on the century-old findings of those meteorologic pioneers, suggests that the summit is at freezing point for two-thirds of the year, has clear visibility for less than a third, and gets as much rain in the 'dry' months (April, May and June) as a large chunk of England gets in an entire year. That hoary quip about Britain's weather, 'eight months of winter and four months of bad weather', is close to the truth in the case of Ben Nevis. When all the factors are considered – wind and rain, cloud and sunshine and temperature – we must conclude that the Ben is usually in its jolliest or least grumpy mood during

June and July. At such a time, mind you, there has to be a risk of running the gauntlet through a mob of tourists – and hill-walkers have no marked affinity with crowds. In summer one would want to be hotfooting it up the old pony track while tuned in to the dawn chorus. But I'd rather take my chances in spring or autumn.

Given the mountain's supreme altitude and the effects of the observatory (that broad packhorse trail, tourism, the foot race, and the exemplary exercise in improvized ping-pong) it is hardly surprising that Ben Nevis has been the scene of some daft stunts, mostly for charity. An old camp-fire song insists that 'you'll never get to heaven in an old Ford car' but one such did get to the top of the Ben in the days when the track was in better condition than it is now. Scot Gunn gave me two more illustrations of British eccentricity. In each case the perpetrator was staying at the youth hostel. 'A big fellow strapped an upright piano on his back and got it to the top – it took him four days – and played it. A couple of weeks later the local council sent him a letter saying the piano had to be removed, so he went up and dismantled it.' Perhaps the council thought the idea might catch on – they didn't want the summit to be cluttered with pianos. 'Another guy crawled up, all the way, on his hands and knees. They both did it for charity.'

That sort of nonsense arouses ambivalent feelings. We all like a bit of fun, especially if a good cause benefits, and out-rageous challenges – even those that involve playing the fool – are in tune with the nation's character and heritage. Moreover, the Ben Nevis stunts have left no visible scars; unlike the mess of ruins on top or the railway up Snowdon. On the other hand it may be argued that no matter how imaginative they may be, attention-grabbing practical jokes are degrading insults to the dignity of Britain's highest mountain. Clowns have no place in church.

The Ben is a cure for hangovers. Philip was now rehydrated. Moreover, he decided that I could be trusted to put in a short stint of educational overtime. The idea was that we should potter down to the Carn Mor Dearg arête to have a look at the cliffs, the Coire Leis, and a route for which he had an affectionate respect – that swinging along the ridges high above the eastern flank of the Allt a' Mhuilinn. Such a prospect would have been a rich reward for the extra 1,000 ft (305 m) of boulder-hopping, but the mission was swiftly aborted because we could not see much. The downward view consisted of shifting clouds and mist veiling hints of mountains that seemed to be in motion, like giants turning in their sleep. The sight might have induced an Impressionist to dance with joy and eagerly unpack palette and paints and brushes. Every man to his trade. Philip and I turned back to the 'stone-age village' and, after our fifty-five-minute break on and around the summit, began the descent.

During the lunch interval I had joked with some Australian about going back by train. We had not been thumping our way down for long when the familiar accent rang out: 'Missed the train, mate?' We also came across an ascending group who were pleasantly confused by the unsolicited company of a liver and white spaniel. This was Misty, who lives at Achintee. It must be doubted if any creature, man or beast, has been more persistently enthusiastic about climbing Ben Nevis. 'She's been in the local paper and is quite a celebrity,' Scot Gunn told me later. 'She must have been up the Ben thousands of times. People bring her back. She must pick them up when they go past the farm. A typical spaniel: they like people. But bitches seldom stray.' Misty does. The Ben is her favourite excursion but she turns up all over the place and is not averse to jumping on a bus. Early next morning, before she took off, I called in at Achintee with the camera in quest of a still. No chance. It was like trying to photograph an explosion in a fireworks factory.

Though not in the Misty class, Philip and I felt lively enough to prance about a bit during our descent alongside the Red Burn. The repeated jarring aggravated the effect of previous exertions and had inconvenient consequences. I began to wonder if medical science extended to knee transplants or, at least, spare parts for the knee's equivalent of shock-absorbers. Maybe the ball-bearings had rusted. Anyway, the protests were keenly felt. If knees had a trade union, mine would have been threatening industrial action (modern usage for industrial inaction) because of intolerable working conditions. When it comes to transport across rocks, Shank's Pony – otherwise known as Walker's Bus or the Marrow-Bone Train – is not the most comfortable conveyance. Split-second demands for agile footwork – for rapid adjustments to correct a slip or deal with persistent vertical or lateral variations in the terrain – come naturally and easily in youth. But when one is poised on or about pensionable age the knees are more vulnerable to the stiffening equivalent of battle fatigue.

In this respect the tourist route up and down Ben Nevis was a more searching test than the steeper but grassier challenge of Corrán Tuathail, which hurt the lungs more than the legs. The Irish summit is also more striking, visually, and more self-contained. An ascent of the Ben from Achintee or the youth hostel concerns two mountains rather than one. For almost 2,000 ft (610 m) the track skirts the western and southern slopes of Meall an t-Suidhe, 'Hill of the Seat', which is little more than half the height of Ben Nevis but provides a formal name for the Halfway Lochan that lies in the saddle between them. It is at this point, near the south-eastern shore of the lochan, that the popular route swings right to traverse the last of the vegetation and invade the screes of the Ben itself. The alternative, as we have noted, is to walk straight ahead between the lochan and the screes: on the path that bends round the north-western extremity of the Ben to the CIC Hut in the Allt a' Mhuilinn. This walk, in either direction, can be recommended to those who feel no compulsion to reach the summit or doubt their capacity to manage it. Ben Nevis thus offers scope, as Snowdon does, to walkers who merely want to capture the flavour of the mountain, to enjoy a glass of wine without emptying the bottle.

Scree slopes are not much fun unless it is safe – to oneself and those in the lines of descent – to do a standing glissade down the loose, gritty variety (rather like skiing down nursery slopes without the aid of skis and snow). We were denied that pleasure. But it was a relief to have a green prospect instead of a grey one, to look across Glen Nevis to the hills of Ardgour and picture, if only in the mind, the landscape beyond: Loch Shiel, with its monument to Bonnie Prince Charlie (who raised an army by gathering the clans at the head of the loch), and the road to the Isles. Thanks to Heather Gunn, we had drinks in hand before we had time to sit down at the Glen Nevis Centre. That was at four o'clock, which meant that our downward progress had taken two and a half hours. Excluding the lunch break, we had been up and down the Ben in less than six hours. This respectable if hardly record-breaking time was achieved at a gentle, sexagenarian pace – but in perfect conditions. All one needs to add is that the uninitiated would be unwise to plan an extended picnic between ascent and descent. On top, it was bloody cold.

Back at the Glenlochy Guest House one pondered the more exotic implications of its business card's reference to 'rooms with private facilities'. The night manager of a hotel in Tehran once woke me up in the small hours to ask 'Is there any other peoples in your room?' Maybe he thought I'd organized an orgy, that one or two ladies in the business of glandular excitement had, by arrangement, climbed up the wall and through the window. I was just taking off my boots (at Fort William, not Tehran) when, again, there came an urgent summons to the telephone. And again one recalled those few days in Tehran and Isfahan when an expected freedom from the tyranny of the telephone was frustrated by a night manager or, more often, by the Ministry of Information's local whizz-kid. Only my wife knew where I was staying at Fort William. Unless she merely wanted a chat, the call was ominous. Perhaps she had locked herself in and couldn't find the keys. Perhaps the house was on fire. Perhaps the dog, while exercising his considerable barking power, had given some passing old lady a heart attack.

The caller was in fact a colleague from way back when: Richard Evans, journalist, author, broadcaster and man-about-tennis. An Englishman born in Paris, he was telephoning Fort William from Stockholm on behalf of the Florida-based Association of Tennis Professionals to commission a programme article for some lavish event at an up-market resort in Australia. I had given up that sort of thing but, standing there in socks and breeches after the descent from Ben Nevis, was so startled and impressed by the cosmopolitan range of Richard's initiative that a negative response was out of the question. Tennis writing is an outlandish trade. I once filed articles from three capital cities – Rome, Brussels and Paris – on consecutive days. And I was phoning a piece from a Sarajevo hotel room at dawn when the smooth flow of dictation was suddenly disrupted by an echoing racket from an adjacent mosque. The copy-taker in London was underwhelmed by this alarming assault on his concentration.

'Jesus Christ! What's happening, Rex?'

'It's a muezzin. He's up a minaret, calling the faithful to prayer.'

'Where the hell are you – Bradford?'

All that strictly needs to be said is that before getting under the shower at Fort William one talked to an irresistibly persuasive friend in Stockholm. Then came a regretful farewell to the Gunns, who had done so much to make me feel at home. Next stop was the Nevis Bank Hotel, for a substantial bar supper and a final natter with Philip, who put away a few pints of 'heavy' while I kept faith with cider. Apple alcohol is good for you. My maternal grandmother, at Wincanton, put away a pint of 'rough' with the bread and cheese every night. She lived to be ninety-four, though she wasn't talking a lot of sense over the last lap. Her daughter became another nonagenarian before being afflicted by a few minor ailments, whereupon Mother announced with evident puzzlement: 'I've had nothing but trouble since I was ninety.' She should have drunk more cider.

Next morning, before the drive home, there were two photographic possibilities to be explored. But Misty would not keep still without a retaining hand and when I drove to Torlundy for a last look at the Ben, hoping for a long shot of its terrible northern face, the mountain was obscured by thick, low cloud. Never mind. The gods had been kind on the day that mattered and the objective of the trip had been achieved. Some thirty-six hours on and around Britain's highest mountain had been amply rewarded, not least in terms of new friends to be cherished and the inviting prospect of two goals for the future: a closer, more detailed look at Glen Nevis and a walk up the Allt a' Mhuilinn. Maybe the cider will keep me going long enough for all that. If not, perhaps you can tell me about it in the next world while we're chatting up the angels or shovelling coal in the basement.

There would be no point in a long peroration about the return drive up Glen Coe amid clouds, rain and echoes; the second crossing of the watery surrealism that is Rannoch Moor, that infinite variety of browns; another look at Loch Lomond and its environs, now drained of colour on a dull morning; misty, gloomy Shap, glimpsed through the windscreen wipers; the retreating football supporters on Birmingham's peripheral M6; and the rest of the long trek that separates Fort William from Midhurst. But you would not be reading this book unless you were a traveller, eternally on the lookout for a congenial village pub in which to take a break. I chanced upon one such at Newbold-on-Stour, on the A34 between Stratford and Shipston. The White Hart did an excellent soup and was a pleasant environment for the relaxing pleasures of a pipe and a pint (by that time one could afford to relax the discipline of temperance). The pub's ambience was quietly, consciously genteel in the middle-class sense and the welcome courteously neutral: that is, neither friendly nor unfriendly. Mind you, casual customers wearing anoraks and breeches are not all that thick on the ground at Newbold-on-Stour and must seem slightly alien. Anyway, I liked the feel of the place and the quality of the soup and was to see more of the White Hart on subsequent trips to Snowdonia and the Lake District.

By quarter past eleven that night I was walking the dog and trying not to feel smug about the fact that in just over sixty-five hours I had driven 1,163 miles and been up and down the highest mountain in the British Isles. Not a lot of people would be daft enough to attempt that. It had all happened so fast that one began to doubt whether it had happened at all. But there were good memories to be savoured, knees to be rested, boots to be cleaned, and fresh horizons to be explored. November was nigh but perhaps Snowdon and Scafell Pike would still be accessible...

Two down. Two to go.

GLOSSARY

The Celts, a tall and fair Aryan race from central Europe, were pioneers in working iron. They began to explore the British Isles in about 600 or 500 BC and in the next four hundred years or so settled down to achieve a dominant influence over the earlier residents (mostly hunters or farmers). As far as we can gather, the Celts were impetuous and generous: fighters, drinkers and raconteurs. Most of us can readily associate these qualities with today's Celtic Fringe, especially the Irish. Contingents of Celts conquered piecemeal and never created a coherent empire. They were driven west or north, or absorbed, by later invaders. But although their language declined in popular usage, it has endured to this day.

That language diverged into two branches: the Gaelic, which sank its roots into Ireland, Scotland and the Isle of Man; and the Brythonic, common to Wales, Brittany and – until early in the nineteenth century – Cornwall, where there are sporadic attempts to bring it back from the dead. It follows that the Gaelic of Ireland and Scotland are closely related.

Relevant equivalents already listed in the Irish glossary – ard, cnoc, coire, cruach, dearg, dubh, and mor – are omitted from this selection of words likely to be encountered on and around the Scottish highlands.

Allt	Stream
Aonach	Ridge
Ban	White
Beag or Beg	Small
Beallach or Bealach	Pass
Ben or Beinn	Mountain; hill
Bothy	Hut; shelter
Cairn or Carn	Hill
Creag	Crag
Druim or Drum	High ground; ridge
Fionne or Fyne	White; glistening
Glas	Green
Lairig	Long pass
Lin or Linnhe	Pool
Mam or Meall	Rounded hill
Sgurr, Stac, Stob	Peak
Shiel	Hut; shelter
Strath	Broad valley

Wales: Snowdon

3,560 ft (1,085 m)

It was 5 November, two days before the Snowdon ascent. My wife, propped up in bed with morning tea and *The Times*, spotted a paragraph bearing the too familiar headline 'Climber Killed'. A policeman with a taste for high places had fallen off Snowdon. It was suggested that he had plunged more than 700 ft (213 m) from a 3,000 ft (914 m) ridge but I never trust round figures, even in *The Times*. Such statistical details were irrelevant anyway, not least to those near and dear to the unfortunate constable. But they impressed Hilda.

'These mountain accidents always get more publicity than the rest,' I said, putting on a reassuring bedside manner. 'He was probably a rock-climber. I'm not. Won't be going within yards of any 700 ft drops.' He was not a rock-climber. Just a hill-walker. This I discovered – eighteen days after that uneasy bedroom chat – while agreeably engaged in conversational drinking with a chance acquaintance in Ritson's Bar at Wasdale Head. Coincidentally, he turned out to be a colleague and kindred spirit of the Snowdon victim.

Anyway, that news item in *The Times* topped up one's natural stock of prudence. It also jogged the memory. I once went up Ingleborough with the hill-walking sage of the North-East, Keith Watson, at a time when the big bumps rising from

105

the Yorkshire Dales were attractively but inconveniently
encased in solid layers of snow and ice. We had no ice axe but
there happened to be a walking stick in the car and this served
as a useful third leg and a means of testing the treacherous
texture of the whiteness underfoot. It had escaped the attention of our respective wives that five days earlier a frozen
corpse had been brought down (the poor chap had been
retreating from the upper slopes during a white-out). By
contrast the 'Climber Killed' paragraph had certainly not
escaped Hilda's attention. Nor had it re-enforced her
confidence that we would celebrate our fortieth wedding
anniversary six months later.

'Will you be going up on your own?'

'Possibly. Haven't made any arrangements. But I may pick
somebody up. In any case, Snowdon is never lonely.' (A white
lie, especially in the context of November.)

'It must get pretty lonely if you fall off it.'

'I'll be careful. Apart from anything else, the book is about
climbing mountains without taking risks. Must practise what I
preach.'

'Be sure you do. When are you due back ...?'

Alannah was more argumentative. Daughters often are.

'You must be a masochist, going up Snowdon at this time of
year.'

'It's no big deal. And I've signed a contract. Made a
commitment.'

'Why go now?'

'The publishers would like the manuscript in April. I have to
do the climbing before I can get on with the writing.'

'So go up by train and walk down.'

'There are no trains up Snowdon in November. They're
bedded down in Llanberis for the winter. In any case, that
would be cheating.'

'Who would know?'

'I would.'

'You should write novels. Then you could make it all up.'

With that we were back onto a familiar, inconclusive line of debate. Writing novels is not my scene. Reporters deal with real happenings, real people – more interesting than make-believe. Why invent a world of fantasy? It is all around us. Most novels, anyway, are imaginative extensions of truths experienced by the author or somebody else. Byron was an oddball but made sense when he asserted that truth was stranger than fiction. There are exceptions to most rules but on the whole reporters and novelists have only one thing in common: they write for a living. How confusing it must be to tread, introspectively, that hazy frontier between fact and fancy. When taking a break from the typewriter novelists are akin to actors going home from the theatre, making an effort of will to switch off the dream machine and come to terms with the everyday world and their true natures. That analogy assumes a clear distinction between dreams and reality, a distinction challenged by such psychological mysteries as alienation and *déjà vu*. The most charming eccentric on the tennis circuit used to be Torben Ulrich, who sported a beard and long, flowing locks. The Dane was a hippy, heavily into Zen Buddhism and all that sort of stuff. He had such a sunny disposition that everyone had an easy and affectionate rapport with the man, if not with the philosophical stars he steered by. When we met for the first time in years he asked how I was.

'Torben,' I said, 'as long as I wake up in the mornings, I'm happy.'

In Torben's company, such a comment was a tactical error.

'Waking up is an assumption,' he responded. 'Maybe we sleep when we think we're awake, and maybe we're awake when we think we sleep.' And off he went, skipping lightly down the strange, intricate byways of logic common to those who live half in this world, half in another. After a few minutes with Torben, one always felt like a rock-climber who had run out of holds.

Alannah never gets anywhere with her advocacy of writing novels as well as reading them. Even when it comes to reading

novels, I remain a comparatively undeveloped area, never
having progressed far beyond Jane Austen, the Brontës and
Thomas Hardy (my great-aunt lived at Dorchester, was
acquainted with Hardy, and thought him an odd chap). But
Alannah made one point – 'go up by train and walk down' –
to which many will relate, not least my brother. 'I can
remember trudging down that Pig track with a tired-out six-
year-old on my back,' he recalls. 'Susan's little legs had
stopped working. That trail was a real mind-breaker. We'd
cheated, though. Went up on the train.' Backpacking a six-
year-old while ascending or descending Snowdon cannot be
recommended. That apart, if one could manage only half the
job rather than all of it, one would rather walk up and take the
train down. Going up is easier on the knees. And the achievement lies in climbing mountains rather than getting off them:
the difference, if you like, between drinking the wine and
savouring the aftertaste while junking the bottle.

The important point is that the options offered by the
Snowdon Mountain Railway are merely the least among
many. One of Snowdon's two most attractive qualities is the
variety of routes and combinations of routes, including
pleasant walks on the flanks to accommodate those who (for
one reason or another) cannot reasonably attempt the summit.
It would be easy to spend the better part of a month exploring
the possibilities. Snowdon's other striking feature is its looks.
Whenever the peak is in view, providing proximate bulks with
an aesthetically satisfying apex, this marvellously spectacular
mountain lights fires within us and clamours to be climbed.
For these two reasons, the diversity of routes plus the visual
impact of their purpose, Snowdon may be given an edge over
the three other mountains discussed in this book. The isolated
pyramid of Corrán Tuathail has a more arresting outline. Ben
Nevis is bigger. Scafell Pike is the highest point of that paradise
for walkers, the Lake District. But when we dispassionately list
and compare all the components of a mountain's appeal to the
general public, Snowdon has to be the overall winner. During

the railway season those components include licensed refreshment facilities in the terminal station, which is a few yards from the actual summit, Yr Wyddfa. And because of the railway, and Snowdon's location in relation to such densely populated areas as the North, the Midlands and London, it is more easily accessible to more people – that is, by comparison with the highest points of Scotland, Ireland and England.

The snag, of course, is that mountains are best appreciated in a measure of privacy – and for much of the year Snowdon is awfully crowded. It has been estimated (goodness knows how) that at the peak of the tourist season as many as ten thousand people may be scattered about that vast mountain in the course of a single day: walkers, rock-climbers, family parties going up and down the railroad, and such special interest groups as photographers, geologists, botanists, and students of social and industrial history. There is plenty of room on Snowdon but going up and down the popular routes can be like taking part in a procession that only needs a brass band to round it off. At such times the swarming mass of humanity on tracks, crags and intervening wrinkles (plus the trains) raises images of a gigantic anthill, with all the ants on the march.

Unless you happen to be guiding inexperienced companions whose presence demands good weather and close supervision, Snowdon is best avoided during the summer. Climb it, instead, in April or September. Leave the October–March period to the winter mountaineers. True, on the strength of an encouraging weather forecast I went up early in November, but that experience confirmed the recommendation just made. Had conditions over the last 1,000 ft (305 m) been much worse, I would have retreated. Such decisions – whether to carry on or turn back – are trickier for the hill-walking rookie, who is also more reluctant to put prudence before valour. When in doubt, retreat. Getting into trouble proves nothing except one's capacity for getting into trouble. That November morning, the upper slopes were sporadically challenging because of poor visibility over an unfamiliar and (at the time) lonely route coated with snow and ice, which concealed the clues a tracker needs. Such circumstances demand a delicate mental balance between discretion and what the Boy Scouts used to call stick-ability. The knack of achieving that balance is simply a matter of experience.

The old Welsh name for Snowdon was Eryri, which refers to high ground and in the form 'eyrie' has come to be regarded as the home address of eagles. The Welsh know the peak itself as Yr Wyddfa: burial mound to you and me (that legendary burial will be discussed later). The word Snowdon is a refinement of an Old English term that travelled through three different spellings before settling into the one we use today. The most obvious and apposite meaning is 'snowy hill-fort'. The neologism Snowdonia was coined late in the eighteenth century, coinciding with the early development of tourism, and was applied to the entire area of the national park designated in 1951. Ascents of Snowdon were recorded as far back as 1639. George Borrow, an author and linguist from Norfolk, was enthusiastic about exploring Europe on foot and writing about his travels. Pushing sixty, he went up Snowdon in 1862 and was grateful to discover on the summit 'a rude cabin' in which refreshments were sold ('Henrietta had some coffee and myself and the guide a bottle of very tolerable ale'). He was not to know that thirty-four years later there would be a railroad up the mountain. One doubts if he would have approved unless he had lived that long – in which case he would have been ninety-three and an easy market for a train ticket. Other than the railroad, the improvement of the access tracks, and Snowdon's increased popularity among a variety of tourists, nothing much has changed – essentially, anyway – since Borrow's days. You must find out for yourself whether the ale is still 'very tolerable'. I have never drunk beer on top of a mountain. Red wine, yes (lightly chilled, inevitably, by the time one approaches Munro level).

An alcoholic analogy is appropriate when one looks at Snowdon on the map. The massif looks like a drunken starfish

because of the curving, rocky ridges that radiate from Yr
Wyddfa: the peak of a range on which five mountains are
clustered. In descending order of altitude these are Snowdon
itself, Crib y Ddysgl or Garnedd Ugain, Crib Goch, Y Lliwedd,
and a southern outlier, Yr Aran. At the foot of the cliffs and
ridges are cwms delightful in their diversity, plus lakes large
and small. The highest, deepest, most unavoidably prominent
lakes are Llyn Llydaw, which is 1,416 ft (432 m) above sea
level and 190 ft (58 m) deep, and Glaslyn, 1,970 ft (600 m) up
and 127 ft (39 m) deep. Other lakes to note, moving clockwise
around the valleys, are Gwynant to the south-east; Dinas;
Cwellyn; and Padarn and Peris in the Llanberis area to the
north-west. In the course of research one chanced upon *The
Lakes of North Wales* by Jonah Jones and read it mainly out of
professional curiosity. How could anyone write an entire book
about the freshwater lakes of what is, after all, a minuscule
portion of the Earth's crust? One stretch of water looked much
like another, I reasoned, and could have only a limited amount
to say to us. But there is a lot more to landlocked water than
meets the eye. Instead of merely skimming through the book as
intended, I read every word – and was grateful to author and
publishers for educating me in such an entertaining way. Even
drainage can be interesting when discussed by an enthusiast
who knows his stuff and can toss a few words together.

Mind you, some of these specialists can be hard to take
when wound up. For example, the first thing a botanist may
tell you about Snowdon is that – in common with the cliffs
above Llyn Idwal, on the other side of the Llanberis Pass – it is
probably unique in Britain in providing a home for a flowering
plant called *Lloydia serotina*, otherwise known as mountain
spiderwort (a word raising ridiculous visions of an arachnid
cabbage). The presence of such vegetation in such a place
suggests that those who potter about gardens and greenhouses
talking to the plants may not be as daft as the rest of us sometimes think. There could be some kind of intelligence inside the
greenstuff. Are we to believe it no more than an accident that

the mountain spiderwort flourishes in such an enchanting environment? Far more engaging is the thought that a plant with a remarkably high IQ, as plants go, had checked all the possibilities before wisely settling on Snowdon as a habitat.

One needs to be equally wary of others with esoteric, rather private passions: for example, those who rattle on, at length and in detail, about how such mountains as Snowdon were formed by volcanic, submarine belches. There is no accounting for the way some folk, harmless fanatics, fuss about the small print of mountain contracts. They scrutinize the leaves rather than appreciating the aesthetic qualities of the tree. If they want to know the right time when walking past Big Ben, they refer to a wrist-watch. You and I, of course, take a broader view. Perhaps a little envious of those better educated in the detail of the natural world, we lay claim to the wisdom that masquerades as a refinement of knowledge. We admire the still beauty of mountain lakes in their greys and blues and greens. We are grateful for the music of the tumbling streams that keep those lakes topped up. Grateful, too, for the bird-song, the pretty little pockets of flowers, and the diversity of colour and texture and line in rock formations. And, yes, we are aware that such pleasures would be enhanced if we knew more about what made it all happen, if we could give this or that a name and a reason, if words beginning with 'bio' and ending with 'ology' meant more to us than Scrabble points.

A naturalist chum, David Tomlinson of *Country Life*, once enlivened a dull match at Wimbledon by giving me a brief discourse on that fearsome-looking thing, the stag beetle. David and Simon Barnes of *The Times* both assure me that a passable knowledge of bird-life is easily acquired and richly repays the effort. The trouble is that the older we get, the wider our vision of the oceans of ignorance opening up before us and the less time we have in which to explore them. So thank goodness for the specialists – except those who are so blinkered that they can talk about nothing except their pet obsessions. The enthusiast who crosses the line into fanaticism achieves a loneliness neither sought nor relished.

By contrast the humble hill-walker is well adjusted, wiser by far, and ever patient when explaining to the uninitiated that the secret of a recreational Utopia lies simply in finding a good mountain, a good companion and a good pub. But we need regular doses of loneliness to keep us happy – and fit company for our kind during the quaffing hours at the end of the day. That sporadic search for solitude is not easily satisfied on Snowdon. The mountain is so beautiful, so accessible, so popular, that loneliness can be guaranteed only in the middle of the night or at times when conditions on the upper slopes can be bloody dangerous.

Snowdon is better looking, more inviting, than Ben Nevis or Scafell Pike. Its steep grandeur is difficult to capture in words. Yr Wyddfa dominates its buttressing satellites but these are essential components of a mighty, thrilling panorama: the horseshoe of ridges and peaks swinging from Crib Goch round to Y Lliwedd. One could gaze at that panorama all day but for the fact that the very sight of it is a visual bugle call to front-line action and sets the blood pounding. There is no resisting the urgent summons to sling on the rucksack and head for the heights, to exchange a Platonic rapport for the pleasures of intimacy. In any case, no choice is forced upon us. The Snowdon horseshoe looks its glorious best at sunrise and sunset. In between, there is plenty of time for the climbing.

The ideal location for savouring the splendour of the horseshoe without stretching a muscle is almost any point on the road from Capel Curig to Pen-y-Gwryd. Capel Curig is a straggling village that took its name from a sainted Celtic missionary who found this idyllic spot in the sixth century and decided that there could be no more suitable environment for a contemplative recluse. Nowadays the village – both remote and busy, if that is not a contradiction in terms – is better known as a road junction and as a tourist centre for walkers, climbers and anglers. The road along Nant Gwyrd is all the more pleasing because for a while Snowdon is viewed across

the waters of Llyn or Llynnau Mymbyr (the alternative use of
the plural Llynnau arises from the fact that a delta almost cuts
the lake in two). That road also passes Plas y Brenin, which
dates from 1800 and served as an inn and a hotel in turn until
1955, when it was transformed into a residential centre for
courses in a variety of mountain activities: walking, rock-
climbing, orienteering, general hill-craft, skiing and canoeing.
The Sports Council handles the instruction, which extends to
associated courses in the Alps.

Generations of walkers, rock-climbers and mountaineers
have travelled to Snowdonia via the Holyhead road, the A5,
leaving it at Capel Curig for the stretch to a further junction at
Pen-y-Gwryd. What happens after that depends on the related
issues of choosing a route up the mountain and deciding where
to bed down. For different reasons two means of ascent, the
easiest and the hardest, cannot be recommended to the general
run of hill-walkers. One is the railway, for the obvious reason
that it has nothing to do with hill-walking. The other is that
classic but demanding ridge walk, the Snowdon horseshoe.
This is exhilarating but strenuous and, in places, exposed: a
scramble calling for fitness, safe footwork, a head for heights,
and fair weather. Do make sure that you have taken the 'in'
out of inexperience before attempting it. Even then, have no
hesitation in turning back if the nature of Crib Goch gives you
second thoughts. From Pen-y-Pass follow the Pig track as far
as Bwlch y Moch and then ascend steeply up the eastern ridge
of Crib Goch to the summit at 3,023 ft (925 m). The nasty bit
is a sharp-edged traverse of about 400 yards (366 m), with
interesting drops on both sides. Use the feet for progress, the
hands for security. A crag called the Pinnacle must be circum-
vented rather than climbed. After that, on to a saddle before
the climb to Crib y Ddysgl or Garnedd Ugain at 3,493 ft
(1,065 m). Join the railway track at Bwlch Glas, stroll up to Yr
Wyddfa, and resist the temptation to turn a break into a binge.
This is no time to impair one's judgement, because there is
more excitement ahead. Follow the Watkin path to the south-

east for a while before clambering up Y Lliwedd, 2,947 ft (898 m) high. Note that Llyn Llydaw is more than 1,500 ft (457 m) below and that the intervening cliffs are renowned among rock-climbing enthusiasts. Except for some ridge-walking that is more or less the end of the horseshoe. The descent can be made down a grassy slope to Llyn Llydaw and the Miners' track or, if you still have energy to burn, via Gallt y Wenallt. Should you be a stranger to Snowdon, don't be cross about those unexplained references to the Pig track, the Watkin path and the Miners' track. Read on.

Our main concern here is with the six other routes, all suitable for walkers and mostly associated with the mining era. The Pig track and the Miners' track both start from Pen-y-Pass and they ultimately merge. Moving clockwise round the mountain, the next popular route is the Watkin path from Nant Gwynant. On the road from Beddgelert to Caernarfon are access points to two more approaches: first the Rhyd-Ddu path, which can be tackled from either Rhyd-Ddu or Pitt's Head (less than a mile apart), and the Snowdon Ranger path from Llyn Cwellyn. The final route, from Llanberis, never strays far from the mountain railway. We may as well deal with this first, because it is the walker's easiest means of ascent but is also the longest – a trudge of about five miles – and the least interesting. The views, mind you, become increasingly rewarding, and for hill-walkers who know their stuff there are demanding diversions to the east: for example, along the edge between the Hebron and Clogwyn stations and, coming back, an exploration of Crib y Ddysgl (Garnedd Ugain) and Cwm Glas, which is embellished by a couple of tarns and is a popular spot among rock-climbers and botanists. The Llanberis path starts near the railway station. It has much in common with the tourist route up Ben Nevis, not least the fact that it was originally a Victorian pony track.

Even such an authority on Snowdon as E.G. Rowland seems to have changed his mind, between one booklet and another, about the correct spelling of the Pig or P.Y.G. track. All we know for certain is that the homophones were coined a century or so ago by walkers and climbers setting out from the Pen-y-Gwryd Hotel, which accounts for the initials P.Y.G. But at about 1,850 ft (564 m) the track crosses the Bwlch y Moch, 'Pass of the Pigs', a name that probably dates from the era in which the multi-purpose, domesticated mammal was being developed from the wild boar. We should be grateful for the pig, rather than making fun of it. After all, it gives us pork, bacon, ham, sausages, bristles for brushes and skin for hides: an admirably wide-ranging contribution to our creature comforts. But Britain's wild or half-wild pigs were heading for the evolutionary exit by the end of the seventeenth century and their pampered descendants, smart animals, are fair-weather breeds: unlikely to get in the way when one is halfway up Snowdon. So what were they doing up there? Welsh pigs are, by tradition, hardier than most. But it is reasonable to assume that Bwlch y Moch earned its name in the days when tough, remote ancestors of the pork butcher's friend were roaming about freely. Toy, if you wish, with further implications: for example, the fact that pig can also refer to an oblong chunk of unforged metal. My own conclusion is that the early Pen-y-Gwryd climbers were the first to give a name to the route (as distinct from the pass) but that the pigs had been up there first and, consequently, have a stronger historic claim to be commemorated via the trivia of spelling.

The Pig track, like the less interesting Miners' track, has the inviting advantage of starting from the Pen-y-Pass car park at an altitude of 1,169 ft (356 m), which reduces the leg-work to a modest 2,391 ft (729 m). The route is shortish but steepish, though never arduous. If new to it, note that the track starts by going off to the right from the south-western corner of the car park; whereas the more obvious Miners' track is straight ahead. With the Pass of Llanberis down on the right and a ridge up on the left, the path winds upwards to the Bwlch y Moch. At this point pause to admire the views and part company with the Crib Goch athletes, who must climb due west. Walk over the pass and then swing right for a spectacular stroll along the southern flank of Crib Goch before joining the Miners' track high above the north-western shore of Glaslyn, a location dominated by Snowdon's eastern cliffs and screes. The track then rises to the right of an old copper mine and zig-zags (be wary of drops on the left) to Bwlch Glas. Here the Pig track joins the Llanberis path and the railway for the final pull to Yr Wyddfa.

The Miners' track is less fun until its separate identity is absorbed by the Pig track. But one does not have to be a student of social and industrial history to enjoy the many visible relics from the mining era of a century ago. The route used to be a cart track on which copper was brought down from the mines around Glaslyn. Llyn Llydaw is crossed at its narrowest section via a custom-built causeway: occasionally submerged, in which case it is necessary to detour round the northern shore. The views are superb but little height is gained until the track veers away from Llyn Llydaw and its ruins and climbs to Glaslyn. The further ascent to the Pig track begins on the far side of a mini-bay. For most of its course the Miners' track is a dull old plod but it is not to be disdained, especially if one has the imagination to picture when and how it happened. The route is best regarded as an easy, alternative means of descent.

The Watkin, Rhyd-Ddu and Snowdon Ranger paths involve more climbing because they start from valleys rather than the head of a pass. The kicking-off point for the Watkin path is a by-road branching off the A498 at Bethania, between Llyn Gwynant and Llyn Dinas. The route ascends via water-falls to Gladstone Rock in Cwm Llan and then heads for the western flank of the craggy ridge between Yr Wyddfa and Y Lliwedd. From the Bwlch y Saethau ('Pass of the Arrows') there is quite a strenuous finish up screes that demand respect. Unless memory lies, it was hereabouts that in 1948 a few chums and I were part of the July swarm of hill-walkers (we were too young to be wise) and had an alarming lesson in the perils of big-rock scree. A group up ahead of us dislodged a boulder three times the size of a football and it came bounding down the slope towards us at an ever increasing speed. Any damage incurred would probably have been terminal. There was nowhere to hide and no more than a split-second in which to take evasive action. All we could do was crouch behind the fragile protection of rucksacks. Luckily, all we felt was the draught.

That day on Snowdon was also the basis of a more gratifying lesson. Our company included a beautiful Austrian student on holiday. She was to marry a doctor and mountaineer who also became a big noise in politics. We kept in touch for a few years and in 1975 the tennis circuit found me in Vienna for a Davis Cup tie. Looking up friends from way back when is a dodgy business. Bonds can rust and break, creating a conversational void. But a journalist's curiosity was decisive and when I called Gerda we talked – about today, not yesterday – until my stock of schillings was exhausted. Next evening Gerda and Eduard and another couple entertained me to dinner at a classy restaurant across the road from the opera house. The lesson was obvious: gamble it may be, but always look up your old chums.

The Watkin path has three historic claims to our attention. It was designed by Sir Edward Watkin, a railway tycoon whose initiatives included a preliminary shot at a Channel tunnel. He retired to Nant Gwynant and owned much of Snowdon's south-eastern flank. Watkin's route to the summit was opened in 1892 by Gladstone, a Liverpudlian who was then two months short of his eighty-third birthday and serving the second of his four terms as prime minister. Gladstone did well to get up to some 984 ft (300 m), whereupon he stood on the rock that now bears his name and addressed one hell of a crowd – considering the location – on the subject of justice for such small nations as Wales. In addition to Watkin and Gladstone, King Arthur gets into the act – as he gets in to so many others.

That guy had more lives than a cat and died more deaths than an unfunny comedian. One legend tells us that he fought and won his last battle on the southern flanks of Snowdon, pushed the harassed enemy down towards Llyn Llydaw, but was fatally wounded when the fleeing army turned on him with a defiant flight of arrows. Thus the 'Pass of the Arrows', Bwlch y Saethau, where Arthur was supposedly interred. Another legend suggests that Yr Wyddfa acquired its name as the tomb of a giant called Rhita Fawr, a nasty piece of work who murdered a few kings and wore a cloak woven from their beards. This was regarded as antisocial. Arthur caught up with the ogre, switched his lights off, and had the baddie buried on Yr Wyddfa.

Of the host of Arthurian stories, those two are the most relevant to our present purposes. The total bulk of quasi-historic tales concerning our chivalrous hero suggests that he put himself about a bit – the Solway Firth, Cumbria, Wales, Swindon, Glastonbury, Somerset, Cornwall, or wherever – at a time when Britain had no sort of transport system. A more plausible line of speculation is that Arthur was a popular name in an era of local rather than national 'kings' whose deeds were confused and fused by later generations. On the other hand Arthur could have been a particularly effective tribal leader, a Romanized Celt, who did more than most to resist Anglo-Saxon invaders in the fifth or sixth centuries. That, anyway, was the basis of the first recorded reference to Arthur, in a seventh-century chronicle. The suspicious feature is that the weight of Arthurian legend never fell on us until the twelfth century, when Geoffrey of Monmouth produced an imaginative 'history' of British kings. Part historian, part novelist, he assembled and embellished a wealth of myths and legends about the big wheels of the fifth, sixth and seventh centuries. Geoffrey did not have many facts to work on but that did not deter him – and the British tourist industry has since had cause to be grateful to a man who regarded known truths as no more than the lower layers of a pile of building blocks.

A reasonably convenient overnight base for those using the Watkin, Rhyd-Ddu or Snowdon Ranger routes is Beddgelert, an attractive village popular among generations of tourists. Set among mountains at the confluence of three valleys, Beddgelert ('Gelert's Grave') became a religious centre after a monastery had been founded there in the sixth century. Gelert or Kelert was probably an obscure early saint buried at the monastic site, but that theory is less appealing and less well known than another: a further example of creative 'history'. Geoffrey of Monmouth would have been proud of it. This hackneyed legend suggests that Beddgelert took its name not from a saint but from a dog – the faithful hound of Prince Llewelyn (1173–1240), the king of North Wales. The story was born in the eighteenth century and is believed to have been the invention (possibly based on a grain of truth) of a local landlord who wanted to drum up business for Beddgelert and his inn. The tale suggests that Llewelyn went hunting and left his baby son in the care of Gelert, the hound. The prince returned to find the place in a mess and the dog covered in blood. Whereupon Llewelyn, jumping to the conclusion that the dog had savaged the child, killed Gelert – only to discover that the hound had in fact saved the baby from a wolf. Remorse insisted on a lavish burial and memorial.

The grain of truth could lie in speculation that such an incident happened: that a brave dog, almost terminally mauled in tackling a marauding wolf, had been on the receiving end of a mercy killing. Such incidents did occur. An uninhibited raconteur would not need much imagination to dress up the story by borrowing the name Gelert and bringing Prince Llewelyn into the act. It is reasonable to assume that although such legends were not immaculate in their conception, a modicum of fact may lurk within them. That which cannot be proved is not necessarily false. Not entirely, anyway.

About three miles out of Beddgelert is a big boulder known as Pitt's Head because its profile, if not its complexion, supposedly resembles that of the statesman. An oddity about the southern and south-western approaches to Snowdon is that Gladstone Rock and Pitt's Head commemorate former prime ministers who, among intimates, probably answered to 'Bill'. The route from Pitt's Head goes to Ffridd Uchaf farm and then east of north to join the Rhyd-Ddu path after about a mile. The busier, alternative start is from a car park just south of the hamlet of Rhyd-Ddu. The ascent is roughly north-east as far as the edge of Llechog, which encourages a necessary swing to the right. Bwlch Main, a well-known saddle, has spectacular drops on both flanks but the path is broad enough to make these a thrill rather than a threat. The Rhyd-Ddu and Watkin paths then merge for the final slog to the summit.

The oldest route may be the Snowdon Ranger path, which starts from a youth hostel on the shore of Llyn Cwellyn. The word 'Ranger' was applied to the first professional guide in the area. The youth hostel is a Victorian building on the site of his original cottage, a location that also served as an inn and as a monastery of sorts (not simultaneously, though one likes to toy with the possibilities – monks have come up with some pretty strong brews). The path starts with a few zig-zags and then heads east for quite a strenuous ascent to a rock-climbers' playground, Clogwyn Du'r Arddu. At Bwlch Glas the Snowdon Ranger path joins the railway and the Llanberis and Pig tracks. In roughly three miles (almost five kilometres), the route rises about 3,100 ft (945 m). Give or take a few trivial statistics and you could say much the same about the Watkin and Rhyd-Ddu paths. And one gets to know Snowdon that much better by going up and down on different paths: for example, Pig plus Miners' or Rhyd-Ddu, Llanberis plus Watkin, Rhyd-Ddu plus Snowdon Ranger, or Snowdon Ranger plus Watkin. Mix your own cocktail to suit your own taste.

My choice of Pig plus Miners' was dictated partly by expedience (I wanted a short, quick, but interesting itinerary that would leave time for the drive home) and partly by the pertinent advice with which Harvey and Rosie Lloyd responded to that stated preference. Harvey, a Snowdon guru, is warden of the youth hostel at Pen-y-Pass. I came down from the mountain with a few awkward questions on points of detail and he had all the answers. Rosie has a bed-and-breakfast place a mile down the road, next door to the Pen-y-Gwryd Hotel, which was closed for the winter. No complaints. She could not have done more to make me feel at home. The youth hostel had an earlier history as a hotel, until 1967, and between them Pen-y-Pass and Pen-y-Gwryd have reputations unsurpassed in the folklore of British mountaineering.

The 277 miles from Midhurst to Pen-y-Gwryd took almost seven hours and a half, and – mainly because of a traffic census and roadworks on the A34 and A5 – was quite a test of patience and temper. Our main roads are continually disintegrating and getting them integrated again seems to be an awfully slow process. There is seldom much evidence that work is actually in progress but it gets done somehow, maybe in the middle of the night. Equally mysterious is the labour of tidying up the heaths and woodlands around Midhurst: work has obviously been done but one never catches anybody doing it. Perhaps those who care for our roads and countryside are nocturnal, like bats and badgers. Always on the night shift.

The only voluntary stop was a break for a bowl of soup and a half-pint at the White Hart, Newbold-on-Stour. This was becoming such a familiar watering-hole that had the car been a horse it would have turned in there without any encouragement from reins or knees or whatever it is the horsy crowd use as a rudder. My wife and I, strolling about Exmoor, once embarrassed a lady on horseback by engaging her in conversation. She had the devil of a job arresting her mount's leisurely gait and explained that she (the rider, not the horse) was still a learner, that she was at ease with the ignition and steering gear but had yet to find the handbrake. And during the modern pentathlon at the Tokyo Olympics a British competitor (I think it was Jim Fox) was dumbfounded to discover that he had been lumbered with a horse which would only turn left. One assumes that he covered the course in a series of small circles, because if left goes on long enough it becomes right. Three left turns add up to one right turn. On balance one has to conclude that George Stubbs and Alfred Munnings were on the ball: horses should be painted rather than ridden. The royal family's allegiance to horse-racing and polo has to be regarded as a hereditary defect of character. But we all have one or two of those.

The day was fine and the forecast suggested that clouds were the only threat to one's immediate purpose in life. That unwelcome hint gained substance after a glorious drive towards the oranges and reds of the sunset and (between Betws-y-Coed and Capel Curig) a first view of the mountains. Dusk did not darken fast enough to obscure the fact that Snowdon's summit was wrapped in what looked like cotton-wool: a lovely sight, but not altogether welcome to a hill-walker who, next day, proposed to do a November solo up an unfamiliar route. Meantime one reluctantly had to accept the fact that, other than to buy an up-to-date map and guide-book, there was no point in exploring the Climber and Rambler at Betws-y-Coed or Joe Brown's shop at Capel Curig: both Aladdin's caves for mountain folk. Reaching the sixties is a mixed blessing. Without being wealthy one has a little folding money to spare but little cause to spend it: because one's hill-walking equipment is already adequate. But the new map was inter-esting. I chucked away the cloth-bound 1947 Ordnance Survey job, which cost three shillings, and replaced it with a more detailed successor for £4.50. The contrast struck me only because of the span of years it represented: so many exhilar-ating days on the hills, yet so many more that eluded me because of the need to earn a living. The point to be made to younger readers of this book is that, even if you are light in the wallet and have to deny yourselves a few creature comforts, always buy the best map you can get. It is your mentor, your guide, and may be your life-line.

Near Plas y Brenin, track-suited youngsters were jogging

along the roadside, dreaming of tomorrows that would demand a reasonable level of fitness. At Pen-y-Gwryd, a bleak and lonely spot in a majestic environment, Rosie Lloyd's place – Hafod y Gwynt, 'Windy Farmhouse' – was easy to find because there is little else to find. The hamlet stands at about 900 ft (275 m) on the site of a small Roman settlement and has not grown much, if at all, in the intervening 1,600 years or so. Other than a hotel, a road junction, a lake, and some defiant woodland, Pen-y-Gwryd consists of next to nothing. But in mountaineering terms it is very big indeed. Like the youth hostel and former hotel at Pen-y-Pass, the Pen-y-Gwryd Hotel (a training base for the first successful Everest expedition, in 1953) is rich in memories and souvenirs of famous climbers who pioneered the craft in Snowdonia and Britain as a whole. You may choose to join the youth hostellers at Pen-y-Pass. If not, Pen-y-Gwryd is an ideal starting point for ascents of the Snowdon massif or, for that matter, the Glyders.

An aside about the semantics: a hafod used to be a summer farmhouse, gwynt is wind, a pen is a top, gwryd has green connotations, and glyder – in the same linguistic family as the clitter on Dartmoor – refers to a jumbled mass of rocks.

Rosie fixed me up with a pot of tea in the drawing-room (as a sporadically pedantic wordsmith I prefer that compound to lounge or sitting-room) and her seven-year-old Border collie, Pyp, made discreet overtures to a potential playmate. Pyp owes her unusual name to the initials of Pen-y-Pass. Rosie makes bobble hats and winters in a chalet at Chamonix, the perfect second home for anyone mainly based at the traditional nursery for those climbing in Snowdonia. Chamonix is renowned as the village from which two Frenchmen – Michel Paccard, a doctor, and Jacques Balmat, a guide and chamois hunter – made the first ascent of Mont Blanc in 1786. That feat, common enough these days, was the first chapter in the history of recreational but (originally) quasi-scientific mountaineering. In the next hundred years most of the major Alpine peaks were conquered. Rosie Lloyd is not the only link between Pen-y-Gwyrd and Chamonix: both memorable names in climbing lore.

Having checked in with Rosie and Pyp I drove back to Capel Curig, where the first priority was to call my wife. This experience was by no means straightforward. There was a phone box tucked away by the roadside but the box was unlit and as dark as the night. The buttons were vaguely visible but the digits were inscrutable. So the car was carefully manoeuvred (twice) until its lighting facilities provided the buttons with a measure of illumination as long as I stood to one side. Such an initiative was both challenging and ludicrous. With the car skew-whiff at the side of the road in the Gwynedd gloom, all that was needed to complete the scene was a policeman ('Good evening, sir. What seems to be the trouble?'). The incident is recorded here because it has happened to you – or will – and these trivial frustrations are moderated when shared. Our loved ones have no idea of the pains we sometimes take when checking that all is well. Mind you, that phone call would have been much less trouble if I'd had the wit to remember that there was a torch in the boot ...

Hilda and Acorn, the Norfolk terrier, were in good form. From my wife's point of view (she was accustomed to hearing hubby's voice down the line from places like Tokyo, Sydney and San Francisco) it was not much more than a local call. Free to look after the inner man, I headed towards the cosy and congenial Bryn Tyrch Hotel for a pint of cider and a bar meal. The latter was such a huge, formidable assortment of cottage pie, salad and chips that one had to make a series of flanking attacks before launching a frontal assault. Two of the waitresses carrying such hefty loads from kitchen to bar had such impressive forearms that it would have been no surprise to learn that they were rock-climbers on a weight-training course. After that meal I didn't feel quite the same man. Thank goodness the Pig track was twelve hours ahead.

Back at Rosie's, the scene could hardly have been more domestic. I lit a pipe and, via television, watched Aston Villa playing football in Milan, which brought back pleasant recollections of both Villa Park and Milan. Rosie was packing some bobble hats. Pyp, having finished a snooze, decided to play ball with me. The quickness of her reactions was astonishing. Even more astonishing was the posture in which, eventually, she went back to sleep – with one foreleg draped round the back of her neck like a lady's boa. There were only three legs where one expects to find four. Dogs are full of surprises, mostly delightful. We used to have an English Setter who, once I'd left the bed in order to make morning tea, jumped into the vacancy and slept on, with one leg round my wife's shoulders. But Pyp is the first recorded case (recorded by me, anyway) of a dog indulging in auto-cuddle.

Rosie produced the kind of breakfast a hill-walker needs, and the sunrise was spectacular. What a lovely November morning it was; and as this was out of season there would be no swarming crowds on the mountain. The Snowdon horseshoe looked wonderfully inviting. At Pen-y-Pass I checked in with Rosie's other half, who had previously been no more than a reputation and a friendly, disembodied voice on the phone. Harvey Lloyd is a native of Connah's Quay in the neighbouring county, Clwyd. He was an engineer with Vauxhall Motors at Ellesmere Port until 1972, when he embraced a radically different lifestyle by moving to Pen-y-Pass ('There were frustrating factors about the job I was doing, and this sounded exciting. I've always been interested in mountains and the countryside in general'). Was he, I asked, a hill-walker, rock-climber or mountaineer? 'I've done a bit of everything.' Had he a favourite route up Snowdon? 'I don't think I have. Whatever comes to mind at the moment.' And his favourite time of year for the leg-work? 'Definitely the winter. The hills are quieter and more challenging, and I'm more relaxed because the hostel is not so busy.' In many ways Harvey reminded me of Scot Gunn at the Glen Nevis Centre. Sound men. I value their acquaintance and am wiser as a result of it.

Across the road is a café and, on the same premises, a sub-post of the mountain rescue organization run from the wardens' centre at Nant Peris. Behind the café is a car park from which, at 9.35 a.m., my modest adventure began. Instantly there was a steepish clamber up a staircase of boulders: a good pipe-opener, warning legs and lungs that this was a working day. Then came a gentle gradient on a well-made track, a tribute to the wardens' service of the Snowdonia national park. Maintaining these paths is a never-ending job: 'like painting the Forth Bridge', as Harvey put it. Throughout the climb I kept noticing unsightly heaps of what looked like garbage bags. 'They're used to carry crushed slate to the mountain paths,' Harvey explained later. 'It's taken up mainly by helicopter.'

In places the rocky track was so well worn that there was almost a shine on it. The angle of ascent was sometimes demanding but never unreasonably so. Nothing strenuous. Nothing difficult. And I was immersed in a lovely loneliness. The air was fresh without being chilling. The blue sky was decorated with a few fluffy clouds. There were still a few vague, insubstantial hints of residual morning mist. Far below was the tarmacadam snake of Llanberis Pass. Not to put too fine a point on it, the gods were smiling on me. Even the inevitable breeze on the Bwlch y Moch was invigorating. On the pass I briefly had the company of a youngish party who were about to tackle Crib Goch. Their number included a couple of ladies whose clothing and footwear suggested that they would have been wiser to stick to the foothills. Up on that rugged and exposed ridge they would certainly need the warm young blood fuelling their endeavours.

Nature's original scene-shifters let their hair down at the Bwlch y Moch. The pass is a point of transition between two worlds. The prospect to the north, across Llanberis Pass to the Glyders, had been enchanting – but second division stuff compared with the awesome magnificence over the hill. This was a close-up of the famous horseshoe. Hereabouts the Pig track was level, easy going, so one could soak in the splendour of the view without taking time off to stand and stare. That section of the path, just inside one tip of the deeply hollowed horseshoe, is about 430 ft (131 m) above the causeway across Llyn Llydaw and commands a view down the length of the lake to the forbidding cliffs of Y Lliwedd, which have attracted generations of rock-climbers. These cliffs provide less scope than most for protective belays. Rock gymnasts often stray off-route, some get stuck, and occasionally there is a fatal fall. Y Lliwedd gives the mountain rescue service plenty of work.

That morning the upper crags were suffused with sunshine and, as there was still moisture in the air, the lighting effects were so striking that they smacked of surrealism. Had such a picture been painted one would have assumed that the artist had taken liberties with the facts. To the right of Y Lliwedd, the pre-eminence of Yr Wyddfa was emphasized by thin cloud and a coating of snow. Alongside the track was more white-ness: isolated chunks of quartzite, reminders of days on the Sutherland hills. Beyond a workmen's shed, an odd structure to find in such a place, one was suddenly poised over the south-western extremity of Llyn Llydaw. Then came Glaslyn – not a pretty sight, but awfully impressive. It lies in a vast, dark pit at the base of Snowdon's eastern face. The lake is almost circular and, given its setting, one could not resist an irreverent analogy with half a water-closet. Associated imagery was probably prevalent in the mining community of old. Soon there was a bird's-eye view of ruins outlining the cottages in which the miners lived during the working week.

Talking of birds, I had company: of a sort, anyway. Herring gulls. 'Sometimes known as kipper gulls,' according to Simon Barnes, my main point of reference when it comes to birds and birders. When talking of gulls forget the 'sea' because the suffix is misleading: they seldom stray far from the shore. The herring gull earned its name by dining off the stuff fishermen chuck away. These renowned scavengers ('brilliant opportu-nists', says Simon) tend to breed on lonely cliffs. Snowdon suits them in both respects: the breeding and the scavenging. There are plenty of walkers and climbers with scoff to spare. So the gulls cunningly suggest that they are half-tamed and simply love people. All they have in mind is raiding your larder. They perch on rocks, let you know they are there, but pretend to be casual. No complaints. Somehow, we all have to earn a crust.

Other than the Crib Goch party and a group of lads who had come up from Llanberis under the aegis of the admirable Youth Training Scheme, plus three chaps I met on the top, the gulls and I had Snowdon to ourselves. No complaints about that, either. Climbing Snowdon on such a quiet day is a rare pleasure, an experience to be cherished. Physically and mentally, one merges with the environment rather than forming an anonymous link in a processional chain. I didn't much like a slight if rocky descent – height lost has to be regained. The clouded crest of Snowdon was even less heartening. And after the junction of the Pig and Miners' tracks the zig-zags on steepening scree presented a few interesting problems: visibility down to about 50 yards (46 metres), plus snow and, here and there, ice. Thus was I deprived of both the aids to path-finding – discernible natural features and, underfoot, indications that anyone had been that way before me. Note that untrodden snow covers all traces of even the most heavily booted hill-walkers. Moreover, I was new to the route.

Now, those of you who are familiar with the Pig track or have climbed it as part of the summer swarm may be surprised that anyone could find it tricky. My situation was different. Awkwardly so. E.G. Rowland (*Hill Walking in Snowdonia*) made this comment about the zig-zags: 'The path here may be missed in thick weather'. He wasn't kidding. I made only one mistake but it was educational and set off a faint alarm bell. There is a brief stretch of clear, wide path alongside a wire fence: protection against drops on the left. At the end of that fence one should (as I discovered later) veer slightly left. Instead I innocently traversed to the right and was soon doing some finger-and-toe stuff on the grassy crags of Garnedd Ugain. The technical challenge was trivial but I had no idea what was below me and it was pretty obvious that this was by no means a popular route. I was beginning to trespass on rock-climber's terrain. It's funny, the things one thinks about in such circumstances. The memory that fell off a shelf in the mind concerned my first grope. This occurred in darkness and the young lady was so flat-chested, so deficient in protuberant way-markers, that one almost had need of a guide. Just another example of unfamiliarity with the route.

In going right I had also gone wrong. But among hill-walkers there is an adage that the man who never went wrong never went anywhere; alternatively, that the man who never made a mistake never made anything. Serious trouble can and must be avoided. The important thing is to keep the brain in gear. Mistakes should swiftly be recognized, accepted, and corrected. Before blundering too far into the fog I retreated to the proper path where I had left it, at the end of the fence, and carefully sorted out the next phase of the zig-zags. Whereupon there was another decision to be made: carry on or turn back. Very much in mind was the thought that one of the purposes of this book was to demonstrate that even a sexagenarian could climb Corrán Tuathail, Ben Nevis, Snowdon and Scafell Pike without risk. And I had been given a warning. On the other hand, risk had easily been identified and evaded. More-over I was not much below the safety of the ridge and railway track and adjacent obelisk and, having come so far, was reluctant to call off the climb. Quitting so soon would simply be chickening out. The conclusion was to press on but leave the options open.

There were no further alarms but, ultimately, Snowdon in November was a bastard. The fierce wind howling and sighing across the Bwlch Glas was the kind that sends brass monkeys rushing to the welders to be reunited with their appendages. Other than the length of a tennis court, if that, one could see damn all. And there was a measure of absurdity in crunching along on ice and frozen snow, through the clouds, beside a railway track incongruously perched at an altitude of more than 3,280 ft (1,000 m). Never mind. The railway took the finding out of route-finding and a yank on the Balaclava produced adequate insurance against frost-bitten ears. Both the Balaclava and cardigan were designed to protect British troops during the bitter winters of the Crimean War. The Balaclava took its name from the town and battle in the Ukraine, the cardigan from the Earl of Cardigan, who led the charge of the Light Brigade. The odd thing, among word-smiths anyway, is that the Balaclava usually retains its initial capital but the cardigan does not.

Such were the ramblings of a disordered mind in the dis-ordered world of that laborious trek to a deserted railway station. And it did not escape my mind, any more than it has escaped yours, that the day's doings had provided some revisional homework in the craft of hill-walking. There could hardly have been a more striking example of the extent to which a lovely morning can turn dangerously nasty on the upper slopes of a mountain. Clouds, visible water vapour, indicate air that is rising and cooling. Their close company is disorienting and unless you know the route like the back of your hand or have a railway track beside you, it is easy to wander off course and, possibly, come down with a damaging bump. On the Snowdon massif there are places where such falls would be like stepping down the lift-shaft in a skyscraper. Or lift-shafts. In Dallas I once went up a skyscraper in which one had to change lifts, or elevators, halfway. On emerging at the summit I was greeted by a handshake from the first man on the moon, Neil Armstrong. I never found out what the hell he was doing there (that is, at the top of a skyscraper) but his presence seemed appropriate.

While plodding through the clouds onto the platform at the railway terminus, amid a silent isolation that was rather eerie, I sensed movement behind me. No, the hairs on the back of the neck did not stand to attention. But the feeling was uncanny, especially when I turned and saw a black dog (it seemed huge) looming out of the fog like a ghost. Was this the hound of the

Baskervilles – that 'enormous coal-black hound' – transported on a time machine to put me in a dither? Nor was I much comforted when, as quickly as it had appeared, the dog vanished into the vaguely moving wall of off-white vapour. But it soon became agreeably substantial: frisking about the summit in the company of two men carrying ice axes. (Mental note: if the only people you meet on summits have ice axes, you could be hovering hazardously on the frontier between hill-walking and mountaineering.) The hound, they explained, was called Mot and one of its parents was a black labrador. They were not sure about the other, which was frustrating. One likes to know about things like that. But on consecutive climbs, Ben Nevis and Snowdon, I had met top dogs.

At 12.10 I clambered onto Yr Wyddfa, the highest point of England and Wales. The stroll up from Pen-y-Pass had taken two hours and thirty-five minutes, a period in which the number of children born in China tends to exceed the total population of Midhurst. Another climber had appeared out of the fog like a spectre. Four men and a dog made fleeting contact with the cairn and trig pillar and then backed off fast, as if taking part in a touch relay, and headed for the lee side of the grey, bleakly functional station building a few yards lower down. There was nothing to see on top and the wind was so strong, so cold, that nobody was inclined to hang about.

For more than a century, until George Borrow's era merged into that of the railway, two huts provided refreshment and shelter – even sleeping accommodation – on Yr Wyddfa. Our gratitude for their demolition must be modified. They could not have been much uglier than their successor, the railway terminus. This visually offensive structure has two redeeming features: during the train season its staff serve the highest pints in the British Isles; and it stands, deferentially, slightly below the summit. I have been in a few barrack rooms but none looked quite as spartan as this place. From the outside, anyway (I probably went inside, back in the summer of 1948, but the memory is blank on the subject of café, bar and souvenir shop

– all staffed, in season, by employees of the Snowdon Mountain Railway). Aesthetically, a chalet-type building would have been much more in harmony with the location. But the station had to be sufficiently solid and secure to defy the perils of winter – the weather, plus break-ins – while unmanned. It looks like a fortress that could withstand a mortar attack and at the time of our visit could not have been more comprehensively closed.

The first person plural was briefly relevant because the four of us, plus Mot, huddled beside the station in a measure of shelter from the wind while we had lunch. Well, hot soup from a flask was not much of a lunch, but it went down well – quickly, too, before the soup could be transformed into vichyssoise by the prevailing temperature and the water dripping on us from long, graceful icicles decorating the guttered eaves. What fun we hill-walkers have. The phantom fourth man kindly took a group photograph before vanishing into nothingness as mysteriously as he had come out of it. Then Mot and his companions set off down that toy railroad while I was making a few notes. The two men had been talking English but, when we parted company, slipped back into Welsh. In November there has to be a fair chance that Snowdon will revert to the status of a Welsh rather than tourist mountain.

For what it's worth I'm told that Yr Wyddfa competes with the head of Glen Garry, in the Scottish highlands, as the wettest place in the British Isles. And even on an otherwise sunny day the summit may be covered in snow and wreathed in cloud. It is reported (again, the facts come second-hand) that on rare occasions the view from Yr Wyddfa may encompass the Wicklow Mountains, the Isle of Man, the Lake District, and even a bit of Scotland. But never expect that sort of thing. Just hope for it. Scenically, these high mountains are to be savoured on the way up and the way down. Anything seen from the summits is a bonus. In preparing this book I stood on four peaks. Only one of them – the lowest, Scafell Pike, climbed on the last day of April – offered a clear panorama of an inevitably breathtaking environment. A 25 per cent success rate is not at all bad. What a joy it must be, though, to stand on Yr Wyddfa and visually appreciate that Glaslyn is 1,590 ft (485 m) below it.

On the way down – follow the railway and turn right at the obelisk – I noticed that, below me, Mot's two companions were rummaging at the side of the track and stowing stuff away. They were collecting litter, even in November. Paper, plastic bags, cans, apple cores, whatever. Such a popular mountain attracts a few yobbos, too thick to consider that they should leave the lovely landscape as tidy as they found it, preferably tidier. But for the wardens' service and the voluntary labours of genuine hill-walkers, Snowdon would begin to look like a rubbish dump.

Mot was bounding along, savouring every moment of freedom. The cloud thinned, suddenly. Distantly, over Llyn Llydaw, sunshine appeared. Down there the weather was evidently even better than it had been during the morning ascent. But there was still work to be done and, as it happened, Snowdon had a little further education to offer. I had decided to descend via the Miners' track but, unfamiliar with the junction of the two routes, began the descent towards Glaslyn too soon and, within minutes, was doing some more finger-and-toe exercises on a steep, greasy mixture of rock and grass. Again, there were no technical difficulties; but again it was obvious that I was gadding about in the wrong area and must retreat to the point of error. Once identified, the track down to Glaslyn was the next best thing to a staircase.

Alongside the lake, walking on level ground was an odd sensation after about four hours on the mountain. For a while the legs felt as if a spanner had been tossed into the works. There used to be an American tennis professional called Jim McManus who was known as the poor man's Rod Laver because, except for different levels of ability, they looked much alike. When Jim retired from the circuit he took up marathon running so effectively that he had a best time of two hours and forty-two minutes. After one such run he was playing some recreational tennis when he discovered that his legs – accustomed to hours of forward motion in marathon training and competition – refused to go into reverse gear when he had to deal with a lob. My own situation was comparatively trivial but if legs could speak, the message coming up from mine would have been rude.

Glaslyn, tucked into the base of Snowdon's mighty north-eastern face, is usually dark, still and forbidding. Until twentieth-century soundings took the fun out of speculation, the lake was supposedly bottomless – and the legendary home of a monster that could have been responsible for the mysterious disappearance, between sunset and sunrise, of sheep and goats that had been wandering about on the shore. Any animals taking high dives from the crags would, one assumes, have floated back into view. So we are left with four possibilities: midnight migrations, rustling, wolves or the monster theory. One thing for sure is that you won't find me looming out of the shadows at Glaslyn in the small hours.

Mind you, the miners actually lived there except when making arduous treks home for a weekend break. In a primitive way the metallic content of the Snowdon massif may have been explored as far back as Roman times. The copper mines we know about were on the slopes above Glaslyn and the ore is the cause of the unusual, bluish-green colouring of Glaslyn and Llyn Llydaw. The ore was transported via cable and buckets down to Llyn Llydaw, where it was crushed and smelted. The mining was never big business but provided productive employment from late in the eighteenth century until 1916, by which time the venture's decline had become terminal. To put that in a wider context, Snowdon's copper-mining industry expired in a year better known for famous battles on sea and land in turn: Jutland and the Somme.

A Land Rover parked at the eastern extremity of Glaslyn confirmed that even the blind, the daft or the drunk could have no further difficulties in sorting out the route. The track down to Llyn Llydaw was broad and neatly manicured. The wardens' service have done a good job on Snowdon. The lower paths are suitable for family outings but, except for the railway, the upper slopes remain challenging for the general run of hill-walkers. Alongside the drop from Glaslyn is a musical stream, rushing and tumbling down rocky ledges. This – the Afon Glaslyn, the river as distinct from the lake – plunges to Llyn Llydaw and is then channelled into a huge pipeline that snakes down to a power station in Nant Gwynant.

Llyn Llydaw is not as wild and awesome as Glaslyn. It is comparatively bland but beautifully located and, in terms of industrial history, evocative. I had already had a taste of that: up by the old mine near the junction of the Pig and Miners' tracks and again (while conducting a one-sided conversation with a supercilious herring gull) down by the ruined cottages beside Glaslyn. The mining remnants on Llyn Llydaw's northern shore are more substantial and the ears of the imagination could almost pick up the thump and clank and hiss of machinery working the ore into a more practical product. How bizarre the scene must have been, a hundred years earlier, on such an afternoon as this: a cool breeze moderated the effect of sunshine, the waters of the lake gently lapped its shores, and the heights of Snowdon and Y Lliwedd were misty and vague but fresh in the memory because of wind and snow and icicles and a dog called Mot. I crossed the causeway, built by the mining company in 1853 with rock excavated from the holes made in Snowdon's eastern flank. The level of the lake had to be lowered and a crude canoe fashioned from the trunk of an oak was found embedded in the mud. That was solid evidence of human history, perhaps prehistory, in an era long before that of mountaineers and miners. Not a lot of people know that 1853 was also the year in which a Red Indian chef invented potato crisps.

On the way down from the Pig track to Glaslyn I had passed an elderly couple descending with care but without difficulty.

e easy way to 'climb' Snowdon from Llanberis.

mechanical 'Yeti' bedded down for the winter.

A morning view of Y Lliwedd.
An expert's comment:
'The range of tones is quite
wide and asking a lot of any film,
with or without a filter'.

Alongside the fogbound summit station of the Snowdon Mountain Railway, with Mot
two Welsh climbers. Note the ice axe - and the ice.

The ruins of former miners' cottages alongside Glaslyn.

A familiar and welcome sight to generations of climbers and hill-walkers: Pen-y-Pass from the Miners' Track.

e Wasdale Head Inn, the traditional nursery of English climbing.

e church and 'climbers' cemetery' at Wasdale Head, where a Viking tradition has en sanctified.

Scafell Crag in late November. A famous access route, Lord's Rake, is glimpsed in the top left-hand corner.

king back up Wastwater, England's deepest lake.

e last of the 'Four Peaks'. Scafell Pike's summit cairn is in the background. Left to ht: David Adams, Margaret Bellamy, the author, Keith Watson, and Brian Hunter.

The cairned route from Lingmell Col down to Hollow Stones offers frontal detail of a rock-climber's playground, Scafell Crag.

They had gone up most of the way I did but at the junction of routes had switched to the Miners' track, cutting out the more arduous ascent to the summit. Even so, their day's labour must have been both testing and rewarding. Alongside Llyn Llydaw two younger couples were enjoying an afternoon stroll. One of the men was carrying a well-wrapped baby. On the entire outing I met only twenty-two people (plus Mot) but in terms of age and physical ability they were a cross-section of the hill-walking community. And it struck me again that Snowdon's vast selection of paths and tracks, scattered over a huge area, had something to offer everyone.

The railway is something else, but relevant. That morning, after breakfast, I had driven down to Llanberis: mainly to acquire a mental picture of the railway's bottom end before climbing to its top end. Llanberis Pass, a desolate defile between Snowdon and the Glyders, drops about 825 ft (251 m) from Pen-y-Pass in little more than five miles. About halfway down is the starting point for a tough route up Snowdon via Cwm Glas. The pass acquired a road, circa 1830, because most of the miners lived in the old village of Nant Peris at the foot of the pass – and it was to Nant Peris (and eventually Caernarfon) that the copper from Glaslyn and Llyn Llydaw was transported. But for almost two hundred years local employment was concentrated at the Dinorwic slate quarries on the slopes that rise to the north from Llyn Peris. The dark terracing of the quarries cut deep wounds into the south-western flank of Elidir Fawr and the vast scale of the disfigurement is awesome. These used to be the world's largest slate quarries and they provided work for about three thousand people in the 1890s. The decline was caused by labour-management disputes, foreign competition, and the development of cheaper roofing materials. Quarrying ended in 1969.

Other than all that, Llanberis is a rambling tourist centre with two lakes: Padarn (the biggest in Snowdonia) and Peris. The names commemorate early Celtic saints. On a rocky knoll, close to the point at which the lakes almost meet, are the ruins of Dolbadarn Castle, which had a lively if rather vague history during the era of the medieval Welsh princes. But the purpose of my fleeting visit to Llanberis was, as I said, to find out a little more about the Snowdon Mountain Railway, which is based across the road from the Royal Victoria Hotel. That railway, its history and its place in the scheme of things, has long been a fascinating if decreasingly controversial basis for debate. We take the line for granted now, just as we take for granted the screening of a motion picture – a movie – before a British paying public. Both innovations occurred in 1896 and, consequently, will soon qualify for centenary celebrations.

A few fast facts. The railway climbs more than 3,000 ft (914 m) in almost five miles. The maximum gradient is 1 in 5.5, the views are marvellous, and the return trip (including half an hour on the summit) takes two and a half hours. The track has a narrow gauge, 2 ft 7½ in (80 cm), and locomotion depends on the rack and pinion principle. In other words, it has teeth. One could say that the trains fight Snowdon tooth and rail. There are ten engines: seven steam (four have been working since the line was opened) and three diesel. Two of the diesel engines were acquired in 1986, the third in 1991. A coal-fired return trip costs the company (not the passengers) about thirteen times as much as an oil-fired return trip. So it is no surprise that the steam locomotives are to be equipped with new boilers and converted into oil-fired steam engines, which sounds odd but can be equated with central heating systems.

Weather permitting, the line is open from mid-March until the end of October, give or take a week or so, but travels only to Clogwyn (two-thirds of the way) at the beginning and end of the season. For obvious reasons the café at the summit, which has upstairs sleeping quarters for a staff of four, is open only during those summer months when trains can lift passengers and goods to the top. In 1990 the Snowdon Mountain Railway carried a record total of 122,700 passengers. In 1991 the fare for the return trip was £12 for adults and £8.50

for children under fifteen. From a marketing point of view the
S.M.R. management consider that 85 per cent of their
customers are interested in climbing a mountain by rail and the
other 15 per cent are enthusiasts for the age of steam locomotion.

The only accident occurred in 1896 on the first run. The
engine, destined for a short life, fell from Clogwyn into the
point at which the Cwm Glas Bach merges with the Cwm
Hetiau ('Valley of the Hats', because a lot of hats were blown
off there and collected and sold by the kind of lads who earn
pocket-money by gathering up lost golf balls). The engine was
swiftly reduced to a heap of scrap metal in the cwm. One chap
panicked, jumped out of a carriage window, fell under the
train, and did not live to tell us about it. Otherwise the
passengers were safe because the automatic brakes worked
efficiently.

There is a school of thought that the railway should never
have been built, that it is an offence to the environment, that
its construction was the equivalent of putting wild animals in
cages. If it did not exist and somebody proposed it now, in an
age when conservation is such a popular social issue, what an
outcry there would be. There would be a similar outcry if
anyone proposed that villages should be drowned and their
human and wildlife communities scattered so that such reservoirs as Ladybower in the Peak District, Haweswater in the
Lake District, and Vyrnwy in Powys could satisfy increasing
urban needs for piped water. We may regret all that. We may
oppose such ventures in the future. But the railway is with us.
The reservoirs are with us. Without forgetting or condoning all
the factors involved in their creation, we should make the most
of the consequences. Ladybower has, for me, been a poignant
example. From childhood I have affectionate memories of
Ashopton and Derwent, the now submerged villages. Even so,
only a bigot could deny that, aesthetically, Derwent Dale has
been enhanced by Ladybower and the older reservoirs north of
it. And only a bigot could close his heart to the beauty of the

colours and lighting effects that illuminate Ladybower and its moorland setting late on a sunny September afternoon.

In short, let us make the best of what we have instead of being obsessively churlish about its origins. There are hill-walkers and mountaineers who are toffee-nosed about the railway and those who use it. But such cynics can have their fun on Snowdon – there is plenty of room – without seeing anything of the railway except for the top bit. And they may live long enough to be grateful for it. Consider how lucky we are, those of us who have two sound legs and enough engine power to drive us to the summit under our own steam. But unlike those four surviving 1896 engines, we lack the secret of eternal youth. If we are spared that long, you and I may eventually have to accept the fact that our wobbly old legs have lost the capacity to pump us all the way up Snowdon. But our interest in sex does not decline at the same rate as our level of performance and it is equally true that, even when infirm, we will still have a yearning for such a climax as Yr Wyddfa. Thanks to the railway we will still be able to satisfy that yearning – and savour the memory of cherished yesterdays.

So let us not be patronizing when, proud of our modest climb, we see the train disgorge its human cargo at the summit station. There will be old folk among them, perhaps arthritic. There will be mums and dads introducing children to the glory of high places. There will be plenty who have never been up a mountain before and want to find out what the experience has to say to them. We may reasonably argue that although all these have paid for the pleasure of standing on Yr Wyddfa, they have not earned it. But we cannot reasonably argue that the railway is a totally indefensible scar on a wonderful mountain.

All that springs from my earlier point that Snowdon – its paths high and low, its railway – has something to offer everyone. But we didn't quite finish my walk, did we? All that was left of it, after Llyn Llydaw, was a saunter down to Pen-y-Pass. The long outline of the youth hostel showed ever more

detail as a long shot gradually became a close-up. How much
that prospect must have changed since the early climbers came
clattering down in their nailed boots to what was then the Pen-
y-Pass Hotel, now the western end of the hostel building. No
doubt the old-timers lit their pipes and sank a pint or two
while discussing the day's doings. I had the same thing in mind
but the café was strictly for non-smoking teetotallers. Were
today's hill-walkers that much different from their pre-
decessors? Not really. There was nothing to be done about the
beer but a bunch of us gathered in the café vestibule (more
heavily populated than the interior), found a couple of chairs
for the ladies, set fire to various forms of dried leaves, and
sipped tea or coffee. I'm not getting involved in the arguments
about smoking, or drinking and driving. But after a day on a
mountain the choice between tea or coffee (or soft drinks) is
not uppermost in my mind.

Our company included a youngster who had come over the
tops from Capel Curig with two superb German Shepherds,
both show dogs. We admired these and for a while the conversation remained on a canine course. A Liverpudlian listened
attentively. He was a little frustrated because he had hoped to
do a solo on the horseshoe but had prudently curtailed his
programme because of nasty weather on the heights. His
contribution to the dog talk was unusually interesting. He and
his father, he said, were ratcatchers. They had a Jack Russell
which had sometimes embarrassed them by showing as much
interest in chickens as it did in rats. This information prompted
four thoughts. One, in Britain there are probably as many rats
as people and it was heartening to meet a man professionally
engaged in adjusting those proportions in favour of people.
Two, the Liverpool connection was appropriate because I
understand that the hefty and aggressive brown rat has
managed to drive the black or ship rat back to cities that are
also ports. Three, one inevitably toyed with the mental vision
of our large and well-muscled companion setting off for 'the
office' in the company of such a diminutive workmate as a

Jack Russell. Four, how odd it is that this fiery little dog – the 'hit man' of the ratcatching world – acquired its name from a parson. Mind you, I have known a couple of parsons who, when sufficiently provoked, could handle themselves well enough to transform muscular Christianity into mayhem.

My round trip, bottom to top and back again, had occupied a total of five hours and twenty minutes, which is probably about average. That included the bizarre break for lunch within range of windswept icicle drippings. After the café interlude I called on the Lloyds, Harvey and Rosie in turn, to let them know that I was down and, mission accomplished, would be driving home that night as planned. Rosie, preparing for the active pleasures of her coming winter in Chamonix, had just got back from a warm-up on the dry ski slope at Plas y Brenin. On the way to Capel Curig I stopped and got out of the car, twice, to look back. The double-take was necessary because I could not quite believe what I had seen the first time and wanted to imprint on my memory the vision behind me. That vision was the pinks and reds of a glorious sunset, with Snowdon darkly etched against the rich colours of its back-drop. The sun sets every day, of course, and newspapers would have the devil of a job coming up with adequate headlines if it didn't. But for me that parting view of the mountain was, and may remain, a unique experience. In its isolation from the rest of life it brought to mind Edward Thomas's charming poem about the sights and sounds of a magical minute at Adlestrop, and Hilaire Belloc's equally evocative lines:

> This is the place where Dorothea smiled.
> I did not know the reason, nor did she.
> But there she stood, and turned, and smiled at me.
> A sudden glory had bewitched the child.
> The corn at harvest, and a single tree.
> This is the place where Dorothea smiled.

There was a familiar pit stop at Newbold-on-Stour for a bowl of soup and a long overdue pint. About thirteen and a half hours after first setting foot on the Pig track I was back in Midhurst (with 584 miles on the clock for the entire excursion) and walking the Norfolk terrier, our resident ratcatcher – but permanently unemployed because there are no rats in the vicinity. The veterans' monthly Stableford at Cowdray Park, a course with some testing bumps on it, was played a week later. We were swapping news on the tenth when I weighed in with the Snowdon story.

'Did you go up on your own?' Jim asked.

'This time, yes.'

'Should you be doing that at your age, especially this late in the year?'

'In principle, probably not. But it was a lovely day, except on top, and I knew what I was doing. The legs are still good. It wasn't tiring.'

Jim thoughtfully selected a four wood for his second.

'Well, maybe we veterans do tend to be over-careful. Perhaps we coddle ourselves too much, too soon.'

I didn't need convincing. Three down. One to go.

GLOSSARY

We have already noted that the Celtic language split into two branches: the Gaelic common to Ireland, Scotland and the Isle of Man, and the Brythonic common to Wales, Brittany and formerly Cornwall. The words Briton and Breton are closely related to Brython and the Old English name for Cornwall, Cornwealas, referred to the Welsh inhabitants of the county – or, if you like, to the regional mixture of Cornish and Welsh blood lines. Geographic proximity was largely the reason for the separate development of two Celtic tongues. Our Irish, Scottish and Welsh glossaries provide obvious examples of divergence from common roots.

The complicated feature of Welsh spelling, for those of us

unfamiliar with it, is mutation: initial consonants change according to the nature of the preceding word. The consonants subject to mutation are b, c, d, g, ll, m, p, rh and t. There is no essential difference in meaning between, for example, bach and fach, ban and fan, coch and goch, or crib and grib. Regard the initial consonant as negotiable and concentrate on the rest of the word.

Afon	River
Aran	Grassy summit
Arddu	Black height
Bach or Fach	Small
Ban or Fan	Hill
Bryn	Hill
Bwlch	Pass; saddle between peaks
Caer	Fort
Carnedd or Garnedd	Cairn; mountain
Carreg (cerrig)	Rock (rocks)
Cefn	Ridge; back
Clogwyn	Steep crag
Coch or Goch	Red
Craig (cregiau)	Crag (crags)
Crib or Grib	Crest; ridge
Cwm	Valley; hollow
Ddu or Du	Black
Dinas	Fort
Drum or Trum	Ridge
Drws	Gap; gate
Dyffryn	Valley
Gallt or Allt	Hillside
Glas	Blue; green
Glyder	Clutter of rocks
Glyn	Glen
Gwyn, Gwen or Wen	White
Hafod	Summer farmhouse
Lliwedd	Crowd; nation

Llyn	Lake
Maen	Boulder
Mawr or Fawr	Big
Moel or Foel	Bare hill
Mynydd	Moorland mountain
Nant	Stream; valley
Pen	Top
Rhinog	Buttress
Twll	Hole; cavern
Uchaf	Higher
Y or Yr	The; of the
Ystrad	Valley; street

England: Scafell Pike

3,206 ft (977 m)

The Wasdale trip was a paradox. It happened too soon and too late. Impatient to tackle the last and lowest of the four peaks, I did not wait until, weather-wise, the fruit was ripe for plucking. Conditions were far from ideal. But the immediate forecast was promising enough to push to the back of the mind a warning that the tops were bedevilled by snow and fierce, bitter winds – and that, the day before my phone call, a couple of hill-walkers had been mislaid. Everything had been going well, other than the day's delay on Corrán Tuathail and that bit of bother on Snowdon. Perhaps over-confident and consequently careless, I was also eager to exploit a now acceptable level of fitness by climbing to the top of England before such mountains were harshly governed by the equivalent of 'winter rules' on golf courses. It was the time of year when wise hill-walkers become wary of high places and leave them to those quasi-masochists who use ice axes and crampons. In short, I headed north about five months too soon and scheduled the climb for about a month too late: 24 November. Never mind. The outcome was to be an educational reminder that in hill-walking, as in competitive sports, an error of strategy can be corrected by a flexible adjustment of tactics.

The day after Margaret Thatcher's reluctant resignation,

even lively little Midhurst seemed to be in mourning: because of damp, grey weather that, before one had been at the wheel for long, degenerated into a fog representing the then prevalent mood of the Conservative Party. And the forecast emitted by the car radio was the familiar stuff about 'heavy rain falling as sleet or snow on high ground'. What the hell. I was committed and might get lucky. The customary break for a 'half' and a bowl of soup at the White Hart, Newbold-on-Stour, featured an immensely dignified Golden Retriever. This ignored me until the food arrived, whereupon its scrutiny was so intense as to be almost magnetic. One half expected the soup-plate to float through the air on a current of will power from one side of the bar-room to the other. After the Ben Nevis and Snowdon trips much of the route (A272, A34, M6) was no more adventurous than a walk round the garden. West Sussex is a delight, a pub-strewn Shangri-la. But it is not ideally positioned for those of us whose hearts sing the sweetest songs only at two or three times the height of the gentle South Downs. If you live near mountains, make the most of them.

The Lake District was neither familiar nor unfamiliar. As a teenager I went over there from Sheffield with a chum in the Rover Scouts for a walking holiday: vaguely memorable because of high passes, relentless rain and bathing trunks. After the first day we put on damp clothes and socks and boots every morning because the drying facilities at the hostels couldn't cope with the density of water in vast quantities of gear deposited by squelching mobs of temporary residents. It may have been on Hardknott Pass, during the mother and father of a downpour, that we met a chap who had devised a solution. He was clad only in boots, socks and bathing trunks. The rest of his clothing was wrapped in waterproofs inside the rucksack. In those days the possibilites of plastic had not been fully explored but there were plenty of alternatives. Our chance acquaintance had been smart: there can't be many hill-walkers with the foresight to pack bathing trunks. In the years of maturity (that is, for post-graduate Rover Scouts) there were

shorter and drier invasions of Lakeland: a lazy weekend break
with my wife, at Keswick, and a four-man ramble that took in
Helvellyn and High Street. The usual rubber-necking. Nothing
had prepared me for the business of getting from the M6 to
Wasdale.

If you have never done it, be warned that navigating around
the south-western corner of the Lake District in the hours of
darkness – while windswept rain is driving the windscreen
wipers berserk – can be a nightmare. It is no help that main
roads and minor roads look much alike, except on the map.
Mind you, getting disoriented on the M25 must be even worse.
One driver, kidding himself that he was heading north,
covered hundreds of miles of the M25, stopped to ask the
police to direct him to the turn-off for Durham, and discovered
that he was only fifteen miles from his home in Kent. Another,
en route from Lancashire to Middlesex, pulled into an M25
lay-by in a state of glassy-eyed confusion almost two days
later. He had been round once too often and was temporarily
witless. But some Samaritan spotted him and called the police.
The M6-Wasdale route is both easier and more interesting: a
series of zig-zags rather than an orbit. But if you are new to it,
as I was, set about the task in daylight. The drive from the M6
to Wasdale Head covers sixty-five miles and should take about
an hour and three-quarters. There are two alternatives. One is
to stay on the M6 as far as Penrith and then take the A66,
swinging south – near Cockermouth – on the A5086 and
A595 to Gosforth. The other, worth considering only in good
weather, is the direct route on an often steep minor road from
Ambleside via the Wrynose Pass and Hardknott Pass to
Eskdale and Santon Bridge.

Gosforth and Santon Bridge are not the sort of places that
figure prominently in Lake District holiday brochures. But the
signposted names ring bells – introductory or valedictory – in
the minds of walkers and climbers who prefer the remote cul-
de-sac of Wasdale to the tourist traps of central Lakeland. That
dark and stormy night the southern approach was confusing:

partly because there was little to be seen except for the cat's-eyes glowing in the reflected glare of headlights, and the roadside hedgerows, grasses and ferns bending in the tug of the wind; and partly because in heading towards Gosforth, which I'd always associated with Newcastle upon Tyne, I had to drive through Bootle, which I'd always associated with Liverpool. What with one thing and another that approach run was quite a test of concentration. An excuse for a brief break was a phone call to tell my wife (and convince myself) that I was 'almost there'. But I was.

You may be a hill-walker to whom Wasdale is an aspiration rather than a memory. If so, you will appreciate that seeing the name in black and white on a signpost, for the first time, inspired a surge of exhilaration. A pilot concerned about a dicky engine once landed with relief at Heathrow. Dissatisfied with an Indian engineer's diagnosis, he sought a second opinion from an English technician. Same diagnosis. Whereupon the Indian gently observed: 'Now you have it in black and white.' Anyway, black on white is reassuring. Any journalist will tell you that black on yellow is easier on the eyes but such distinctions did not colour my thinking during the ascent to Wasdale. It was a wild night. Windswept leaves rushed down the road towards the car like a Cup Final crowd bursting out of Wembley. The contest between rain and windscreen wipers was fierce, the way ahead vague and threatening.

Second hand, one had a rough idea what to expect next. Such weather, such darkness, sharpened the challenge of that first acquaintance with the undulating contortions of the narrow road alongside Wastwater's western shore. But as Marcus Aurelius pointed out, we can survive anything except death. At 6.45 p.m., with 369 miles on the clock, I pulled in at the Wasdale Head Inn car park and dashed through the rain into the sanctuary of Ritson's Bar for cottage pie and a pint. The inn was closed for the winter (except for a couple of weeks after Christmas, which lunatics on the loose consider a good time for climbing mountains) but its public bar was not. There was a welcoming fire and the place was busy with fresh-faced young walkers and climbers. The walls were heavily adorned by evocative museum-pieces – photographs and primitive mountaineering gear – from the days when climbing itself was young, and specialized clothing and equipment had yet to be developed. The contrast between then and now was strikingly evident. One had only to compare that evening's customers with the garb worn by early climbers: pictured in photographs taken by the brothers George and Ashley Abraham of Keswick, those renowned pioneers in the practice of climbing with cameras. But the old-timers would probably have felt very much at home in the ambience of Ritson's Bar as I found it: that is, out of season, with the summer invasion a thing of the past and the future.

In short, history was all around us. The Wasdale Head Inn is the mother-church of English climbing. More than a century ago its resident employees included a guide, a Frenchman called Pierre Gaspard. His professional labours must have induced less athletic clients to 'gasp 'ard' and make the pun with such irritating regularity that Gaspard may have been tempted to nudge them over some convenient crag. '*J'en ai assez*!'

For a few years it seemed that Seatoller, in Borrowdale, was as likely as Wasdale Head to become the recognized nursery of English climbing. The clinching factors in that rivalry were the personality of Will Ritson and, in 1856, his initiative in getting a licence and calling his popular farmhouse the Huntsman Inn (now the Wasdale Head Inn). In those days many farmers brewed their own ale, so Ritson's transition to the formal status of landlord was no big deal. Ritson was a pipe and pint man. He was also a farmer, fox-hunter, fell-walker, wrestler and raconteur. And a liar. Cumbrians, like most country folk, have a gift for taking straight-faced liberties with the truth. In such a confusing never-never-land, Ritson was king. He knew a lot and invented a lot. Fluent and witty, the man had opinions on everything and in his vast command of fact and fancy he recognized no distinction between the two. He claimed that before the farmhouse was transformed into an inn his guests had included William Wordsworth. Knowing what we do of both (Wordsworth was a local man and put himself about a bit), that could have been true.

What is certainly true is that the upper-crust nucleus of Britain's early climbing community found Ritson to be an eccentric and richly entertaining host. Class distinctions were more marked in that era and one can imagine the scene as academics, scientists, writers and artists gathered round the fire with Ritson and supped their ale in a fug of tobacco smoke. If only the ensuing cross-talk had been recorded! At ease on his home ground, Ritson met all of them on equal terms. There were no social barriers. They had fun together. It's reported that Ritson once observed: why go to London to see the sights when so many of the sights came to Wasdale to see him?

Ritson died at the age of eighty-three in 1890, a year otherwise remarkable for the opening of the Forth Bridge and the introduction of goal-nets at football grounds. He is commemorated via the bar, via Ritson's Force (a nearby waterfall, up Mosedale Beck), and via a 'Biggest Liar In The World' contest held every November at the Santon Bridge Inn. The bar and waterfall keep his name alive and the lying competition does as much for his spirit. It's a light-hearted amateur event and such 'professionals' as lawyers and politicians – regarded as experts at bending the truth – are barred. In Ritson's time it was a local boast that Wasdale had England's highest mountain (true), deepest lake (true), and smallest church (untrue) – and the world's biggest liar (unattested). That was the Ritsonian style: wrap up fact and speculation in one playful, plausible package and, if you have the will and the wit, tie it with the bright ribbons of fantasy.

Refreshed in stomach and spirit, I popped round the corner to check in with Sandra and Michael Naylor at Middle Row, where bed and breakfast had been booked in advance. Back in

Ritson's Bar, I sank a few bevvies in congenial company. This chance acquaintance had known the chap who, eighteen days earlier, had fallen off the Snowdon massif with terminal consequences. My companion reasonably insisted that 'Climbing is no more dangerous than crossing the road', which you and I know to be true. As the chat swung this way and that it became clear that on one subject my drinking partner was unusually reticent. He made no reference to his job. Curiosity overcoming decorum, I finally asked: 'What do you do in the way of earning a crust?'

Silence. Just a guarded look. But I persisted.

'For Christ's sake, are you a tax inspector, a traffic warden, or what?'

The choice of labours mockingly associated with catching people out was deliberately provocative. And it worked.

'A policeman.'

'Why be shy about that?'

'It tends to be a conversation-stopper.'

'Don't see why. Are you on the beat or stuck in a station?'

'CID.'

Whereupon I dropped the subject, because it was obvious that the man did not want to talk about his job and would not have told me much anyway. Gently moving away from it, he said that he worked in Birmingham but lived in Solihull. When he was in his middle thirties, he said, his wife told him that he needed an interest outside his work. He tried canoeing but spent so much time underwater ('playing submarines') that his enthusiasm was dampened. So he took up back-packing, found that it suited him, and enjoyed getting away with friends. They found their own way about the mountains, sleeping in tents or whatever was available. In the absence of fins and gills, walking the tops made more sense than spinning underwater from a canoe.

Years earlier I had done some hill-walking with adventure training instructors in the Metropolitan Police, though few of the chaps I met were native Londoners. Provincial forces tend to raise their eyebrows at some of the methods the Met get away with but one assumes that special problems demand special solutions. That area of debate is a hot potato and I don't know enough to make it digestible. What I do know is that it took hours of leg-work and bar-room companionship to put the Met men at ease with the outsider in their midst. At that time the Met were getting some unflattering publicity. The bobbies on duty with me over Dartmoor and the Glyders horseshoe confessed that, at first, they had suspected that even a hill-walking sports writer might be 'Big Brother' sneaking in at the back door.

It's easy to understand why the police think twice about getting chummy with strangers when it comes to trade talk. There is so much scope for compromising indiscretions. The police are like ministers of the church (and perhaps doctors and the royal family) in that they can only be completely at ease with their own kind. On the whole policemen and clergy-men – and, yes, the royal family too – are no better and no brighter than the rest of us. But they are committed to trying harder, to maintaining an unusually high standard of personal conduct. They are expected to be good in the old-fashioned sense of the word, to play the game of life on the side of the angels. The two professions must consort with the devil, who sometimes pops up within their own ranks. When the clergy fail in their struggle with incipient villainy, the police take over. To stretch a point, one could call it the difference between admonitory and executive functions in the war against evil.

As youngsters most of us regard the police as caring, worldly-wise and reassuringly avuncular. Forty or fifty years on, we become worldly-wise and avuncular ourselves but still expect the police to be caring and reassuring. Television series often depict the police as irritable and morose, even uncouth: not necessarily the kind of people one would invite to tea. But TV series, like the media as a whole, tend to reflect life only in its darkest colours. The job the police have to do must certainly harden their sensibilities and make them cynical.

Consider the company they repeatedly have to keep, the nasty situations they must confront. Most working days, they have to deal with the more vicious or distressing consequences of human nature. They are not supermen, nor saints. But most of them are doing the best they can to make society more comfortable for the rest of us. Speak as you find: and I have never found the police to be anything but sympathetic, even when calling me to order for a couple of motoring offences.

In the days when the artist Stanley Spencer was living at Cookham we moved into a new house in the village. The garden was an uncultivated wasteland and getting rid of the stones cost me a lot of sweat. I got home from work late one evening and, by the light from the kitchen window, spent an hour or so on the then daily chore of digging a deep 6 ft trench. This activity attracted the attention of our village bobby, who propped his bike by the gate, strolled down the path, and shone his torch on the scene.

'Good evening, sir. May I ask what you're doing?'

'Digging a grave for my wife.'

He caught on instantly.

'Got room for mine?'

In short, I respect the police for the job they do and the kind of people they are. Those I've met, anyway. And one could hardly wish for better company when walking the hills or putting away a few bevvies – exercises that, in different ways, tell us a good deal about our companions.

That evening's two sessions in Ritson's Bar compensated for the taxing chore of getting there. At Middle Row, my home for the night, the Naylors and their children were unexpectedly tanned (unexpectedly because this was Wasdale and 23 November). They were just back from a holiday in the Canaries. Michael is a nephew of Joss Naylor, the most extraordinary human product of Middle Row, or Wasdale, or for that matter the Lake District as a whole. That opinion is not lightly advanced. William Wordsworth was born about 14 miles away (22.5 km) at Cockermouth. He was hot stuff and we can all quote him, but only his most bigoted devotees would claim that he was in a class of his own. Joss Naylor was. No doubt about it. The fact that both came into the world in the same remote, thinly populated area is a reminder of the old joke about an American tourist who turned up in just such an environment and made himself an easy target for the local brand of humour by asking:

'Any big men born around here?'

'No. So far, only babies.'

Naylor emerged from the womb into Middle Row in 1936, a year also remembered for the short and uneasy reign of Edward VIII and the outbreak of civil war in Spain. As a fell-runner, this sheep-farmer took endurance running through barriers of time and motion that might have induced even the legendary Paavo Nurmi to check his life insurance. But just as Wordsworth had more publicity because he was a poet, Nurmi had more publicity because he ran in the spotlight of the Olympics. Their fame spread far beyond poetry and the Olympics and both remain household names. Naylor has more in common with Arthur Newton, whose character and career inspired even the modestly talented Rex Bellamy to collect a few cross-country prizes as a schoolboy. Newton and Naylor were both farmers who became record-breaking endurance runners in their thirties and (by contrast with Wordsworth and Nurmi) turned on its head the biblical cliché that 'a prophet is not without honour, save in his own country'. In their own 'countries' Newton was, and Naylor is, spoken of with awe.

The *Evening Standard* columnist Neil Allen was formerly a colleague on *The Times* and remains a good chum. An athletics specialist, he was an exemplary captain of *The Times* reporting teams when I was posted to the Tokyo and Mexico City Olympics as an odd-job man and 'colour' writer. Neil has sorted out for me the dimly recalled details of Newton's career, and stresses the point that Newton's philosophy and methods influenced succeeding generations: particularly the thinking of Arthur Lydiard, a New Zealand marathon runner who achieved renown in the early 1960s when coaching those illustrious Olympians, Peter Snell and Murray Halberg.

Newton went to school at Bedford, where he was not much interested in competition but enjoyed running on his own for anything from fifteen to twenty miles. Later he went to South Africa and, irked when the government of Natal wanted to take over his farm and transform it into a native reserve, desperately needed to publicize his cause – and decided that he had to make a name for himself. His schooldays were twenty-odd years behind him but the time was ripe for competing – and winning. So he went into training and entered for the Comrades Marathon: more than 54 miles (87 km) over tough terrain from Pietermaritzburg to Durban, passing the eighteenth mile at 3,000 ft (914 m). Definitely a Naylor-type challenge. Newton was inexperienced but canny. He began slowly but won by more than half an hour.

That was in May 1922. Newton was hooked. The land dispute receded into the background and he was soon travelling the world – for example, the 100 miles from Bath to London in fourteen hours and six minutes – as a full-time endurance runner with sponsors and back-up teams. His helpers used to bring along a wind-up gramophone, because Newton liked to listen to classical music when taking a roadside break. I've come across two other great athletes who practised or trained to music; but Jonah Barrington (squash) and Joe Frazier (boxing) found that beat music best suited their purposes. Mind you, Barrington enjoyed Mozart's company when refining drop shots and I once caught Frazier hammering a punchbag while tuned in to 'Try A Little Tenderness'.

Newton believed in a long, gradual build-up to the peak demanded by any severe competitive test. He advocated heel-and-toe running over the marathon distance, 26 miles and 385 yards (42.7 kilometres), suggested 1,300 to 1,400 strides to the mile, and considered that the long-distance men should always run at 20 to 25 per cent below the maximum pace within their capacity. In short, he used his brains as well as his will. Somebody needed to. The original marathon runner, back in 490 BC, was a Greek soldier who is reported to have dropped dead when he finished the course. Newton was not around to give him a few tips. Nowadays the name Arthur Newton seldom rings bells – even Joss Naylor had never heard of him – but for almost seventy years endurance runners have benefited from Newtonian principles.

In the Lake District sheep-farmers and fox-hunters (who worked on foot because horses are no good on crags) had to work it out for themselves. For more than twenty years Naylor was not even a joke as a prospective record-breaker when it came to running over hills and mountains. He had spinal problems from the age of nine, had an operation at twenty, spent eight weeks in a surgical jacket, and later 'got knocked up and had two more do's', as he puts it. The medical advice was that he should do something less strenuous than sheep-farming and fell-running. On the other hand he was a stringy, rawboned man who carried hardly an ounce more than the task of locomotion demanded: he was almost 6 ft tall but weighed only 9 st 7 lb ('I'm still about the same').

Naylor went to school at Gosforth and at fifteen became a shepherd, working for his father and other farmers. In 1962 he married and successfully applied for the vacant tenancy of Bowderdale, an isolated farm even by Wasdale standards (it's about two-thirds of the way up Wastwater, at the foot of Over Beck). Most of the 140 acres consists of grazing high on the fells and some of the stock has to be sent down the valley for winter pasturage. Joss and Mary have two daughters, one son, eight dogs (six work and the other two 'have been pensioned off'), and have built up the original tenancy flock of sheep from 150 to between '450 and 500', mostly Herdwicks. The Naylors also have a self-catering cottage for the use of tourists. In 1976 Joss was awarded an order of chivalry, the MBE. In 1979 he took a second job: shift work on the fuel inlets at Sellafield, Britain's first nuclear power station.

A note about Herdwicks and sheep-farming on the fells. The

hardy Herdwicks ('herd' speaks for itself and 'wick' refers to a farm or other settlement) have been Lake District natives for so long that nobody is quite sure how long. The breed was domesticated by Viking settlers and later became big business for the monastic empire based at Furness Abbey, north-east of Barrow-in-Furness. During the last seventy years Herdwicks have been re-enforced by Swaledales: a Yorkshire breed, as the name implies. The great thing about both breeds is that they stay on their own patch, with a homing instinct that cuts down the need for retaining walls or fences. Little Bo-peep must have drawn the short straw. Had the lass been working with Herdwicks or Swaledales she would have had a pretty good idea where to find them. But upland sheep-farming is a demanding and dodgy business and an economist tells me that the future looks bleak because, in his opinion, subsidies are unlikely to be raised. He thinks lower ground can accommodate all the sheep we need. The National Farmers' Union, on the other hand, insists that there is no writing on the wall:

> Hill-farmers have often gone through bad patches and they're going through a bit of a bad patch at the moment. In the last year or two sheep profitability has fallen, both on the lowlands and the hills. But it's agricultural policy, government policy, and European Community policy to provide special subsidies – over and above the normal subsidies – for sheep and cattle farmers on the hills. That's partly economic, partly social (to maintain rural communities), and partly environmental. There's no danger of sheep vanishing from high places.

If we live long enough we may find out whether we should believe the economist or the NFU. Meantime, it is safe to assume that Joss Naylor did not go to Sellafield because he thought what marvellous fun it would be to work longer hours, doing two jobs instead of one.

To get back to Naylor the fell-runner (with a history of back trouble), he ran his first race, from Wasdale Head, at the age of twenty-four. He entered late, ran in boots, got cramp, and retired after eight miles. He had a lot to learn and made no great impact until he was in his middle thirties and created some startling records ('Training made the difference'). The big years, record-wise, were 1972 and 1973, a period over-lapping his thirty-sixth birthday. As a hill-walker – past, present, or prospective – take care, if you will, to absorb the details. They put our own little adventures into perspective and give us the measure of a man whose feats were almost super-human.

In the Lakeland Classic, a 24-hour race, Naylor reached 72 summits over 2,000 ft (610 m) and covered 108 miles (174 km), including 38,000 ft of climbing (11,582 m), in 23 hours and 11 minutes. Note that although Naylor has not run a marathon on the roads he has broken long-distance road records and, in the Lakeland Classic, ran the equivalent of four marathons in a day – over strenuous terrain. With the help of drivers and timekeepers (and this was before the M6 provided a convenient link) he took only 11 hours and 54 minutes to surmount Ben Nevis, Scafell Pike and Snowdon, starting at Fort William and finishing at Caernarfon. And on a particu-larly nasty and murky day ('It was like running in the dark') he ran from the top of Snowdon to the top of Foel-fras in 4 hours and 46 minutes. That little jaunt took in 14 summits over 3,000 ft (914 m) in a mountainously compact area incorpor-ating the Snowdon massif, the Glyders and the Carnedds. Try walking it. You may reasonably deduce that Naylor was the first example of bionic man.

This was mind-boggling stuff. The news spread. Great endurance runners lay awake at night, toying with the thought that they might, after all, be mere novices. Naylor ran in Colorado, Switzerland and the home of the marathon, Greece. But unlike Newton he remained a farmer who ran as an amateur. And in his middle fifties he's still at it, still setting up the odd record ('I run two or three big races a year'). In

1990 he ran over the tops from Ullswater to Wasdale in filthy weather, taking only 11½ hours to cover 47 miles (76 km) that included 16,500 ft (5,029 m) of ascent. That was for charity. 'It was a nice thing to do.' You will have gathered that Naylor does not suffer from vanity. With a record like his, there would be no point in it anyway. He admits what he has done, confirms this or that fact, but has no taste for verbal garnish unless the occasion demands it (he has twice won that 'Biggest Liar In The World' competition). Which takes us back to Wordsworth and invites flippant speculation. We have a pretty good idea what would have happened had Naylor and Wordsworth taken one another on at poetry and fell-running. No contest. But if they'd had a play-off, at story-telling, the betting odds might have been slightly in Naylor's favour.

It is more to the point to wonder what might have happened if Newton, Nurmi and Naylor (all at their best, of course) had clashed in a three-event series: that is, at fell-running, a road marathon and one of the longer Olympic track events. We shall never know. But there is a yardstick by which we can measure Naylor against Olympic long-distance heroes of much the same era. That yardstick is a mountaineer and fell-runner better known for winning the 1956 Olympic steeplechase: Chris Brasher, latterly a journalist, businessman, and joint founder and director of the London marathon. As an endurance runner Chris not only saw the great Olympians in action: he also found out, the hard way, about Naylor and his kind. So tune in to the man's conclusions:

'At his best, in the 1970s, Joss was superior to any other long-distance runner I have known. As a fell-runner he burnt them all off. They couldn't hold him.'

And how did Naylor compare with Emil Zatopek and Vladimir Kuts?

'We often talked about that – and we rejected them all. Joss was better than Zatopek, Kuts, Coe, Ovett ... There was only one man in his class and that was "Wilson" of *The Wizard*. You had to go into fiction. What Joss did was unbelievable, but you knew it had happened because you were there.'

So how would Naylor have fared at the marathon, or at the long-distance track events?

'He would have been the absolute star.'

That is just one man's opinion. But Chris Brasher knows what he is talking about. He is among the host of outsiders who have been attracted to the increasingly popular sport of fell-running, which used to be the exclusive preserve of local shepherds, fox-hunters, guides or whatever. 'The difference between the Lake District and Wales,' Chris says, 'is that the native farming community of the Lake District have always been interested in sports – guides' races, hound-trailing, wrestling ... They appreciate fell-running.'

Arthur Newton and Joss Naylor have provided a long if irresistible digression from the purpose of that first night at Wasdale Head. But as I settled down to sleep in Naylor's birthplace (no easy task, because the room was chilly and wind and rain were buffeting the window) it struck me that celebrity status is, at best, an uncertain guide to merit. Consider the examples we already have: Newton, Nurmi, Naylor. Or the public reputations enjoyed by soap opera actors and actresses and chat show hosts compared with the private reputations of such self-effacing altruists as Albert Schweitzer and Mother Teresa. Or the publicity accorded to the IRA compared with that accorded to the voluntary life-saving work of the lifeboat and mountain rescue services. Publicity is the key. Celebrities are celebrities only because they get more publicity than the rest of us.

In the small world of tennis and its glitzy awards banquets I often had the 'treatment' but was always aware that this was an accident that could have happened to anyone, that it happened to me only because I spent thirty years writing about the game for a distinguished newspaper. It's gratifying to be fêted and pampered – but one should never take the fuss seriously. Adlai Stevenson, the best president the United States never had, got it right: 'Flattery hurts no one – that is, if he doesn't inhale'. We defer to those who know more about a particular subject than we do but, socially, we should respect everybody but defer to nobody. Everyone is important. No one is very important. The VIP tradition is the biggest load of codswallop in English society, even when one is on the receiving end. But politicians and the like are treated as if they had done something special. Good souls though they may be, most of them have done very little.

Next morning it was evident that rain had indeed fallen as snow on high ground – and the grey sky looked loaded with bad news. The bedroom window offered a frontal view of the day's climb and the white tops were attractively off-putting: that is, easy on the eyes but discouraging for anyone aware that getting up there in snow and wind and November would not be a lot of laughs. Never mind. I would give it a go, keep the brain in gear, and retreat if discretion demanded that. In the fields across the lane from Middle Row were sheep and cattle and, joyous sight, Border collies at play. These smart and agile dogs were bred for work and thrive on it. One tends to think of them as permanently intense, hard-eyed, and it is always good to see them romping about and having fun together before heading for the 'office'.

There were a few other guests, all young and mostly beefy. Sandra Naylor did us proud at breakfast, which included a pleasantly unfamiliar component: potato cake. Then it was time to take a closer look at the day – and at Wasdale, which had so far been an unseen presence, a picture in the mind. The first stop was the Barn Door Shop, which occupies one end of an old barn – the outer walls have provided many a visitor with climbing practice – between Middle Row and the inn. The assistant's slight accent rang faint bells, echoes of the tennis circuit. He turned out to be a South African, Eugene du Preez, who had been working there since 1989 – though as far as he was concerned Wasdale was not even a rumour when he first headed for Europe. After two or three years in the East End of London his wife became disenchanted with the place and took a job at the Outward Bound Mountain School in Eskdale. 'She dragged me away from London kicking and screaming. But before coming here I'd been working at any job I could find: on building sites, or whatever.' The South Africans I've met have all been outdoor types and Eugene looked totally at ease in the kind of gear he was selling. Even so, Eskdale and Wasdale Head must be a hell of a contrast with the East End of London.

Across a field, hidden among yews, was the tiny parish church: about fourteen yards by five (much the same in metres) and seating thirty-nine – that's the figure I've been given, anyway, and it would have been pernickety to fuss with a personal estimate. Legend has it that the original building was constructed from the timber of a Viking longboat and since 1977 the church has been dedicated to the patron saint of Norway, King Olaf II. The point of the dedication is that Wasdale Head was first settled by Norse invaders, who cleared away the boulders – debris from the crags – and provided the hamlet with excessive material that was tucked into uncommonly thick walling. Most hill-walkers and climbers probably find the churchyard even more interesting than the church, because the epitaphs provide terse, tantalizing hints of the way lives can be lost on the fells and the cliffs. Those tombstones should be required reading for recruits to Wasdale and hill-craft. They give a new meaning to the words inscribed on countless war memorials: 'In memory of the fallen'.

That little cemetery was not consecrated until early in the nineteenth century. Before that, corpses had to be carried over Burnmoor to Boot, in Eskdale. Other ancient tracks came down to Wasdale Head from the Black Sail and Sty Head passes. What a busy settlement it must have been in the days of drovers and packhorse teams and smugglers. In the sixteenth century the hamlet had eighteen farms with common grazing rights on the fells. The number was down to eight by 1800 and has since been halved. Nowadays this isolated community might go to pot but for its reputation among those with a yearning for the hills and crags. Even in November the place was spattered with cars, tents, Land Rovers, dormobiles and brightly coloured anoraks. But Wasdale Head is no tourist centre in the wide sense and the Barn Door Shop is no general store. All is geared to the needs of walkers and climbers. There is nothing much else to do. If you want more, go somewhere else. But if you want more you would not be reading this book.

Wasdale Head is not the only starting point for an ascent of Scafell Pike or, for that matter, Scafell, which is slightly lower but more challenging. The Pike has more in common with Ben Nevis than it has with Corrán Tuathail or Snowdon, because it is a bump on the landscape rather than a sharply defined peak. But in terms of routes, which can be linked to provide contrasts between ascents and descents, it has most in common with Snowdon. Working clockwise around the mountain, the 'base camps' for the popular approaches are Borrowdale, Langdale, Eskdale and Wasdale Head. Note that the following rough guides refer only to Scafell Pike, and that hill-walkers who fancy their chances of scrambling between the Pike and the temptingly adjacent Scafell by the direct route (from the crest of Mickledore) are asking for trouble. Leave that exercise to the rock-climbers.

There are two main paths from Borrowdale. Both begin at Seathwaite, which all the available evidence suggests is the wettest inhabited place in England. The theory of evolution suggests that, a few thousand years hence, the populace will be born with webbed feet. Rain is just as frequent elsewhere but plunges onto Seathwaite in such heavy quantities that it should be measured in feet rather than inches. To be more precise, getting on for 11 ft (335 cm) a year. That is a lot of water. Seathwaite, obviously, is directly in line with the overflow pipe from the celestial cistern. But hill-walkers do not go there for the purpose of taking a cold shower. The idea is to pursue either of two routes to the top of England and come back via the other route. Alfred Wainwright's preferred approach – and he knew the Lake District better than most hill-walkers did, or do – was via Stockley Bridge, up Grains Gill, left on the Langdale path, right on the track to Esk Hause, right again up Calf Cove, and then left on a south-westerly course between Broad Crag and Ill Crag. It's plain enough if you have a decent map and know how to use it. The other route swings right from Stockley Bridge and winds up past Taylorgill Force and Sty Head Tarn to Sty Head, where a variety of paths converge. The one you need goes left, towards Langdale, and then right, along what is known as the Corridor Route for reasons that soon become evident. An interesting sideshow is the head of Piers Gill, a nasty place where damaging things have happened to the unwary.

The Langdale approach is a slog up Mickleden and Rossett Gill and past Angle Tarn, turning left about a mile after the tarn to join Wainwright's Esk Hause route. There are options, but ignore them until you know the lie of the land. The southern line of attack, from Eskdale, is recommended to those who like to know about Romans and/or railways. There is more than one way of tackling this long climb. But try following the Esk from Brotherikeld and forking left to Throstle Garth and Great Moss. Then cross the Esk and take your pick from the Mickledore and Little Narrowcove paths – or clamber over the summit of Pen.

Before setting off, have a look at what's left of the Roman fort known as Hardknott Castle, which has been excavated and partly renovated. Built about AD 130 on behalf of the emperor, Hadrian, this is an impressive reminder of the Roman road that linked what is now Ravenglass with what is now Ambleside, where it joined Roman routes between south and north. Hardknott was no settled community and in view of its bleak isolation one can understand that. In such an environment the Romans were simply concerned with garrisoned communications. Hardknott is an evocative example of the garrisons. If it fits in with your arrangements one means of access to the area is the seven-mile Ravenglass and Eskdale Railway, which terminates south of Boot. This narrow-gauge venture was inaugurated in 1875 to transport minerals to the coast. The mines near Boot are now derelict but the line still carries passengers up and down the valley. Good luck to it. There are not a lot of remote places in which the Roman and railway eras linger shoulder to shoulder as if thrown out of a time machine for a blind date.

From Wasdale Head there are two much trodden routes. The longer but easier and more varied approach is via Burnthwaite and Lingmell Beck (not to be confused with Lingmell Gill to the south). Then either of two paths on the southern slopes of Great Gable lead up to Sty Head and a choice between the Corridor route or – if you feel ready for more – a detour past Sprinkling Tarn and round Great End to Esk Hause. The short, steep, direct ascent is via Brown Tongue and Hollow Stones, a mess of jumbled rock from which one can go straight up Mickledore or swing left to follow a cairned, less demanding path towards Lingmell Col before turning right up to the summit.

By this time you know me to be a straightforward, uncomplicated chap with a naive belief in the truism that the shortest distance between two points is a straight line. Consequently I had provisionally decided, before this first look at Scafell Pike, that although Brown Tongue had no kind of reputation for charm it was unavoidable if one's sole purpose was to ascend the Pike quickly and without fuss. But it seemed a good idea to check with an old chum, Ronnie Faux, a mountaineer who finds that a home in the Eden Valley is a reasonable base for his labours as northern correspondent of *The Times* and also leaves him perfectly poised to explore recreational possibilities during days off. Ronnie and I shared a hotel room for three weeks at the Mexico City Olympics and discussed a project which we provisionally labelled The Times Popocatepetl Expedition. The idea was abandoned when we established that 'The Smoking Mountain' was 17,520 ft high (5,340 m) and was also 40 miles away (65 km), a combination of logistic problems that clearly could not be solved in any free time we might have fitted in between breakfast and lunch. I'm not in Ronnie's class anyway. He has climbed extensively in Europe and joined the Army Mountaineering Association's successful 1976 Everest expedition to cover the venture for *The Times* and co-operate on a book. What mattered, though, was that he knew the Lake District. So I called him and explained that the object of the exercise was to get up Scafell Pike while observing a principle familiar to all journalists: keep it short and keep it simple.

'That's easy,' he said. 'Go up Brown Tongue and Mickledore and turn left. There's a good pub at Wasdale Head'.

Well, yes. Thanks, Ronnie. Positive and to the point, if sparing on detail. At least he had ticked my homework.

It was ten o'clock when I emerged from the little graveyard and set off down the valley. There is a path from the inn to a bridge at the bend in the lane. There is another path that crosses Lingmell Beck and goes south along a hillside to Lingmell Gill. But I was not thinking about paths or, for that matter, about anything. This was a time for feeling rather than thinking, a time for soaking in the unfamiliar, awesome splendour of Wasdale. So I just toddled down the lane towards the head of Wastwater, turned left past the parking area and camping site at Brackenclose, engaged legs and lungs with the lower reaches of Lingmell Gill, and marvelled at what was already no mean assault on the senses.

Wasdale is some cul-de-sac. Frank Smythe described it as 'the grandest scene in England'. The obvious components are the lake, the screes and the terminal range of mountains – Red Pike, Kirk Fell, Great Gable, Scafell Pike and Scafell – that loom over and around the walled fields enclosing the tiny hamlet of Wasdale Head. Wastwater is 3 miles long (5 km), half a mile (almost a kilometre) at its widest, and getting on for 260 ft deep (79 m). At its deepest point the bed is more than 50 ft (15 m) below sea level. If you react to deep water the way I do, that hardly bears thinking about. The screes plunging straight into Wastwater's south-eastern shore (there is no shore in the accepted sense) are even more intimidating because they drop about 1,800 ft (549 m) in half a mile – as we know, less than a kilometre. Now that, if you like, is steep. In short, England's most famous screes dive frighteningly into its deepest lake. Most of us have had some fun on scree slopes but you wouldn't catch me on the Wastwater screes unless somebody was willing to put up a three-figure contribution to the Search and Rescue Dog Association and engage the likes of Joss Naylor as a minder. Plus a lifeguard.

In youth I had an unsatisfied yearning to explore a secluded Swiss valley called the Lötschen Tal, because books and maps indicated that it had no exit and not much of an entrance – and that, consequently, it had eluded the advancing tide of civilization and in many ways remained almost medieval. The tantalizing thing is that walking and climbing holidays have taken me within a few miles of the Lötschen Tal's extremities: first to the vicinity of the Finsteraarhorn, to the north-east, and then up the Val d'Anniviers, to the south-west. We never had the time and opportunity to find out how much substance there was to my mental picture. Maybe it was just as well. Reality usually fails to measure up to our dreams. But that morning – musing in the lonelier, more compact environment of Wasdale – I thought of the Lötschen Tal again and concluded that I was savouring its spirit if not its scale.

There is hardly room to get into Wasdale and most of us approach this secluded corner of the Lake District via the coastal routes: the back door, so to speak. And alongside Wastwater the winding road (one of those officially classified as 'generally less than 4 m wide', about 13 ft) is squeezed between lake and hills. That slightly claustrophobic drive is an exemplary argument for sobriety – especially on stormy nights when wind-tossed foliage is dancing across one's line of vision. In daylight the end-of-the-world feeling is, if anything, enhanced: because one can see the lake, the flanking heights, and the gigantic natural wall (Kirk Fell and Great Gable) that terminates the dale with an awesome finality.

From Lingmell Gill I had a lateral view, rather like sitting a few rows up behind the umpire's chair at Wimbledon. And it struck me that in England there could hardly be a wilder setting for farmers, walkers and climbers. Civilization has touched Wasdale without grasping it. Again one must stress the diversity of its components: the lake, the screes, the mountains, and the hamlet of Wasdale Head that puts a full stop to a valley with nowhere else to go. Wasdale is not pretty. By no means. But a bunch of other adjectives came to mind and may hint, inadequately, at its nature – magnificent, dramatic, barren, forbidding, savage, challenging. Even that overused word, unique. I was a happy man, totally at one with the environment. The Lötschen Tal may have disappointed me. Wasdale did not. It was everything I had expected. Perhaps a little more, because the sense of belonging had been missing from the menu composed in the mind.

On the other hand, there was Brown Tongue to negotiate. This is, indeed, shaped like a tongue, its tip the point at which two streams converge. Brown Tongue rises and spreads between them. One engages it via some undemanding rock-hopping across Lingmell Gill. There is only about half a mile (less than a kilometre) of Brown Tongue but it is irritating and boring, except for the views of the craggy barrier ahead and the valley receding behind you. The relentlessly steep ascent is a plod up a mixture of grass and what might best be described as granulated scree. If you don't know the bloody stuff, imagine climbing upstairs – in a skyscraper – on ball-bearings. You may reasonably assume that on Brown Tongue my ardour cooled. Moreover, I was leaving the sunshine below, climbing into wind-driven sleet, and becoming aware that the wind and the white-coated tops spelt trouble.

At the top of Brown Tongue I was crunching through snow and skipping over ice-coated rocks. This was the edge of Hollow Stones, which would be more accurately named if the words were the other way round. It's a slightly concave mass of boulder scree dominated by the intimidating cliffs from which the scree came: Scafell Crag on the right and, straight ahead, the long wall incorporating Pulpit Rock and Pikes Crag. Between them is the saddle of Mickledore. The slope up to Mickledore was so beautifully yet ominously caked in virginal snow that I decided to take the easier, safer route to the left, towards Lingmell Col – but couldn't sort it out. Even the cairns were obscured by the snow. With the wisdom of hindsight I confess that only a fool could miss it. But other newcomers to the spot need to know that the place to aim for is a dip at the left-hand (northern) extremity of the frontal cliffs. I didn't know that; and the dip was invisible anyway, because of the sleet and the mist. There was nothing for it but to follow the advice of Ronnie Faux and tackle Mickledore head on.

Now, even a hill-walking rookie knows that walking through knee-deep snow is tiring. Even more so if deepening snow is perched on scree at an angle equivalent to the roof of a house and any protruding boulders are coated with ice. The wind was fierce and cold. Ahead, a small cloud swirling off the ridge between England's highest mountains told me that conditions up there were, shall we say, dangerously turbulent. And the sky was leaden. If ever there was a time to pause for thought, this was it. So I paused and thought – and studied a remarkable close-up view of that rock-climber's playground, Scafell Crag. This is so sheer that the prevailing whiteness could cling only to ledges and gullies, bumps and wrinkles. The mixture of rock and snow defined every detail, exposing the main features with such clarity that it was like looking at a familiar black and white photograph – so familiar that without taxing the memory I could put names to all the famous bits. Newcomer though I was, there was again that odd sense of being at home if temporarily unwelcome. Windswept snow was billowing off that forbidding face like steam from the spout of a kettle.

Looking backwards and downwards I saw three figures struggling slowly up the steep and stony defile of Lord's Rake:

the only avenue by which hill-walkers can explore Scafell Crag. Given the snowy background and the distance between us, they looked like exclamation marks. Their progress was so arduously painstaking that a series of exclamation marks and asterisks would probably have represented their feelings pretty accurately.

It was rotten luck, plus optimistic planning, that having had company up Corrán Tuathail and Ben Nevis in decent weather I had eventually climbed into wintry conditions and dodgy visibility during these November solos on Snowdon and Scafell Pike. During that pause for thought, maybe 100 ft (30 m) from the crest of Mickledore, there were several factors to consider. It would clearly be tiring to get up what was left of that steepening slope of snow and scree. How much energy would be left in the tank for the last slog through a violent wind, over unfamiliar and boulder-strewn terrain to the summit? Then there would be the task of getting down when presumably weary and possibly disoriented. On the other hand, having come so far (first from Midhurst, then from Wasdale Head), I was reluctant to quit.

While this inner debate was going on, somebody turned up – an apparition that would not have been much more startling had it been a yeti. About half my age, he said he was a local man 'out for a walk', a comment I digested with a generous pinch of salt because his gear included an ice axe and crampons: equipment not commonly associated with going 'out for a walk'. Poised uneasily on the sharp incline, with boots and calves buried in snow and the wind whistling around us, we discussed this and that as if huddled around the fire in Ritson's Bar. The previous week, he told me, a friend of his had snapped an ankle on the summit plateau when a gust of wind had blown him over at a time when the relevant foot happened to be wedged between rocks. This information was not reassuring. My chance acquaintance said I had about half an hour's work ahead of me and, bless his heart, added that he had nothing special in mind and, if I wished, would keep me company: 'And I won't leave you alone on the mountain'.

That, I said, was a kind thought. Privately, I concluded that even a sexagenarian hill-walker should not impose on a stranger for care and maintenance. 'You push on,' I told him, 'I'll probably go down. I've had a good look at the mountain, I've enjoyed it, and I can come back another day.' So he wandered upwards into snow and wind and nothingness and I rounded off the inner debate with some clinching arguments. I had no wish to risk adding to the list of hill-walking casualties and (ultimate humiliation) demanding attention from the voluntary rescue services. And although one could think of worse terminal homes than that intimate climbers' graveyard at Wasdale Head, I was in no hurry to move in. The difference between a live hero and a dead fool is often marginal. Finally, I was acutely aware of the overriding principle behind this book: that the highest mountains in Ireland, Scotland, Wales and England can be climbed safely and without too much effort. Beyond that, I had nothing to prove. To have pressed on would have betrayed the purpose of 'Four Peaks'. Have I not stressed the importance of recognizing danger and retreating to avoid it rather than advancing to embrace it? You would not think much of me if I failed to practise what I preached.

From the moment I had looked out of the window at Middle Row and considered the snow and wind on the tops, it had been evident that my modest venture was no more than an even-money bet, that a reconnaissance (which it turned out to be) might be the best one could hope for. Now there were only two sensible objectives: a pint and a pipe in Ritson's Bar. Failure? No. To get down from a mountain in good health without troubling the rescue crews is the only success that matters. My brother, a kindred spirit in both senses, absorbed the disappointing news and sent a comforting note from Toronto: 'Wisdom and experience dictated a strategic withdrawal. I would have done the same. No use pushing your luck. Scafell Pike will be waiting for you, next time.' It was, too – and that was the most consoling thought of all. The excitement

of driving up Wasdale the previous day had been moderated by a twinge of regret because this trip was intended to be
the last phase of an exhilarating quadripartite adventure that I
was reluctant to put behind me. Instead, I felt like a child who
had taken the last chocolate out of the box and been told to
put it back for future delectation. What a joy it would be to
renew the rapidly forged bond with Wasdale ...

At 12.20 p.m. I turned my back on Mickledore and began
the retreat. The upward tracks left by me and that friendly
'yeti' had been effaced by wind-blown snow. On the upper
section of Brown Tongue, patches of grass were so neatly and
prettily encrusted with ice that it was easy to imagine them
chopped up and used as paperweights. Then it was back down
that slippery, tiresome scree, with the snow and the wind a
receding memory and Wasdale a lovely picture opening out
before me. Later came a black mark, in the form of a black
labrador, for Ritson's Bar. The poor thing was tethered outside
in light rain and a chilly breeze, because dogs were barred.
Around Midhurst, my wife and I patronize only those pubs
where dogs are welcome. Our Norfolk terrier is partial to a
drop of cider or Guinness. Wasdale Head is not on the list of
places we might visit as a threesome. Anyway, I gave the
labrador a tickle and a few words of sympathy, went inside,
and by 2.40 p.m. was enjoying a pint and pipe. Half an hour
later I was on the road and marvelling at those astonishing
screes across the lake. By 12.35 a.m., with a total of 745 miles
the clock, I was back in Midhurst and resigned to a winter's
estrangement from hill-walking.

It is no coincidence that the Lake District is both the highest
chunk of England and the wettest. There are only four mountains that, in Scotland, would be classified as Munros: Scafell
Pike at 3,206 ft (977 m), Scafell at 3,162 ft (964 m), Helvellyn
at 3,116 ft (950 m), and Skiddaw at 3,054 ft (931 m). But
much of the associated terrain consists of bumps and ridges
that surpass 3,000 ft (914 m) without achieving the status of
peaks and the entire area is dotted with hills more than

2,000 ft high (610 m). In short, there are lovely walks, long or short, at every level and in every type of scenery one expects from a land of lakes and hills. The beauty arises from the contrast between the mostly bare heights and the lush greenness of lake-studded valleys. Let us be grateful for the rain rather than waxing peevish. But for the proximity of high ground to the weather blowing in from the Atlantic's little brother, the Irish Sea, the Lake District would not be the compact wonderland that it is. The only oddity is that, namewise, there is only one 'lake' in the area: Bassenthwaite Lake. In suffixal terms the rest are 'waters', 'meres' or 'tarns'. But that peculiarity – a Lake District with only one 'lake' – is a legacy buried in the dialectic history of a once-remote land that was a law unto itself. As a walker, note that the climate is usually mild in the valleys but cold, windy and often wet on the heights.

The first inhabitants to make much of an impression, more than 2,000 years BC, were the Stone Age hunters. The possibilities of metal had yet to be exploited, so tools and weapons were made out of stone, especially flint. Axe heads and spear heads were roughed out, high on the hills, before being taken to coastal settlements for polishing – and mounting on wooden shafts. The finished products were transported by boat to other areas of Great Britain and also to Ireland and Brittany. Traces of those ancient axe 'factories' can still be detected in the Langdale region and almost 3,000 ft up (914 m) on the southern and south-western flanks of Scafell Pike and Scafell. But that sort of research is strictly for the enthusiastic experts who know where to look and what to look for. Most of us are content to accept the fact that, 4,000-odd years ago, our playground was a workplace.

The Celtic farmers moved in next. Then the Romans, who were mainly concerned with defence and communications on the edge of their empire but, in the process, opened up the heart of the Lake District. From the fifth to the seventh centuries, give or take a few generations, they were succeeded by the Anglo-Saxons. A more enduring influence was that of the Scandinavians – otherwise historically labelled as Norsemen, or the warrior-seamen known as Vikings – from the eighth to tenth centuries. They turned up from their Irish, Manx and Scottish colonies to raid and plunder but felt so much at home in the environment of mountains, lakes and sea that they settled: clearing the valleys, cultivating the land, exploring the diverse possibilities of sheep, and bequeathing a rich vocabulary of their native language.

Border warfare between England and Scotland overlapped the era dominated by the Cistercian order of monks based at Furness Abbey, where the abbot reigned as a sort of feudal lord. The monks were wealthy property-owners. Via Herdwicks, they made the wool trade big business. They left us sheep-walks, packhorse trails, bridges and rudimentary walling (though most of the dry-stone walls familiar today date from the eighteenth and nineteenth centuries). They smelted iron ore, laying the foundations for the mining age in which iron, copper and slate became industrial commodities in the Lake District. They also created a network of tracks from which drovers and smugglers were to benefit. Given the fact that their overt priority was religion, the monks were good businessmen. They worked on the side of the angels but they knew how to make ends meet – with an overlap in their own favour.

From the eighteenth century onwards another contemplative order, with no fixed base or orientation, introduced the tourism that is still with us. These were the aesthetes – writers, poets and artists – and, from the nineteenth century, the climbers, whose aestheticism (if any) tended to take a scientific or recreational bent. The literary types and the artists made the Lake District fashionable among the educated classes and did much to popularize the concept of hill-walking for pleasure. The pioneer was a Londoner, Thomas Gray, best known for the first verse of his 'Elegy'. Gray's most finished prose work, the *Journal*, published four years after his death, was an account of his tour of the Lake District in 1769. That remote corner of England was no longer a secret. Gray had let the cat out of the bag.

In 1817 a literary magazine, *The Edinburgh Review*, printed a disparaging article which contained the first reference to the relevant poets as 'The Lake School'. At the time this was basically a threesome – William Wordsworth, Samuel Taylor Coleridge and Robert Southey. But a promising young poet called Percy Bysshe Shelley briefly got into the act when he spent the 1811–12 winter at Keswick after he had been sent down from Oxford for too publicly arguing the case for atheism. It was friendship, rather than the Lake District, that drew the poetic nucleus together. Wordsworth and his sister Dorothy had been born at Cockermouth and settled at Grasmere for more than eight years in what had formerly been an inn. They were swiftly joined by their West Country friends, the Coleridges, who rented a house at Keswick. Three years later, in 1803, the Southeys moved from Somerset to Keswick in order to rejoin the Coleridges – not least because the husbands got on well and the wives were sisters. Southey stayed there until his death forty years later but Coleridge, disliking the climate, headed for the Mediterranean sunshine after less than four years in the Lake District.

Wordsworth owed much to Dorothy's devotion and vocational help: she had a sharp eye for detail and a knack of expressing what she saw. Because he was born and buried in the Lake District, produced the hackneyed but wonderfully graphic 'Daffodils', and could loosely be described as the headmaster of 'The Lake School', Wordsworth is the poet most closely associated with the subject of this chapter. In geographic and literary terms, anyway. When it comes to hill-walking, Coleridge is the most significant figure. True, his best known poem is a mystery concerning an ancient mariner and an albatross. What matters to our present purpose is that Coleridge was king of the poetic hill-walkers. The first Lake District climb on record (one assumes that shepherds were

already familiar with the tops) was Coleridge's ascent of the
Scafell massif in 1802. For three years he was an enthusiastic
and seemingly inexhaustible walker who often climbed alone
and was not afraid to take chances. Maybe he took one too
many. His health broke down and for the rest of his life he was
a semi-invalid.

One has to suspect that the Lake District did poetry more
good than it did the poets and their kind. Dorothy
Wordsworth was mentally ill for the last twenty years of her
life. Coleridge was an opium addict. So was the essayist
Thomas de Quincey, who rented Dove Cottage, at Grasmere,
when the growing family of Wordsworths moved to larger
premises in 1808. Coleridge also hit the booze; and his
marriage hit the rocks. Southey and a later arrival, John
Ruskin, worked awfully hard and, eventually, were fatally
afflicted by softening of the brain. The lives of the Lake District
literati also featured an assortment of marriages and liaisons
and generally wayward conduct that gave poetic licence an
entirely different meaning. Southey and Wordsworth, who
succeeded him as Poet Laureate, were comparatively solid
citizens. Southey was particularly kind and generous in caring
for others. Wordsworth went to France as a young man, sowed
some wild oats with the connivance of a lady who was
teaching him conversational French (yes, we've heard that one
before), and thus acquired an illegitimate daughter. But
Wordsworth, later married, never severed the French connection. He continued to show supportive concern for the
consequences of his French lessons; and Dorothy, who must
have been a sister in a thousand, regularly corresponded with the
mother, Annette Vallon.

'The Lake School', doubtless inspired by their environment,
hinged on Wordsworth and Southey and was responsible for a
diverse and distinguished output for about forty years. It was
too famous to die with its founders. The literary tradition was
maintained in different ways at different times in different
Lakeland locations by Matthew Arnold, Harriet Martineau,

Ruskin, Beatrix Potter, Arthur Ransome, Hugh Walpole and Alfred Wainwright. Ruskin is not light reading. But this aesthete, philosopher and philanthropist was uncommonly versatile in his range of interests and was a pioneer of the conservation movement. We are told that his marriage was annulled because he did not amount to much between the sheets, and that his correspondence suggested a suspicious but probably harmless affection for teenage girls. Maybe that had something to do with the air and ambience of the Lake District. Note that Martineau, sometimes, and Potter and Ransome, more often, wrote stories for the delectation of the young.

Of the twentieth-century writers associated with the Lake District, Potter and Wainwright are particularly interesting. Both fell for the place while on holiday and later settled there: Potter west of Windermere at Sawrey (near Hawkshead, where Wordsworth went to school) and Wainwright at Kendal on the A6. I discovered neither until I was too old to be enchanted by Potter's stories for children and too experienced in hill-walking (and too far from the Lake District) to feel a compelling need for Wainwright's companionable guidance. But one can never be too old to appreciate the painstaking craftsmanship with which Potter created fantasy out of the countryside's wildlife and Wainwright shared his affection for the hills and his exhaustive knowledge of those he knew best. From all accounts Potter and Wainwright, for all the gentle humour of their work, were not the jolly, gregarious types who make a party swing. But posterity does not give a damn about that. They were not in the business of founding charm schools.

Potter had something in common with the Brontë sisters, born little more than a generation earlier, in that her response to a rather austere domestic regime was to invent a world of make-believe: in Potter's case, the origin of the profitable and much-translated 'Peter Rabbit' series. At thirty-nine she had made enough money to buy Hill Top Farm at Sawrey, which was a far cry from Kensington but was already a second home because of family holidays. Potter worked there for eight years and, in all weathers, walked the hills and let her fancy roam. Her cultivated mind was at once imaginative and precise, a rare blend. She made up stories, knew how to tell them, and gave animals individual characters to which children could easily relate. Woven into the text were drawings and water colours that combined artistic flair with delicate accuracy of detail. In short she was one of those multi-talented people who give most of us every reason to be modest.

In 1913 Potter married a local solicitor, William Heelis. She also became a farmer, a respected breeder of Herdwicks, a shrewd businesswoman, an acquisitive landowner (the royalties on her books were pouring in) and a familiar figure – in clogs and sloppy tweeds – at agricultural shows. And the creative juices dried up. Hill Top became a museum piece belonging to a dream world Potter had invented and Mrs Heelis had deserted. Her home was now another farmhouse, Castle Cottage across the road. She lived two lives, was successful in both, died in 1943, and left her property to the National Trust. Her diaries, published in 1966, had been written in a code that was not easy to unravel – further testimony to the range of a remarkable intellect.

Wainwright, too, illustrated his work with meticulous care. He also shared Potter's affection for the Lakeland countryside and left a legacy that will be cherished by generations yet unborn. Comparisons must end there. Wainwright made his name by writing guide-books: unique but, nevertheless, guide-books. Later he expanded his geographic and to some extent his literary range. But his reputation is solidly based on a series of seven pocket-sized volumes covering the entire upland area. Their nature is summed up by an explanatory note on the cover of the example beside me as I write: 'A pictorial guide to the Lakeland fells, being an illustrated account of a study and exploration of the mountains in the English Lake District. Book one: The Eastern Fells'. The bald precision of the language takes one back to the kind of books mountain men were writing when Wainwright was, as they say up north, 'nobbut a lad'.

Wainwright was born and brought up at Blackburn in modest circumstances. He left school at thirteen and became an office boy in the town hall. Bright and diligent, he studied hard, became a fellow of the Institute of Municipal Treasurers and Accountants, and also had a spell in the surveyors' department – useful grounding for the guides that were to earn him renown. At twenty-three he had his first holiday in the Lake District and knew where his future had to be. But he was thirty-five when he moved to Kendal and forty-one when he became borough treasurer in 1947.

A pipe-smoking, contemplative man, Wainwright was fascinated by Ordnance Survey maps and fish and chips. In his spare time he travelled about by bus, wandered up and down the hills, and devoted the winters to capturing what he had seen. His pen and ink drawings were based on his own photographs. In 1952 he decided that – for his own pleasure, with no thought of profit – he would walk every Lakeland hill and use his notes and drawings to produce a series of guide-books. The task took him thirteen years. His guides were copied by a local printer and, later, published by the *Westmorland Gazette*. Wainwright's calligraphy was as neat as his drawings and the special feature of his guides is that every page was done by hand – both text and illustrations – and then photographed. As a journalist, he would have been hot stuff at page make-up.

Those guide-books are packed with detailed information. But the text is couched in such genial, conversational terms that it is not easy to picture Wainwright as the intensely private, rather lugubrious man he was. At the office he was respected, but punctilious and rather aloof. Unassuming, he lived simply and devoted most of his royalties to the animal rescue charity he and his second wife helped to found. Wainwright was most at ease when alone on the hills. The snag was that he became a legend among hill-walkers when he still had a lot of hill-walking to do. His reputation, plus the preference for his own company, explains why he tended to avoid chance meetings with his kind. He once admitted that he became 'furtive' in the cause of making himself elusive. The paradox was that although Wainwright was wary of other hill-walkers he did more than anyone else to attract them to the Lake District tops in thousands: and thus was his own worst enemy when it came to preserving the solitude he craved for his own sake and that of the environment.

In a way I felt sorry for the man. Most of us can enjoy casual acquaintances – on the hills or in the bar later – because nobody knows or cares who we are. There is no special interest in cultivating, or avoiding, anyone's company. Wainwright was denied that *laissez-aller*, partly because of his fame among hill-walkers and partly because of the kind of man he was. Late in life he achieved an uneasy compromise with the publicity media. He had mellowed – and there was money to be made for the animal charity. But he remained self-conscious about the 'Alfred' and preferred 'A.W.'

Wainwright was creative not in the task he set himself but in the way he did it. There are plenty of guide-books about but no others quite like his. Any rookie planning a hill-walking holiday in the Lake District would be perverse to ignore Wainwright's wise counsel. When he died in January 1991, at the age of eighty-four, the sage had a clean slate with the land-lord of the Border Hotel at Kirk Yetholm (near Kelso), the northern terminus of the 270-mile Pennine Way. Wainwright wrote a guide to the Pennine Way and offered to buy a pint (amended to half a pint in later editions, because of the rush) to anyone who walked all the way from Edale and turned up at the Border Hotel with a copy of his book. But there could be no check on whether claimants had done the walk or any part of it. The unscrupulous could get off a bus and collect a pint or a half as long as they had Wainwright's book with them. The positive comment to make is that, at worst, Wainwright was promoting and subsidizing the sales of his book and simultaneously encouraging people to walk the Pennine Way.

I'm familiar with several sections of the Pennine Way but have no wish to spend a fortnight slogging from Edale to Kirk Yetholm or vice versa. On the other hand I was determined to get up Scafell Pike but, like a superannuated greyhound impatient to totter out of the trap, waited five months until the weather got its act together. Second time around, the trip could not have worked out better. Its objective was achieved in the company of two old friends and two new ones, all of whom decided that the occasion justified an awkward cross-country trip from the lower reaches of the Tees. Their presence gave the day's ups and downs a party flavour, which was additionally gratifying to me because it was the ideal way to round off this 'Four Peaks' venture.

The old friends – we had walked many a mile together over rough country in rough weather – were walker-writer Keith Watson, whose work has much in common with Wainwright's, and that dynamo of the diabetic world, Brian Hunter, a self-styled 'geed-up Geordie' otherwise known as the mad mullah of Sedgefield. The new friends were a retired civil servant, Margaret Bellamy (no relation), and the youngest member of our assault team, David Adams, a 10 st driver of heavy goods vehicles. The David and Goliath story, updated. Some of the men clambering in and out of HGV cabs prompt the question: how can so little control so much?

One says 'assault team' only because it seems an appropriate cliché. There was no way we would have passed muster as candidates for an Everest expedition. Our combined knowledge of the route was sketchy. Only three of us were sound in wind and limb: and less sound than we had been twenty or thirty years earlier. We could all be loosely labelled as something ending with 'ic': anankastic (Keith, a compulsive perfectionist), arthritic diabetic (Brian), asthmatic (David), geriatric (me), a 'put-me-down-as-an-erotic' (Margaret). We should have alerted the mountain rescue people, engaged the services of a travelling doctor, and carried next-of-kin tags so that any bodies left by the wayside could be parcelled up and posted to the right addresses.

The wonder was not that the return trip took us almost seven hours and a half – six hours should be plenty – but that we came through a delightfully rewarding day undamaged. There were those among us who had to fight the good fight against discomfort and/or self-doubt. But our rather queasy quintet demonstrated – as I hope this entire book demonstrates – that you do not have to be a superman, or superwoman, to climb mountains. It is simply a question of pacing yourself so that at all times you have reserves of physical and mental energy. These are related. The approach of exhaustion, or the onset of self-doubt and barely controlled fear, have similar effects in that they erode confidence and the capacity for clear thinking.

The drive from Midhurst to Wasdale Head took less than eight hours. There was mist and rain in the Midlands and Lancashire. Alongside the A595 in Cumbria the lambs looked damp and puzzled and slightly resentful. The womb had been cosier. During the approach to Wasdale the mountains looked vague, insubstantial, as if painted by a water-colourist who had used too much water. There was no hint of snow on the tops but that did not mean much because one could not see the tops in any detail. The minor road flanking Wastwater was blocked by sheep. Three dogs were at work, earnestly, giving 100 per cent because they could not give more. This was Joss Naylor's empire.

It was the fag end of April but the south-western corner of the Lake District had escaped the first flood of tourist traffic and I had been grateful for that. The Romans opened up the heart of the Lake District and, skipping a few centuries, tourism has been encouraged by the artists and literary giants, by the age of the motor car (the M6 made the area a practicable weekend retreat, even for Londoners), and by Wainwright, who little knew that he was proving the old song's argument that 'you always hurt the one you love'.

The consequences of tourism have been good and bad.

Good because the city folk have found out what is what in the way of aesthetically satisfying recreation and, in consequence, have enhanced local possibilities for income and employment. Bad because outsiders buying second homes for occasional use have pushed up prices – inducing many indigenous young families to look elsewhere for homes – and have also de-activated (from Monday to Friday, and throughout the winter) shops and schools and social functions in a host of once-busy village communities. Bad, too, because in summer the mostly narrow and winding roads tend to be choked with traffic; and because some popular footpaths have become scars on the landscape thanks to spreading erosion.

The rights and wrongs of all this could be debated at length. The solid point to make is that the social and economic struc-ture of the Lake District has drastically changed since the days of William Wordsworth and Will Ritson. What matters to you and me is that although the Lake District can be hell for motor-ists it remains a paradise for the happy wanderer – using paths pioneered by sheep and shepherds, drovers and packhorse trains, monks and miners. So dump the car – and forget about it until you have to go home.

The Wasdale Head Inn, closed for the winter during my first visit, was now open for the season but not yet busy. Ideal. It was my kind of place, and everything one expects of a remote hotel tucked among mountains. There was a comfortable, homely ambience about it, arising to some extent from a wealth of panelling – oak, pine, whatever – which gave the public rooms a warm, welcoming character. Paint and plaster could not have done that. And the walls were so abundantly adorned with mountain photographs that one felt outdoors even when indoors. The staff were relaxed and friendly, yet efficient, the menu and wine list a cut above those on offer at many more pretentious and expensive hotels, and the 'mod cons' exemplary. It hardly needs to be added that from every window the views were inviting reminders of one's purpose in being there. I have stayed in some of the world's most sumptuous hotels but will remember none with more affection.

Mind you, such responses are coloured by motives. The Wasdale Head Inn scored bonus points because I was there for personal reasons, to climb a mountain. That was not the same as living in luxury while earning a living by telling readers of *The Times* how well or how badly the likes of Stefan Edberg and Steffi Graf were playing tennis. In total, I have spent almost ten years of my life living in this or that hotel room. They become home for a few days, maybe a week or two. One settles in. Then one packs and leaves. I always pause at the doorway to look back at a 'home' that, suddenly, has become just another bare room in just another hotel. There is a little sadness in all such partings. Well, not quite all: I could never turn my back on New York too soon.

Brian Hunter had arrived a day earlier and was staying up the lane at Row Head. We had a bevvy in Ritson's Bar and dinner *en suite*, at the inn. Brian's professional experience at a teaching centre for nurses had given him a specialized insight into the functions and malfunctions of the human body, not least his own. He is a diabetic with arthritic problems in the knees and feet. 'I always have my diabetes under control and I can cope reasonably well with pain.' But, unfit and aware of it, he had taken the precaution of devoting a day to a training walk on the hills around Wasdale Head. He wanted to accustom himself, particularly his knees and ankles, to the jarring pressure of climbing and descending a mountain. 'I was aware,' he told me, 'that the Scafell Pike climb – and, more so, the return – would be somewhat painful. Yesterday's walk was an essential part of my preparation, to let body and mind know what to expect. My muscles, sinews and disadvantaged areas of my body became suitably sore. This condition, I dreamed, could only be salved by the attentions of a 5 ft 10 in, blonde, double-breasted Swedish masseuse. Sod the expense. But in Wasdale there are not a lot about . . .'

When climbing the likes of Scafell Pike such men do not go through the pain barrier. They live with it. They submit to hours of slow progress that will hurt – all the time, but especially when thumping downhill. So why do it? 'I admit to getting a bit chuffed when I succeed in such things,' Brian said. 'My kind of madness has a purpose – not personal gratification, but improving the lot of those less knowledgeable than I am about diabetes. It's a big thrill when I get letters from young people and parents asking for advice, as I often do.'

Next morning, at breakfast, there was a tea-strainer on the table, a refreshing reminder of the days when tea did not come in bags. For company there was an economist on assignment at Whitehaven and delighted to be based at Wasdale Head (he had been 'almost raised' on Cader Idris, had a special affection for the Rhinogs, and organized walking holidays from Machynlleth) and a couple of Munroists who, having climbed all 277 of the over-3,000 ft (914 m) peaks in Scotland, were now engaged with the equivalent English, Welsh and Irish summits. Modest and low-key, as most mountain folk are, they quietly suggested that bagging all the Munros had been no big deal because they had lived in Scotland for twenty-five years. Rubbish. Munroists may be the last to admit it but they are a special breed: immortalized in the publications of the Scottish Mountaineering Club.

The postman was wearing walking boots. That made sense on the kind of round he had to make: a scattered farming community in a soggy, stony valley. Brian and I champed at the bit, waiting for the rest of the team to complete a cross-country drive that must have started at cock-crow (Margaret, Keith and David made a demanding day trip of it, travelling pretty well from the North Sea to the Irish Sea and back again and, halfway, assuming a vertical posture long enough to get up and down Scafell Pike). Eventually Keith's lean, familiar figure emerged from a car. It was good to see him again. He is a sensitive, caring man and as walkers and writers we have much in common. The bond has been strengthened by days of plodding communion that has never needed a lot of verbal garnish because we have always been so much at ease with the

environment and each other. Since our last joint acquaintance
with the hills we had both become a little greyer but, inside,
many a bottle of the 'sweet wine of youth' (that's Rupert
Brooke, not me) had yet to be uncorked. Wild, high places
keep all of us young. The well of enthusiasm never dries up.
The hills are like Paris – eternally refreshing, rejuvenating, no
matter how well we know them.

Keith introduced us to Margaret and David. There was not
much of Margaret but she looked sturdy and businesslike: the
kind of walker who might regard Scafell Pike as no more than
a warm-up for a stiffer challenge. David commanded respect
for a different reason, because he was still working out the
equation between asthma and hill-walking. To some extent he
was a younger equivalent of Brian in that he had something to
prove to himself and, by example, to others similarly harassed.
Before leaving the car David made use of an inhaler. This, I
learned later, induced a sense of foreboding in Brian, who
knew more about the implications than I did and was aware of
the respiratory and possibly mental problems that could
confront an asthmatic during a steep ascent.

We were on our way soon after eleven o'clock: a late start, but
more than adequate for our purpose. It was the lambing
season. Jet fighters screaming low over the fields prompted the
angry thought that although one sympathizes with people born
without brains they should not be sitting at the controls of jet
fighters. I was over-reacting. But maybe Joss Naylor was being
excessively tolerant and discreet when he told me later: 'They
serve a purpose and don't interfere with anybody. The sheep
have got used to it.' He could be right. But I can't believe that
screaming jets do a lot of good to the morale of newly-born
lambs or heavily pregnant ewes.

That abortive November 'recce' had made me familiar with
two-thirds of the direct route. This I envisaged in three
sections: Brown Tongue, fork left to join the Corridor Route at
Lingmell Col, and then turn right up the boulder-strewn dome
of the summit. It makes sense to break a task down into

distinct but related components, to set oneself intermediate goals. Reaching a peak is merely the culmination of a series of subsidiary triumphs, some of which are more arduous than the glamorous bit at the top. Plenty of Wimbledon champions have had comparatively easy finals after going through the fires of hell in earlier rounds.

From the foot of Lingmell Gill the vast wall of crags on the skyline looks bleak, terminal and awfully impressive, especially to newcomers uneasily aware that the summit is beyond that wall and about 500 ft (152 m) higher up. Whether that prospect is exhilarating or intimidating depends on one's experience and one's knowledge of the terrain. The ascent is hackneyed but first-timers alone on that western approach can still feel the pioneering spirit surging within them. What was left of the morning was sunny and clear, if cool, as we began to grind our way up Brown Tongue (Brian: 'Anybody going up Brown Tongue is going to wish they hadn't bothered'). Lots of people are in trouble after a short acquaintance with Brown Tongue and it was certainly not designed for the comfort of asthmatics. David's respiratory system was soon under stress and evidently it was serious. He was cream-crackered. Keith stayed with him while the rest of us, farther up, found grass-cushioned perches and admired the downward view of Wasdale. Would David go back or carry on? It must have been touch-and-go.

In such circumstances others in the party have to find a balance between caring encouragement on the one hand and, on the other, a fussy excess of sympathy that can be counter-productive, making the ailing climber feel worse rather than better. The safety of everyone is of paramount importance. A walker in trouble should never be left alone on a mountain unless he or she is too damaged to move and has only one companion, who must fetch help. But David was not too damaged to move; and there were five of us. Had it been necessary, one of us would have gone down with him. It was not necessary. David had the recovery time he needed and, that crisis behind him, bravely pushed on – and went well on the upper slopes.

Brian was slightly alarming company on Brown Tongue because he made a lot of noise during the ascent, shouting this or that piece of nonsense. Keith and I were aware of the wild streak in him but this was a bit much. Was he going bananas? Was his system running short of the sweetstuffs, fruit juices, or whatever it is that diabetics need to keep them on an even keel? But Brian knew what he was doing. He explained later: 'My expostulations in guttural Geordie were a well-tried way of getting my lungs into a good rhythm for breathing in the maximum amount of air at the difficult bits. It works.' He might have warned us. His roaring progress must have scared the hell out of any wildlife in the area. And over dinner that evening Brian said that, while sitting and looking at the day during David's stationary torment, he had been having dark thoughts of his own: 'Coming down was in my mind, especially when I saw the rocky bits and the snow. I've always had a penchant for slipping about in such conditions. The possibilities of falling maybe make me too careful – and the niggly knee syndrome acts as a brake anyway.'

What with the asthma, the arthritis, the diabetes, the combined accumulation of birthdays, and the fact that we were none too sure of the route, there were moments when it seemed no more than an even-money bet that all five of us would totter to the top of England and down again. Not without distressing repercussions, anyway. But we did. Full marks to the heroes of the climb, David and Brian. It just shows what can be done with the right blend of madness and guts.

At the top of Brown Tongue we accidentally split up. Margaret, Brian and David veered right, towards Mickledore, Keith veered left in a successful search for the cairned route to the col, and I stood on a rock midway between them – trying to keep everyone in sight and feeling that, in the shepherding league, I had to be down there with Little Bo-peep in the

relegation zone. In decent visibility these divergent paths
should be easy to find. And on the brow of Brown Tongue,
where it merges with Hollow Stones, adjacent large and small
cairns indicate that a choice must be made if it has not been
made already – right towards Mickledore or left towards that
dip at the left-hand extremity of the frontal wall. We took the
easier route, to the left. I don't know what anyone else was
thinking but it struck me that the steepish clamber to Mickledore was a pleasure Brian and David should be spared.

Brown Tongue was the heart (and lungs!) of that climb. The
rest was comparatively easy because of the cairns and the
gentler gradient. On the other hand, slogging up a vast
boulder-field in a fierce and bitter wind, with snow and ice
underfoot, was not exactly a walk in the park. Keith gave me a
wry grin and muttered: 'Snow. Ice. A typical Bellamy walk . . .'
He has a long memory. Our joint hill-walking ventures have
always occurred outside the season of summer and tennis –
when I have been preoccupied with earning a living. By 2.45
p.m. we were shivering alongside the trig pillar and war
memorial plaque on the summit's massive cairn. Nothing gave
me more of a thrill than the sight of young David coming over
the last rise and I hurried back over the boulders to shake his
hand. Climbing Scafell Pike is no big deal but that sort of thing
was a new experience for him and, given the asthma, his was
quite an achievement.

It was cold. Very cold, because of the wind. But the day was
sunny and clear, the views superb. We looked around us at
Great Gable, Sty Head Tarn, Great End, Broad Crag, Ill Crag
and – distantly – almost every prominent height in the Lake
District. The details were exposed in a clarity tinged with gold.
Getting there had been no piece of cake but our labours were
richly rewarded. Was it on such a day, I wondered, that
William and Dorothy Wordsworth and their guide stood on
this same spot in 1818? Scafell Pike ('Sca' has Norse origins
and refers to steep rock or a bare summit) is bulky rather than
handsome. It is a star to some extent upstaged and obscured

by its supporting cast; or, if you like, a self-effacing prime
minister dominating more striking personalities in his cabinet
team. But Scafell Pike is as high as England goes, it is hemmed
in by crags that demand respect, it can be a dangerous place to
get to or from, and on good days (like that with which we were
blessed) it commands a panorama that catches the breath.
South-west of its terminal bump is Broadcrag Tarn, at 2,746 ft
(837 m) the highest in the Lake District. The mountain is also
reported to be the haunt of a rare and presumably perverse
sub-species of spider classified as *Eboria caliginosa*. But not a
lot of people climb Scafell Pike in search of spiders.

The dome has much in common with the uppermost layer
of Ben Nevis in that it is a jumbled mass of shattered rock, a
barren wasteland with a few dry-stone shelters hinting at a
ruined hamlet from way back when. But although our Stone
Age ancestors worked in the area, they had more sense than to
live over the shop. The shelters are simply wind-breaks and,
even in that limited function, imperfect. We invaded a small
one – it was full of us – and sat down to lunch. Then I passed
round the Valpolicella: a custom of mine when perched on top
of mountains with companions who have put up with me
without becoming audibly grumpy. At one point, while Brian
was fumbling about for some elusive item in the overspill of his
impedimenta, Margaret innocently asked: 'Can I hold
anything for you?'

We let that pass. Men are pretty quick to jump on double
meanings, intentional or not, but we did not know Margaret
well. She seemed proper and might even be prim. We had no
wish to embarrass the lady. In mixed company most men steer
clear of the kind of humour associated with the oleaginous Bob
Monkhouse, whose act often implies that wit begins and ends
in the middle – or, more precisely, immediately below or above
it. In short, below-the-belt comedy. Smut. Our discreet caution
about the range of Margaret's taste in comedy was swiftly
dispelled when I went outside for a pee. It was terribly cold. In
such temperatures a man's reproductive organ diminishes close

to the point of no return. I was unzipping when Margaret's voice came over the wall with a wickedly demure enquiry:

'Can you find it? I've got nice warm hands ...'

I wish I'd been smart enough to ask her if she had a pair of tweezers, but we seldom think of the best lines when we need them. Anyway, no riposte could have matched the uproarious effect of Margaret's question.

Briefly, we discussed the route down. All else being equal, anyone who has gone up via Lingmell Col should go down via Mickledore or vice versa, for the sake of variety. But in our case all else was not equal. Brian was game to tackle the Mickledore descent but his knees and ankles are not the ultimate in flexibility. Keith and I thought it wiser to settle for the devil we knew: back the same way. Let me make it clear that Brian and David were reticent about their special problems, did not invite sympathy, and would not have welcomed it. Nor will they thank me for bringing up the subject here. I do so partly because the rest of us knew and cared and made allowances (without, I hope, making it obvious), but mainly because the way Brian and David coped with their handicaps was exemplary and deserves publicity, not least among those similarly afflicted.

We picked our way down the rocky dome of the summit and soon had the wind, snow and ice behind us. The westward descent was a visual delight because the sun was heading for an embrace with the horizon out to sea. The lighting effects made strange and wonderful adjustments to the surface of Wastwater and the hills around it. A few perfectly white clouds embellished the sky like angels' lingerie hung out to dry. It was the last day of April and one could hardly imagine a lovelier afternoon. Moreover, much of the descent from Lingmell Col to Brown Tongue took us straight towards the awesome 500 ft (152 m) precipice of Scafell Crag, which geological evolution designed for the recreational pleasure of rock-climbers rather than hill-walkers. If you put your mind into a dreaming mode it is easy to picture the pioneers of British climbing, complete with tweeds and pipes, clinging to this or that protuberance as they sorted out routes more than a century ago. Near the foot of Lord's Rake a cross is carved in the rock. It commemorates four men who fell to their deaths in 1903.

By comparison the ball-bearing route known as Brown Tongue could almost be described as a ramp for the use of the aged and infirm, which to some extent summed up the composition of our team. In the valley, tiny lambs walked tentatively, learning the trick of it. By 6.30 p.m. we were downing well-earned pints in Ritson's Bar and Margaret, Keith and David were tucking away mountainous meals in readiness for the drive home. Our little venture had not amounted to much, certainly not by Joss Naylor's standards. But by our own standards a worthwhile goal had been achieved, and we felt good about it. The valedictory line in the 'A-Team' television series says it all: 'I love it when a plan comes together'. That thought tempered the regret of parting. The trio of cross-country travellers drove off towards the sunset and Brian and I repaired to the inn to discuss the day's doings at leisure while we digested a cracking dinner and a bottle of wine. Red, of course. White is for ladies and fish.

Next morning I drove Brian over to Penrith, where he had a 'house call' to make in the diabetic cause. On the way it became evident – and this was no surprise in view of the location – that the loveable if unlovely Border terrier was a popular breed in the area. I was not to know it but at much the same time our Norfolk terrier was slamming the door behind my wife and locking her out of the house, thus scripting a hilarious carnival that featured kind neighbours, step-ladders, fence-hopping, and a generally bizarre exercise in re-entry. You probably know the feeling. Most of us have occasionally had to endure a lock-out, with or without the help of a dog. Anyway, that little domestic drama, plus the story of a quasi-decrepit 'assault' team's modest conquest, gave us plenty to talk about that evening in the bar of the Noah's Ark at Lurgashall. The homecoming had but one hint of sadness and that was private. It was with a sense of closing a chapter – nay, a book – that I cleaned the Brasher boots and tossed hill-walking socks and underwear into the dirty-linen basket. Suddenly I felt a long way from the mountains. Corrán Tuathail, Ben Nevis, Snowdon and Scafell Pike were now memories rather than challenges.

Four down. Nowhere to go.

On the other hand, the legs were still sound, the heart still young, and the highest mountains were not the only bumps on the landscape ...

GLOSSARY

An English glossary is not the superfluity it may seem. Every historically self-contained patch of the country acquired, in addition to standard English, a small vocabulary peculiar to itself. During a geographically divided youth I picked up a few words and corruptions of words almost exclusive to Somerset and Yorkshire. Your own examples depend on where your roots happen to lie. The Lake District – and to some extent adjacent counties – is particularly interesting in this respect. The Celts left a small linguistic mark. Far greater and more enduring has been the influence of the Vikings who invaded and settled the land. They implanted a version of English academically known as Old Norse.

The word 'fell', an anglicized version of Norse and Danish terms, demands special attention because of the confusion it can cause. It refers to a hill or to high moorland. In and around the Lake District, but nowhere else, a hill-walker is known as a fell-walker. To talk of fell-walking in other parts of the country would be precious and pedantic. One would be using a word alien to the context of, for example, the Peak District. Throughout this book I have used the hill-walking compound for the sake of consistency. Everyone knows what it means because it speaks for itself. Fell-walking is a regional term for the same thing.

In addition to Norse words, the following list includes relevant interlopers that have so far escaped this glossarist's net.

Arête	Ridge
Beck	Stream
Cam	Ridge
Col	Pass
Dodd	Bare, rounded summit (often subsidiary)
Fell	Hill; high moorland
Force	Waterfall
Garth	Enclosure
Gate or Gait	Way or path
Gill or Ghyll	Ravine with stream (possibly dried up)
Grice, Grise or Grize	Wild boar; pig
Hals or Hause	Pass; ridge; defile
How	Low hill
Ill	Steep; savage; dark
Keld	Spring
Knott	Rocky outcrop
Man	Summit; cairn
Pike	Peak
Raise	Cairn; top of ridge
Rake	Slanting passage or ledge
Rigg	Ridge; hill
Sca, Scar or Scarth	Steep rock
Stickle	Sharp peak
Stile	Peak
Sty	Ladder; steep pass
Tarn	Mountain pool
Thwaite	Clearing (often in wood)

Higher Education For Walkers

The double meaning in this chapter title incorporates a sound analogy: walkers who head for the heights need more special-ized knowledge (and equipment) than those who take a walk in the park or along some much-used bridle-path, or around a golf course. At the same time there is no need to regard hill-walking as an esoteric recreation demanding a prolonged course of study and a massive investment in appropriate clothing and auxiliary kit. Walking is a natural function. Barring accident or inborn disablement, we do it all our lives until the ultimate rot sets in. Physically, going up and down mountains differs from everyday walking only in that heart, lungs and legs continually have to cope with terrain roughly equivalent to a mixture of shattered, rocky stairways and often slippery ramps. The challenges and hazards of hill-walking lie in dealing with that physical stress – and with sorting out a route and adjusting to rapid changes in temperature and, probably, visibility. In short, hill-walking is more testing and potentially more dangerous. Note the 'potentially'. Don't take chances.

These days I live a long way from the tops and seldom have a chance to climb anything that could reasonably be described as a mountain. While researching this book I remembered a lot and learned a little. While reading it, you may have reacted in a similar way – unless you happen to be new to hill-walking, in which case you may have remembered a little and learned a lot. When I was still playing squash and earning a crust as a long-serving chronicler of the professional game, our club captain dug me out of the bar and asked me to watch him in action for a while. Something had gone wrong with his game, he said, and he could not work out what it was. From the viewing gallery it was easy to spot the fact that he had become lazily forgetful about one of the fundamentals of squash – the importance of swiftly regaining position, just behind the T-junction of lines, between shots. In the same way I find that every time I go hill-walking some basic lesson is remembered, brushed up or re-learned. The notes in this chapter will, I hope, serve as an *aide-mémoire* to those whose experience and instincts need a nudge; and a grounding for those who have just discovered, or are about to discover, the joy of mountains.

A friend took up hill-walking in his late sixties after retirement, and it was gratifying to show him, and his wife, a few tricks of the trade during a tops walk in the Peak District. Most of us start about fifty years earlier. Whatever kind of hill-walking the novice has in mind (gentle slopes or the rough stuff), experienced advice is a short cut to wisdom. This advice may come from a companion who knows his stuff, from organized group walks (for example, with a rambling club), from a residential holiday course at such outdoor centres as Plas y Brenin, or from the vast literature on hill-craft. Those of us brought up among the larger lumps on the landscape, as I was, should be grateful. Anyone reared south of a line between the Severn and the Humber needs a more carefully calculated education, though no hill-walker underrates Dartmoor when it is in a bad mood – and its bad moods are unpredictable.

Given an adequate introduction to hill-craft, anyone can safely roam the Peak District, the Cheviots, the Ochil Hills, the Pennine Way, and a bunch of accommodating Munros. It is simply a question of selecting goals within one's known capacities – and I stress the word 'within'. Never be tempted to take on more than you know you can safely manage with something to spare. That limit will gradually be extended. But don't rush it. On mountains, one must always be in control of the circumstances, relating one's abilities and experience to the terrain and the weather. If the circumstances control you, somebody else may have to pick up the pieces.

This book is for hill-walkers, who have no need for ropes, pitons, ice axes or crampons: the gear needed by rock-climbers and winter mountaineers. The hill-walker goes up and down without the aid of such equipment. It may be that you move on from hill-walking to the more specialized crafts of rock-climbing and winter mountaineering. That depends on age, agility, personal ambition and, obviously, the proximity of rocks and mountains. I flirted with rock-climbing and rope technique for a few years, at rookie level, but never became hooked. I have also used crampons during a glacier scramble in the Bernese Oberland but, again, this flirtation carried no prospects of a marriage. In short, rock-climbing, snow and ice work, and for that matter long expeditions involving bivouacs have never lit the fire of enthusiasm.

At the same time these pursuits could be regarded as natural extensions of, or digressions from, hill-walking. You may want to find out what they have to say to you. If so, you will need technical and tactical knowledge that must be acquired under the supervision of experts. That is outside my area of competence. But whatever your ultimate preference may be, a basic education in hill-craft – and that education is, I hope, emerging from the pages of this book – is a prerequisite. I have known only one exception to that rule: a gymnastic eccentric who used to drive his jeep to the very foot of the crags on Stanage Edge, in the Peak District. The rest of us loosened up with a pleasant stroll across the moor from Hathersage. Not him. A blinkered obsession with rock-climbing closed his mind to the wider possibilities of rough country. He even resented walking from one climb to the next.

There is no hard and fast definition of a mountain. The generalization widely accepted in the British Isles is that if a hill rises beyond 2,000 ft (610 m) and has a summit enclosed on the map by a single contour line, it is a mountain. This argument gains weight from the fact that, mainly because our islands are not all that far from the Arctic, severe changes in climate – and possibly terrain – tend to occur at about the 2,000 ft level. It is reasonable to suggest that at the same transitional altitude a hill becomes, by our standards, a mountain. On the other hand I could never regard my old stamping ground, Kinder Scout at 2,088 ft (636 m), as a mountain. Just as a massive lump of peat and scattered outcrops. Visually, the more modest Peak District eminence of Shutlingsloe at 1,659 ft (506 m) is much more striking. Scot Gunn, at the Glen Nevis Centre, often refers to Ben Nevis – our supreme summit – merely as 'The Hill'.

Our conclusions must be subjective gut reactions. My own is that nothing under 3,000 ft (914 m) deserves to be classified as a mountain. That was the altitude governing the research of Sir Hugh Munro when, in 1891, he produced a tabulated list of the highest lumps of Scotland. He was a founder member of the Scottish Mountaineering Club and its third president, tried to climb every mountain on his list, but was frustrated by death – which has a ruinous effect on many ambitions. The first Munroist, who took ten years to climb the lot, was Archibald Eneas Robertson, the parson at Rannoch. That was in 1901. It was twenty-two years before the next Munroist emerged: another parson. The breed have always worked and played to the principle that they have friends in high places.

Munro-bagging has since become a popular recreation among mountain folk. After much classification – an attempt to distinguish between isolated peaks and subsidiary bumps – there are now 277 recognized Munros. These, plus the twenty-four equivalents scattered about Wales, Ireland and England, are what I call mountains. The rest are open to debate. Frankly, I am not overly concerned with defining what is or is not a mountain. Nor am I concerned with pot-hunting. In the course of half a century of hill-walking I have been up a lot of Munros and similar heights outside Scotland but never bothered to count them. At the same time Munro-bagging must be a wonderful incentive for the young to put themselves about in the right places. For the purposes of this book, let me suggest that the hill-walker graduates in three stages: first, up to 2,000 ft (610 m); second, up to Munro level; and third, beyond that. When you climb beyond 3,000 ft (914 m) and stand in a bitter wind on a jumbled mass of rock broken up by the progressive action of frost, you have climbed a mountain.

At the age of sixty-two I faced, for the first time, the prospect of playing thirty-six holes of golf before tea, on one of the toughest courses in England. A friend, with a status loosely equivalent to that of Wodehouse's 'Oldest Member', suggested that I should take a spare pair of socks, eat and drink with moderation during the lunch break, and carry a note of my next of kin. 'You could be giving advice to a hill-walker,' I told him.

Let us, first, discuss the question of clothing. In Wasdale one day I met a chap who, though he had nothing more testing in mind than a day's hill-walking, was equipped as if for Everest or a moon landing. He bulged. He walked like a robot, because his clothing was so thick and all-encompassing, his rucksack so huge and heavy. There are times for that sort of kit but this was not one of them. Just as the newcomer to golf can get by with four clubs, a few balls, and shoes that give him a firm foothold, the newcomer to hill-walking need invest in no more than boots, anorak, Balaclava, and a lightweight rucksack. The only other clothing needed – probably the anorak, too – can be disinterred from wardrobe or drawers.

I was brought up in the age of walking boots nailed with clinkers, tricounis and/or muggers. Clinkers were the most suitable for hill-walkers. They gave us a marvellous grip that, on any surface, inspired confidence. But compared with today's unnailed, slickly bonded models, they were inevitably heavier and less waterproof – and tended to scar the land-scape. The only comparative disadvantage of the modern moulded, ridged soles is that in my experience they are not quite as secure as nails on greasy surfaces: for example, wet or mossy rock. In every other respect today's boots are better: lighter, more flexible, and more waterproof. And as has been strikingly demonstrated by the refinement of climbing ropes, strength is not necessarily related to weight. Beware of heavy-weight boots. When buying your first pair of hill-walking boots, impose on some experienced acquaintance to help you make a wise choice. Take two thickish pairs of socks with you and wear them when trying on the boots, which should be at least a size larger than your everyday shoes. There must be a little room to spare, enough to wiggle the toes, but on the other hand you don't want so much freedom that the feet slam into the toes and heels of the boots on rough going. These days, you are unlikely to find walking boots without sewn-in tongues, which are essential to waterproofing. Boots should be comfortably snug around the ankles; if the boots are too loose in that area, they invite the abrasive entry of grit and associated garbage.

All that is quite a lot to remember, so take your time about the choice. Adequate boots need cost no more than a good pair of shoes. Which reminds me that when flying about the world and travelling light (while eager not to miss the chance of a decent walk), I always wore a pair of strongly made shoes with formal uppers but solidly ridged soles. They were equally suit-able for social use and most forms of available hill-walking. As a last note on boots, take care of them. After use, wash off the mud. If the boots are made of leather, wait until they are almost but not quite dry and then rub in some waxing. I do this with a combination of fingers and a soft toothbrush (all toothbrushes are soft by the time they have been dismissed from the bathroom). Pay particular attention to welts and seams. Waxing keeps boots flexible and waterproof and extends their lifespan. And never dry or store your boots near a radiator. That kind of heat is bad news for leather.

I have three pairs of hill-walking boots, old friends who have been kind to my feet. Thanks to proper care, all the uppers look as though they have not been out of the shop for much more than a year (the extremes of the soles give the game away, but there is still a lot of tough walking left in them). Do I need to add that you should never go hill-walking on smooth soles unless you have a death wish and intend to fulfil it in a spectacular way?

As for socks, the important thing is cushioning comfort. Some people prefer two thick pairs, others one thick pair and one thin. Whatever, get some wool around your feet, for insulation and warmth and to absorb any sweat. My own combination of socks depends on the fit of the boots I happen to be using. Maybe two thick pairs, maybe one thick and one thin. I use breeches with a thick pair of long socks – the inner socks – tucked into them. Some people imprison trousers into over-socks. Others use gaiters. I'm not sure about gaiters and have never worn them (not as a civilian, anyway). They do keep water and snow and granulated irritants out of the boots, but can be fussy to put on and take off and can also be sweaty. For hill-walking purposes I'm happy with breeches and an outer pair of socks loosely folded over the boot-tops. How much coddling do we need – a synthetic bag from head to foot? If so, maybe we should stay indoors. But mine is an old-fashioned opinion. Regard gaiters as optional.

I have paid much attention to boots and socks because safe, comfortable footwork is essential to hill-walkers. Carry some plasters. You may never need them (I haven't) but your companions may. Blisters or blackened toe-nails are not a lot of fun.

Headgear – at the other extremity – can be desperately important. The biggest concentration of blood vessels close to the skin occurs in the head. Consequently the head is the main vehicle for the body's heat loss and needs special care. The best headgear is the versatile Balaclava, possibly with a small peak.

It's light, comfortable and warm. Bobble hats are fun, and almost as effective as the Balaclava. Forget about hats with brims. Sooner or later the wind will steal them. The hands, like the head, must be kept warm. I'm a hands-in-pockets walker but there are times when the hands are needed for balance or support, for consulting a map or taking a photograph, or for rummaging about in the rucksack. Nowadays there is a wide choice of specialized gloves but I have never had cause to try them. Putting on and taking off gloves can be a nuisance, especially in strong winds. One does not have to do that with half-fingered gloves, or mitts, which I recommend from experience. They keep the hands reasonably snug and the exposed fingers are always free to fiddle about with zips, camera buttons, or whatever.

There are three general points to make about clothing. It must breathe, or you will be uncomfortable and may ultimately sink under the weight of your own sweat. It must be loose-fitting, so that one's circulation and freedom of movement are not inhibited. And in order to retain body heat it must incorporate insulation: in this respect wool is an admirable component and several thin layers of clothing are more effective than one thick layer. I usually wear thermal underwear for the higher and colder walks. Always pack a spare sweater, wrapped in a plastic bag to keep it dry. The effort of walking keeps us warm but that sweater (alternatively, a light waterproof) will be useful during a lunch break – and as we rise in the world, the temperature falls.

Note that because of underwear, shirt, one or two sweaters, or possibly a jacket, all of them fitting loosely, the outer (anorak) layer needs to be roomier than most everyday models. There is some confusion between the anorak, parka (both of Eskimo origin) and cagoule (French for a monk's hood). The cagoule tends to be knee-length and that idea does not commend itself. Such a garment may either restrict movement or flap about around the thighs. On the other hand one's anorak (the word is more fashionable than parka, which means much the same) should cover the bum. A waist-length anorak may be fine when walking about town but is not the best choice for mountains. You may already have a suitable anorak. If not, buy with care, paying particular attention to roominess (wear a jacket or a couple of sweaters when trying on the anorak), to length (over the bum but not the thighs), to the hood (essential) and to zips – which I prefer to buttons or press-studs because they are easier to handle and tend to be more weatherproof. My favourite anorak happens to combine zips and press-studs.

Trousers or breeches? Trousers will do for a start. Breeches need not be part of the beginner's investment but later on you may decide in their favour, as I did. Meantime, dig out an old pair of trousers that are reasonably hard-wearing yet comfortable when wet or dry, in hot weather or cold. With those reservations, the material is not important, though personally I'm less than enthusiastic about wet corduroy.

Given the fact that the anorak should offer a measure of protection against all but the worst weather, waterproofs (like breeches) need not be an item on your initial shopping list. It depends how much you can spend. But lightweight waterproofs can be very useful: as protection against rain and wind, as an extra layer of insulation, or simply for sitting on.

As for the rucksack, much depends on the kind of walks you have in mind. Those who intend to bivouac or to go on tour without a car need a large, framed rucksack. For the rest of us a lightweight 'day sack' will suffice. Such a rucksack is necessary anyway, because even Pennine Way walkers and the hardy folk who roam mountains for a week or more will also spend a lot of time on less demanding, day-long walks. Why carry a suitcase when you can make do with the equivalent of a modest hold-all? My brother and I have affectionate memories of the heavy, canvas rucksack, complete with frame, which we used in youth. That sort of thing now qualifies as a museum piece. Today's rucksacks give us all the advantages of that old friend at half the weight. My own is the most basic type of

framed rucksack, weighs only 26 oz (737 g), but has only once
– during that flight to Killarney for the Corrán Tuathail climb
– been packed to capacity. Be content with that sort of thing: a
lightweight job with two or three zipped pockets. If you can,
take an experienced walker with you on the shopping trip.

All this has indicated, I hope, that the newcomer to hill-
walking need not fall out with his or her bank manager. It may
be that wardrobe and drawers already contain an anorak and
socks suitable for the purpose, in which case spending can be
restricted to boots, Balaclava and rucksack. Be wary of laying
out a lot of money before you know what's what. Just get the
basics, do some exploratory walks, notice what the experienced types are wearing, browse around the specialized
equipment shops, and then find a carefully considered compromise between your financial resources on the one hand and your
tastes and ambitions on the other. Take your time about it. Be
wary of fancy gear at fancy prices.

This is as good a time as any to bring up the subject of
colour. My blue rucksack (at the time I had little choice, and
colour was low on the list of priorities) is slightly embarrassing
because I was brought up in an age when dull colours were *de
rigueur* among hill-walkers – so that we would merge with the
landscape and would not startle wildlife and mar the scenery
for other walkers. Nowadays bright colours are the thing.
There are hill-walkers whose gear makes them look like traffic
lights on the blink. There is something to be said for this:
bright colours are fun and have practical value to mountain
rescue teams searching for the lost and the injured. But there is
a compromise between yesterday's conventions and today's. It
still makes sense to wear dull colours and merge with the landscape. It also makes sense to ensure that the rucksack contains
some item – perhaps the survival bag or that spare sweater –
vivid enough to attract attention in emergency. There is a place
for gaudy clothing but that place is not in wild, high country
unless you get into serious trouble – which will never happen if
you have been reading this book attentively . . .

Survival bags? Get one, as soon as you emerge from the supervised rookie phase. They are large, heavy-duty plastic containers which retain body heat if one happens to be stranded overnight at high altitude. I have never needed mine, except for sitting on, but once considered the possibility when coming down from the Five Sisters of Kintail in almost desperate circumstances. The survival bag is a form of insurance, especially when climbing alone. True, climbing alone defies the unwritten rules. But occasionally we all do it: as you will have noted from the Snowdon chapter and my first go at Scafell Pike.

On mountains it is not only more comfortable to be warm and dry – it is also a damned sight safer than being cold and wet, which causes a loss of body heat and may induce hypothermia, which can kill. The symptoms of this condition are pallor, shivering, clumsiness and irrational thinking. If it gets that far, instant action – in terms of shelter, dry clothing, warmth and any hot drinks available – is essential. But do not let it get that far. Act on the first hints, which may be weariness and declining morale in damp, cold conditions. At that stage food can be a fast, effective remedy: especially energizing sweet stuff. The question of appetite is irrelevant. The victim – it may be you – will probably have no taste for food but should eat anyway. I have been in that situation, or approaching it, a couple of times, and have forced down a Mars bar or some Kendal mint cake, though I had not the slightest interest in either. But I knew what was happening – and how to deal with it. On the Five Sisters of Kintail I once went so far as to feed Kendal mint cake to a brave but weakening Gordon Setter. Learn from my experience (and that of countless others) rather than your own. If tired and cold and depressed, eat. You may not want to, but eat anyway. The mind may not crave for nourishment but the body does.

Physical problems, bad enough in themselves, can also affect one's capacity for thinking quickly and clearly. That leaves us vulnerable to even more trouble. Accidents can occur: perhaps from slipping on a greasy or loose surface, perhaps from getting lost, perhaps from such bad luck as getting hit by a falling rock. Even a sprained ankle, not all that serious in most situations, can have nasty repercussions on a mountain. One needs two sound ankles, not one. There are heart attacks, too, usually arising when the unfit, overweight or aged take on too strenuous a task. A basic knowledge of first aid should be part of the school curriculum and the hill-walker's rucksack should contain such items as plasters and bandages. In the event of a fall, the victim must be kept still and warm until a rescue team turns up. A small quantity of a hot drink may help, but not alcohol, which is incompatible with the anaesthetics or drugs that may be needed later.

Rescue teams do not come out of the blue. They have to be fetched, or summoned by means of a torch or whistle. Once beyond the need for experienced companionship, always pack a small torch (check the battery before you leave, and take a spare) and a whistle that can be heard a long way off – shops specializing in mountain gear stock suitable models. The distress signal is six blasts of the whistle or flashes of the torch, at ten-second intervals, for one minute. Then pause for a minute before going through the same routine again. Keep at it. You may need that spare battery. The response you hope to hear or see is three blasts, or flashes, at twenty-second intervals for one minute. As before, a minute's pause before the signal is repeated.

Don't be put off by all this stuff about the things that can go wrong and the ultimate recourse of a distress signal. They simply come under the heading of background knowledge the wise hill-walker needs to have. You may stay out of trouble yourself but could come across others who have got into it. As hill-walkers go I'm pretty long in the tooth but have never had an accident and never needed the first aid kit or the torch and whistle (correction – I once used the torch when consulting a map at twilight). And it was as one of the rescuers, rather than the rescuee, that I played a minor role on the end of a rope in my only experience of mountain rescue – a sobering, educational, painstaking exercise that, between the fall and the ambulance, occupied seven hours. Getting a stretcher-borne casualty gently down a mountain, often inches at a time, demands infinite care and patience. And the people who do it, day or night (perhaps both), are volunteers taking time off from their jobs or their hours of leisure.

The maddening thing is that these good folk are often called out on false alarms, or to rescue fools. Except in the case of a genuine, unavoidable accident, calling on the mountain rescue services has to be a disgraceful humiliation for any hill-walker. There are certain precautions we can take. Don't climb alone unless you know what you're doing. Even then, leave a note of any identifying features (for example, the colour of your ruck-sack and anorak), your intended route and the estimated time of return. Pack a torch, whistle, map and (when you can use it competently) compass. Have something brightly coloured with you, to help rescuers locate you – or whoever else is in trouble. Ensure that footwear and clothing are adequate for coping with tough terrain and climatic extremes, even if the valleys promise fine weather. Until you are safely down, always keep some food and fluid in reserve for emergency use: the fluid because anyone stuck on the tops for too long can become dehydrated. Finally, don't forget the survival bag and some first aid kit.

Sounds worrying, doesn't it? But we have to prepare for the worst while taking care to avoid it: the care including a decision to retreat at the first sniff of serious trouble. The fact that I have stayed out of trouble has nothing to do with luck or being smart. It has simply been the result of getting a solid grounding in hill-craft from more experienced companions and, after that, recognizing my limitations and showing unwavering respect for the mountains and the kind of weather they attract.

The rescue teams are drawn from every walk of society remotely connected with mountain communities: farmers, deerstalkers, policemen, the armed services, hoteliers and others associated with tourism, and so on. They can be called out at any hour of the day or night. The team assembled depends on who is available and on the nature of the incident: a climbing acccident, exposure, a general search, or whatever. They may need an RAF helicopter, perhaps a boat, perhaps dogs and handlers from SARDA (the Search and Rescue Dog Association). And while the men are out on the tops, perhaps at night and in bad weather, some of the wives and girlfriends may be back at the rescue post – tuned in to the radio link, making sandwiches, and worrying.

Note that the rescue teams and SARDA are voluntary services. Somehow they have to raise funds for the wealth of expensive equipment needed. Lifeboat crews come into the same category: putting themselves at risk in order to save others. There are a legion of other voluntary organizations, giving their time for the good of society. Our honours' system seems to me to smack of a creeps' charter, with additional hand-outs to those distinguished in their professions. Can there be any point in awarding titles or orders of chivalry to people who merely did the jobs they were paid to do? If we must have an honours system the voluntary services should be recognized more often and more prominently.

My favourite charity, because of a special affection for dogs and wild, high places, is inevitably SARDA, which works in harness with mountain rescue teams. You could call SARDA a service within a service. A handler must have had at least a year's experience of mountain rescue and a dog has to pass basic obedience tests before moving on to severe assessment trials and, if it is up to the job, training courses. There is no restriction on breeds – ability is what counts – but the rescue dogs are mostly German Shepherds, Labradors or Border collies. They are family dogs, kept at home except when on duty. Their great advantage is the ability to home in on wind-borne human scents. That makes them key components of rescue teams at night or in bad conditions: for example, snow or poor visibility. A dog can smell what a man cannot see.

Pending the arrival of expert help, keep any casualty still. If there is any chance of a broken limb or internal damage, movement may make the injury a lot worse. Sprained ankles are an obvious hazard. Avoid them by taking care with your footwork on awkward terrain. If they happen anyway, keep the boot on – firmly laced – and add any available bandaging material, wrapped around and above the sprain. Loosen up if swelling occurs. Once down, have the ankle checked for possible fractures.

Our school soccer coach used to elicit stout-hearted deeds from commonplace material by telling us, before a big match, that he expected us to finish up with a VC or a blanket. And you have all heard about the manager who insisted: 'Football isn't a matter of life and death – it's more serious than that'. Those sort of comments may do for soccer, which is not a life-threatening sport. But they have no place in the hill-walker's philosophy. Danger is never far away and its proximity is exhilarating. The trick is to keep it at a safe distance. We don't play leap-frog on top of the Empire State Building. We don't walk, blindfolded, into heavy traffic. We don't stand too close to the decapitating threat of big swingers on a squash court. Edward Whymper, the Matterhorn man, put it as well as anyone: 'Remember that courage and strength are nought without prudence, and that a momentary negligence may destroy the happiness of a lifetime'. And although Frank Smythe was discussing a craft more hazardous than hill-walking, he made a sound point with exemplary baldness when he wrote: 'Mountaineering is at variance with gravitational laws. For this reason it demands a never-ceasing vigilance.'

At some length we have already referred to fear. I return to the subject because its effects, we gathered later, had much to do with the Glyders accident that educated me in mountain rescue. The victim was a young man with a holiday group. He was not accustomed to scrambling over rocks in high and often exposed places and eventually his nerves were stretched to breaking point (the cumulative consequence of prolonged fear). He blacked out, fell, and bounced down a scree slope like a rag doll. That victim got off lightly, with only a week in hospital and no lasting damage. But what an awful warning that was to all of us. Courage, the control of fear, is a form of mental energy and one's stock of it – like one's stock of physical energy – is limited. It needs replenishing with rest and refreshment. So persistent fear is itself dangerous, quite apart from the fact that it is not fun. At the very least, it impairs judgement. Avoid fear by avoiding danger. Let the admirable Smythe have the last words on that subject: 'The man who experiences fear on a mountain should not seek to conquer fear by going on, he should eliminate it by going back ...'

Dodgy situations, if any, tend to arise from sloppy route-planning, inefficient map-reading and path-finding, poor visibility, sudden storms, or plain foolhardiness. There was an incident on Snowdon, remember, when I wandered off course for a few minutes. I was unfamiliar with the route and, because of snow on the ground and fog around me, needed a second shot at sorting out the way ahead. That sometimes happens and need cause no concern as long as one quickly corrects the mistake. If you are in a hole, stop digging. Before setting off on a walk over terrain that is new to you, study the route thoroughly, in advance, with the help of a map and possibly a guide-book. Make a mental or written note of the contours and the natural features – lakes, rivers, ridges, cliffs – that will be passed or crossed when you have walked, say, half a mile east or a mile north. If any one of those features fails to become visible when it should, return to the preceding feature and check the route. You will probably be passing the time of the day with other walkers. Many of them will know their way about and can confirm or correct your path-finding.

If tempted to cut corners, remember the Spanish proverb: 'There is no short cut without a lot of labour'. Nor should you be tempted to improvise a downward route via one of those innocent little mountain streams that gurgle out of the rocks at high altitudes. Such streams have spent thousands of years carving ever deeper, ever wider cracks down to the valleys. They travel with increasing force, taking big drops in their stride and producing a slimy, green coating on enclosing walls of rock. The consequence, like as not, will be plunging, crashing torrents negotiable only by water and birds. One makes such an error only once. I have done it; and it was the only time I have ever faced the possibility of spending a night in a survival bag near the top of a mountain. That would have been no big deal for me. I had all I needed, including emergency rations. But there was no way I could have let the hotel staff know that I would be out overnight. They might have alerted the rescue services.

So don't try to be clever. Mountains are not the place for it. When planning a high-level walk there are five questions to be asked and answered: where are we going, how do we get there and back, how much time will it take, is the trip safely within the capacity of the least robust member of the party, and does it finish near a decent pub (even an indecent pub) during opening hours? That last question is not entirely a joke. You will have earned your pint and will need it.

If there is a convenient path, use it – and the middle of it, not the fringes. Otherwise you will be widening one scar on the landscape or helping to create a new one. This has additional importance when crossing farming land. And keep yourself oriented. You may need to remember the route back. Some simple advice once appeared in blank verse in a scouting book: 'Be particular, when passing corners, to look back and observe the aspect of the scenery when viewed from the opposite direction to your route'. There is nothing profound about that. But it makes sense and is worth lodging in the memory.

When it comes to estimating the time needed, give yourself a reserve supply of daylight: an emergency ration, as it were. There are respected formulae for working out an overall time on the basis of distance covered in relation to feet or metres ascended or descended. But I'm no mathematician and have never needed to be. There is an easier method: allow a day-long average, breaks included, of one hour for every two map miles. Make a slight adjustment to the estimated total time if the map tells you that, overall, the going will be more or less arduous than the norm. That system has never let me down. Give or take half an hour, it has been pretty accurate. It needs to be, because timing affects a variety of arrangements at the end of the day: eating and drinking, transport, accommodation, and so on. If excessively late, we cause anxiety to those expecting us, who may even decide to come out and look for us.

Keith Watson once led Brian Hunter and me from the High Force Hotel to Dufton over the Upper Teesdale section of the Pennine Way. The conditions were wintry – snow, ice and a chilling wind – but Keith had done his sums right. He had arranged for a friend to pick us up at Dufton and, having covered about sixteen map miles in seven hours and a half, we turned up early. In view of the whiteness and the wind, our gallant chauffeur was agreeably surprised. No hill-walker himself, he was equally surprised when having generously produced a large flask of hot coffee, he was offered a choice of Valpolicella or whisky in return. Given our premature arrival and the nature of the goodies travelling with us, he no longer had cause to doubt the sanity of hill-walkers.

The maps to use are the Ordnance Survey Outdoor Leisure series bearing the mysterious figures 1:25,000, which simply means that one unit on the map is equivalent to 25,000 units on the ground. That translates into 2½ in to the mile or 4 cm to 1 km. The less detailed 1:50,000 Landranger series provides broader pictures of this or that area and is more readily available. If necessary, wait until you get into the vicinity of your walk and then pop into a mountaineering equipment shop, which is sure to stock the relevant 1:25,000 map. A transparent plastic map case is worth the trivial cost.

Before tackling a long drive we check the route: road

numbers, main towns, whatever. This practice is even more important when hill-walking. Competent map-reading and route-planning keep us on course and make life easier. And maps are fun. If unfamiliar with them, first study all those notes and little symbols on the covers and in the margins. Once that information is imprinted on the mind, the nature of the chosen route becomes an open book. You know in advance what lies ahead, even though you may never have been there before. That is wonderfully gratifying for the rookie because he or she has, so to speak, passed an examination. The homework has been effective.

The snag, of course, is that occasionally we walk into mist or, even worse, fog. That is no intimidating problem if we know the route well and can check off familiar natural features as we go along. But it can be hazardous if the terrain is new to us and offers no help in the way of obvious paths and identifiable crags or watercourses. That is when we need a compass. My brother and I were once caught on Kinder Scout – a bare, peaty plateau – in thick fog. But we knew the compass bearing we needed to stay on, and did so. It was a slow, painstaking business that stretched our patience. One of us stood still, checking the compass and ensuring that the other, moving ahead, stayed on the correct bearing until he was almost out of sight. At which point the compass-bearer moved up to join the leader and the process was repeated. And repeated. And repeated. We were covering maybe 30 yards (27 m) at a time. But we got across, and down, safely. The same system applies with a larger party. They should keep close together in an arrowhead formation, with the navigator at the back.

The compass scored another bonus point one day when I was alone, except for a Gordon Setter, in that high semi-wilderness east of Derwent Dale in the Peak District. I knew the terrain vaguely, from youth, but when fog descended I had to make a choice between memory and instinct on the one hand or, on the other hand, the compass. I trusted the compass and that decision saved me a lot of time. Other than those two instances I can't recall using the compass much except for routine checks that I was on course. Mine happens to be an antiquated model, a paternal relic from the First World War. It has answered all the questions asked of it but if planning long expeditions over high, wild, trackless country I would invest in one of the more sophisticated modern compasses. In extreme cases, the efficient use of a good compass can mean the difference between life and death.

Eventually, the magnetic variation will be down to zero. At present, depending on where you happen to be in the British Isles, magnetic north will be between 4 and 7 degrees west of true north. This means that when the compass settles it will point 4 to 7 degrees west of the vertical lines on the map. So spread out the map, put the compass on it, and allow for the magnetic variation. When everything is lined up, the map is set. Use a pencil or some other straight item to link your location with the next objective – then look up from the map and examine the terrain that is an extension of the pencil line. That is the way you have to go. This is only a rough guide to compass-work. Practice is essential and you can get this on clear days when you know where you are and can see the way ahead. Check all that against the information the map and compass provide. Incompetent use of a compass can be as dangerous as not using it at all.

Some people wander off course even when the sun is visible. In that case, the wrist-watch is useful. Deducting an hour in summer time, point the hour hand towards the sun. An imaginary line bisecting the angle between the hour hand and the figure 12 points south. Similarly (again, deducting an hour in summer time), you can be reasonably confident that the sun will be east at 6 a.m., south-east at 9 a.m., south at noon, south-west at 3 p.m., and west at 6 p.m. Digital watches were not made for hill-walkers. And if you intend to spend a lot of time on high, desolate places and carry neither compass nor watch, I hope you have a companion with more sense.

During the busy summer season and to some extent in

spring and autumn, nobody needs a compass on the popular routes up Ben Nevis, Snowdon and Scafell Pike. Wherever and whenever, that basic information on compass-work may be surplus to your requirements. It depends what you have in mind. But there is no harm, is there, in knowing more than we need to know?

So let me chuck in the fact (which you could probably live without) that mist has to be reclassified as fog when visibility is less than 1,093 yards or a kilometre. One or the other can be a recurrent hazard on high ground. It is just a question of moist air moving upwards and getting, shall we say, clotted. Even more important, because it is a more consistent phenomenon, is the drop in temperature. Everybody knows that it's hot in hell but the corollary – that one needs to wrap up well if moving in the opposite direction – gets less publicity. We may reasonably assume that underneath those white nighties the angels are wearing thermal underwear. The British Isles lie at much the same latitude as Moscow, the Bering Sea and Hudson Bay, none of which is renowned for the prevalence of heat waves. When they're as close to the Arctic as we are, our friends from the Alps no longer scoff at such superficially modest altitudes as 2,000 ft (610 m), because from that level upwards we can offer them conditions appropriate to three times that height in their homeland. If you are going much above 2,000 ft on these islands, be prepared for snow, ice and cutting winds – which introduce the chill factor (increasing the effect of low temperatures). As a rule of thumb, the temperature falls by about 1 °F during every 300 ft (91 m) ascended. Ultimately it can get a lot worse than that because of the chill factor. So don't forget that spare sweater or windproof.

For almost forty years the chore of earning a living has usually restricted my hill-walking to the fringes of winter. No complaints. The heights are less crowded in spring and autumn and one should, anyway, enjoy them in all seasons. But one has to be ready for such things as verglas and graupel. Verglas (it comes from French) is a film of ice on rock and can be treacherous on two counts. It may look like wetness, no more, or it may be disguised under even the lightest coating of snow. Graupel is a German word indicating frozen rain, or snow-flakes. It's a kind of soft hail that does not bounce. Imagine coffee granules, but white. In my experience verglas is particu-larly deceptive. If it fools you and abruptly reduces you to a recumbent position, be grateful that the reduction has not taken you a few hundred feet lower down the mountain.

It has already been made clear that the hill-walker who needs an ice axe or crampons has picked up the wrong exami-nation paper and should toss it over to those willing and able to deal with it. So I am not going into the appropriate tech-niques for cutting steps or arresting a fall with the help of an ice axe. You and I don't have one. On the other hand we may occasionally need to go up an icy slope. Keep moving. To stop is to risk an exciting reminder of the worst throws we ever made at snakes and ladders. Kick in with the toes of the boots when going up, with the heels when going down. If traversing across an icy slope, kick in with the sides of the boots, using a staccato sawing action. Such exercises are tiring for the lower leg. They also defy the general hill-walking principle that, whenever possible, one should plant the entire sole on the ground in order to gain the maximum grip.

There are three other points to be made about staying healthy in health-threatening conditions. Snow covers paths and obscures or disguises natural features. If there is the slightest prospect of a white-out, a blizzard, get down as fast as safety permits. And note that the pretty stream you crossed on the way up may be transformed into a powerful, impassable torrent by heavy rain. Never underestimate (many have done so to their cost) the hazardous fury of a flash flood.

One thing for sure is that we have to deal with scree slopes. Not to put too fine a point on it, these can be bastards; and big-rock scree can also be dangerous unless treated with care. The trick is to go up side by side in case any rocks are dislodged and start plunging downhill before you can grab them. But you will be sure to grab them, won't you, because there may be other hill-walkers, perhaps out of sight, lower down? Scree slopes, consisting of rock detritus, tend to be tedious, tiring and time-consuming. The lower sections are usually granulated and slippery, the upper sections steeper and composed of larger rocks. If you want good samples of both, go up Brown Tongue, across Hollow Stones, and up Mickle-dore. All scree slopes are unstable and demand careful footwork – and the kind of vocabulary many of us pick up in the Army. You could say that they are the bills we pay for the fun we have.

I had a Christmas message from a South African tennis player who had retired from the professional circuit and told me how much he was enjoying hours of 'relentless relaxation' on the Cape Town beaches. And it struck me that without being aware of it he had encapsulated the nature of the happy hill-walker's pace. Don't hurry but seldom stop. Obviously one stops occasionally, to take a photograph or exchange a few words with other walkers. But as a general guide one should be stationary for no more than a total of, say, five minutes in any hour – except during the lunch break, which inevitably breaks one's rhythm. Whether one is going upwards, downwards or sideways, a consistent rhythm is less tiring and ultimately more productive than changes of pace. Take an example from tennis or squash. At a persistently steady pace one can play without stress for an hour, maybe two. But five minutes at a really hot pace, or variations between the extremes of pace, can leave one in no condition for anything except intensive care. It is the same with hill-walking. Take your time. Look around you. Leave plenty of energy in reserve. But keep going. Shorten the stride on steep terrain. And never forget that the pace you set must be comfortably within the capacity of the slowest component of your team.

If a hill-walker cannot tolerate his or her own company, the chances are that others will find it equally difficult to tolerate. Walking alone is, within reason, recommended. There are no caring, conversational distractions. All the senses are alert to the sights and sounds and feelings that come to us in high, lonely places: the clouds and the almost-silence, the soft sighing of the wind, the burbling music of infantine streams, the crunch of boots on rock, the subtle interplay of light and colour. Equally, it is a joy to share all that with kindred spirits as long as they don't talk too much. Hill-walkers commune with nature rather than with one another. It is safer to have company. As for numbers, some people are content to be lost in a crowd but most of us go to the heights because we want to get away from all that. If pressed for a preference I would say a maximum of four: because that is a compact load for car or dining table, provides a variety of conversational pairings during the walk, and ensures at least four rounds of drinks. You will not, of course, get involved with anyone likely to disappear to the lavatory when it is his or her turn to 'shout'.

One's companions may include children or dogs, who have something in common in that they need a special time allowance so that they can explore private adventures. As a rough guide, children can walk as many miles as they have years. Dogs tend to cover about three times as much ground as we do and should not be allowed to burn up too much energy at the beginning of a day's hill-walking. They must also be kept under close control so that they do not frighten sheep. Too much prancing about on rocky ground can tear a dog's paws. And I have learned, the hard way, that it is not easy to lift a 5 st 7 lb Gordon Setter over a series of high stiles – and even less easy to catch that 5 st 7 lb when it is commanded to jump down into one's arms from one rocky ledge to another. Remember, too, that dogs are dependent on the water you carry for them, because there is none of it about at high altitudes. If rooming with a dog at a hotel or bed-and-breakfast place, pack a towel, brush and bedcover.

What else should one pack? We have already discussed most of the essentials. The rucksack is your wardrobe and pantry and general storage unit, but beware of putting more into it than you need. Just imagine yourself carrying a boulder on your back up a steep scree slope when the wind is blowing in the opposite direction. If that picture does not impress you, pack the rucksack to bursting point and lug it up Brown Tongue or Ben Nevis or those hanging corries on Corrán Tuathail. You will curse any weight that was not essential to your purpose – and you will not make the same mistake again. Pack ruthlessly but with care, stuffing the exterior pockets with the items you may need most often: light snacks, the camera, a bag for litter, and unless it is dangling in front of you, a map. As for the inside of the rucksack, ensure that everything that needs to be kept dry – food, spare sweater, torch, tobacco and matches – is wrapped in one huge plastic bag or a series of smaller ones.

When taking strenuous exercise one does not need a lot of solid food, which would impose unnecessary stress on a body that already has enough work to do. But I would not go far without a flask of hot soup, a couple of oranges or apples, and chocolate, boiled sweets or health snacks. I save myself trouble by keeping a checklist permanently in a rucksack pocket. It includes such odd items as a spare bootlace, first-aid plasters, a garbage bag, a dish and food for the dog (if any), and toilet paper. I have never needed a crap when hill-walking but one has to be prepared. Bury it. A rucksack checklist saves a lot of thinking time. One packs faster and more efficiently.

After a good breakfast the hill-walking rule is to eat little, often, and wisely. A nibble or a munch. Something light and nourishing. I'm a great believer in oranges: sticky, but food and drink in one. As for alcohol, a beer (if available) or a nipperkin of red wine goes down well with lunch. But serious drinking must wait until the end of the day. On the hills one has to be wary of alcohol because it can impair the judgement and also causes a loss of body heat and a measure of de-hydration. We don't need any of that. We do need clear heads, neat footwork, warmth and non-alcoholic fluids. To re-coin the old saying, abstinence makes the heart grow fonder; and once safely down in the valleys, the intensity of our self-discipline can be relaxed. There is no need to be frustrated if a 'boomerang' walk begins and ends in a pub-free zone. The trick is to set off with a can of beer or cider apiece and deposit these in some convenient stream where prying eyes will not spot them. By the time you get down from the tops and open the cans, the contents will be cold enough to satisfy even an Australian's pernickety taste.

Talking about coming down, this takes about two-thirds of the time it takes to go up. Usually, anyway. Not always. There is a delightful old story of adjacent notes in a hotel visitors' book. Both concerned the famous Pinnacle on the Crib Goch scramble.

First entry:

'We ascended the Pinnacle in five and a half minutes and found the rocks very easy.'

Second entry:

'I descended the Pinnacle in five and a half seconds and found the rocks very hard.'

Index

Packed with information, this book is also anecdotal and discursive. The following index, though comprehensive in all that concerns its main theme, omits several passing references to locations, people, and subjects.